MINDFUL TEACHING WITH TECHNOLOGY

MINDFUL TEACHING WITH TECHNOLOGY

Digital Diligence in
the English Language Arts, Grades 6–12

Troy Hicks

Foreword by Lesley Mandel Morrow

THE GUILFORD PRESS
New York   London

Copyright © 2022 The Guilford Press
A Division of Guilford Publications, Inc.
370 Seventh Avenue, Suite 1200, New York, NY 10001
www.guilford.com

Printed in the United States of America

This book is printed on acid-free paper.

Last digit is print number: 9 8 7 6 5 4 3 2 1

Library of Congress Cataloging-in-Publication Data is available from the publisher.

ISBN 978-1-4625-4803-3 (paperback) — ISBN 978-1-4625-4804-0 (hardcover)

To Ty,

Thank you for listening, for providing insight,
and for asking the difficult questions.

Love, Dad

About the Author

Troy Hicks, PhD, is Professor of English and Education at Central Michigan University, where he teaches master's and doctoral courses in educational technology. He is also Director of the Chippewa River Writing Project, a site of the National Writing Project. During the 2020–2021 school year, Dr. Hicks served as the leader of a Teaching with Primary Sources grant through the Library of Congress and as coeditor of the *Michigan Reading Journal.* A former middle school teacher, he is a recipient of the Teacher Educator Award from the Michigan Reading Association, the Excellence in Teaching Award from Central Michigan University, and the Divergent Award for Excellence from the Initiative for 21st Century Literacies Research. An ISTE (International Society for Technology in Education) Certified Educator, Dr. Hicks consults with educational companies and nonprofit organizations and presents regularly at national educational conferences. He is the author of numerous books, articles, chapters, blog posts, and other resources broadly related to the teaching of literacy in our digital age. His website is hickstro.org.

Foreword

When I was an undergraduate in a teacher education program, we had to learn about audiovisual aids, or AV for short. We learned to thread a 16-mm film projector, use an opaque projector, and operate a tape recorder. When I began teaching, change was always a constant. The photocopy machine replaced the mimeograph machine, and we had to learn about transparencies for overhead projectors. We had slide and filmstrip projectors and then VCRs and VHS tapes, which eventually we transferred onto DVDs. Now *everything* is on our computers.

With the wonderful software we could use to enhance our instruction, computers were an exciting innovation. Nothing, however, has changed us more than the Internet. AV has turned to IT, with the endless possibilities of information technology. The arrival of the COVID-19 pandemic in 2020 changed the role of technology in the classroom from another tool to supplement instruction to an absolute necessity. Who had ever heard of Zoom? Now there will probably never be a "snow day" again at school (so sad!) as we will just go remote for the day. If you are absent, what you missed can be played back because it was recorded. If you are sick in bed, you can still watch school in real time with the provision of virtual learning. It isn't a matter of whether we should use technology in school; rather, we *must* use technology. But we must also do so with *diligence* and *mindful teaching*.

In *Mindful Teaching with Technology: Digital Diligence in the English Language Arts, Grades 6–12*, Troy Hicks helps us deal with the challenges and opportunities for creativity that coexist in this time of multimedia and teaching the language arts. The premise of the book's title is relevant now and forever, as we must always be diligent when using digital tools and must always engage in mindful teaching with technology. Without a doubt, the pros and cons of technology are here to stay. With technological change happening faster than ever, it's not surprising that teachers often find this process unsettling. However, in this book, Hicks makes dealing with these changes feel easy.

This outstanding book will serve those of us who have been teachers for a long time and don't feel all that confident with technology, as well as those who played with an iPad in their baby stroller. It is filled with the best ways to combine reading, writing, listening, and thinking together—as we have done in the past when teaching the language arts—but now with the wonderful digital tools we have at our fingertips.

Each chapter in this book follows a similar outline, which creates a comfortable environment for readers to learn to enhance our instruction using technology. Chapter 1 lays out the author's definition of *digital diligence* as "an alert, productive stance that individuals employ when using technology . . . for connected reading and digital writing, characterized by empathy, intention, and persistence." He discusses the best ways to use virtual and face-to-face learning, and how to combine synchronous, asynchronous, and hybrid instruction. Even remotely, with Zoom and similar programs, we can see each other, hear each other, and work in small groups at the same time. This book explains how teachers can manage it all.

When I began reading, I expected to find a volume filled with strategies for teaching the language arts. The book is this and much more. It deals with so many important elements that need to be discussed with students but may not seem like the teacher's responsibility. If not ours, then whose? Hicks explains how students need to—and can—maintain privacy when using technology, given our awareness of how easily files can be accessed. He describes how we can help our students to practice digital diligence by knowing how much time they spend in their virtual lives and taking responsibility for this. As humans, we need to socialize in person and be physically active. Students must know that it is important to maintain that type of active life alongside their virtual lives, including how (and how much) to use social media in a safe, dignified manner. The book emphasizes that what young people do with social media can follow them the rest of their lives and potentially be detrimental. Another important area of focus is helping students understand that what they find on the Internet may not be true, real, honest, worthy, and so forth. Students need to be sure their sources are reputable and scrutinize what they read in a diligent manner. This book shows teachers how to guide them toward these goals.

Hicks carefully describes evidence-based best practices in teaching writing and reading. He provides teaching points and useful resources throughout, as well as dialogue for teachers that will help students analyze and think more critically. After having read the book, I am eager to try some of the methodology with my undergraduate and graduate students. This well-written book is filled with resources and crucial information for those who will be using digital tools in teaching the English language arts.

Thank you, Dr. Hicks, for writing it!

LESLEY MANDEL MORROW, PhD
*Distinguished Professor and Director of the Center
for Literacy Development
Rutgers, The State University of New Jersey*

Preface

Toward a Definition of Digital Diligence

While there are many dates that one might choose to indicate the beginning of a significant shift in public opinion, October 26, 2018, was a touchstone in our current conversations about the role of technology in our children's lives. As more parents, educators, psychologists, and other concerned members of the general public were increasingly talking about issues of "screen time" and "digital distraction," *The New York Times* released three related articles whose headlines themselves captured the zeitgeist and, in a paradox, cast Silicon Valley executives as hypocrites ruling the empire they had built.

Nellie Bowles, a veteran tech reporter, offered the following three pieces, framed with black-and-white photo illustrations created by Tracy Ma. The titles themselves are stark enough, though the images associated with each are just as bleak:

- "A Dark Consensus about Screens and Kids Begins to Emerge in Silicon Valley" (2018a)
- "Silicon Valley Nannies Are Phone Police for Kids" (2018b)
- "The Digital Gap between Rich and Poor Kids Is Not What We Expected" (2018c)

In each of the three pieces, Bowles describes how technology executives—increasingly worried about the insidious effects of the devices, apps, and websites they had been peddling—were caught trying to keep their own children's lives device-free. Citing examples of Steve Jobs, Apple's legendary CEO, who kept his own children away from iPads, as well as Bill and Melinda Gates, who kept their own teens away from smartphones, each of Bowles's examples builds on the next, documenting the conversations that Silicon Valley parents were having to try to find balance between the positive and detrimental aspects of technology in their own, and in their children's, lives.

The overall effect: Parents who see the insides of the tech industry are quite cautious about when, why, and how they allow their children to use devices. In the third piece, "The Digital Gap between Rich and Poor Kids Is Not What We Expected," Bowles summarizes her findings in a concise, if perhaps exaggerated, manner:

> It could happen that the children of poorer and middle-class parents will be raised by screens, while the children of Silicon Valley's elite will be going back to wooden toys and the luxury of human interaction.

This series of articles came at a moment, in late 2018, where Pew Internet's annual reporting on Internet access and device usage showed nearly ubiquitous access and use across socioeconomic boundaries.

For instance, as of June 2019, though not everyone had broadband Internet and some users were "smart phone dependent" in their connections, Pew reports at that time noted that "the vast majority of Americans—97%—now own a cellphone of some kind" and that "today, nine-in-ten American adults use the internet" (Pew Research Center, 2019). Pew is careful to report that, even with such high rates of Internet usage, "adoption gaps remain based on factors such as age, income, education and community type." And, as educational technology historian Audrey Watters reminds us, the same Pew data demonstrate how the tech elites are, indeed, allowing and encouraging their own children to use devices, connect to the web, and stay engaged, despite the stories they might tell the media (Watters, 2019, entry 98).

From this collection of inconsistencies, questions emerge:

- What accounts for this hyperbole, hypochondria, or outright hypocrisy?
- How is it that, in an age of digital saturation, we find ourselves saying one thing (for ourselves and for our children) while doing another?
- And, despite these seeming contradictions, what can be done?

We know that people are using the Internet more and more, and often through their smartphone. And we know that concerns about when, why, and how (let alone how much) we use our devices have shifted public discourse about technology, and even introduced concepts like "technology addiction." There is a groundswell of concern about the ways in which we are using our devices, and the ways in which children are learning how to use these devices in school. These were the "before times," the questions we were asking in 2018 and 2019.

Now, as I finalize this book in 2021—after an election as contentious as ever, filled with outright falsehoods and misinformation in all forms, let alone amid a global pandemic—schools around the country and around the world are faced with an impossible balancing act of deciding if and how to open, or if they should offer entirely virtual instruction, and when to toggle back and forth between the two.

This conversation about *whether* we should be teaching students to use technology, explicitly, as part of our K–12 system has now been compounded with the fact that we will, most likely, be *required* to teach more and more within digitally mediated spaces, through both what we typically call *asynchronous* (or "anytime") and *synchronous* (or "real-time") modes of delivery. Even when our schools get back to something resembling "normal," many students will likely still opt for online instruction.

It is with these questions and this context in mind that we begin our exploration of what it means to teach and learn with what I define as *digital diligence*. In some ways, I have been exploring these questions for my entire career. As educational historian Larry Cuban reminds us, we have all seen many instances in which ed tech has been "oversold and underused" (2001) and, before that, the idea that constancy beats change when it comes to teaching with tech (1986). As it happens, Cuban still blogs regularly about these issues, and a link to his site—as well as other sites mentioned here in the Preface and through the entire book—can be found on this book's companion website (hickstro.org/digitaldiligence).

Cuban's constant refrain can be summarized quickly with the aphorism "The more things change, the more they stay the same," and he argues that one of the primary drivers for using technology in schools is not any high-minded goal toward innovation. Instead, he concludes, "the rationale for giving devices to every student and teacher has shifted from linkage to student outcomes to the simple fact that all standardized testing will be online" (Cuban, 2020b). In a separate post, he argues that "remote instruction in sharply reduced fashion will remain in public schools as the default option for teachers to use when students cannot attend school" (Cuban, 2020a).

I agree. In an era when many schools are now forced to explore fully online instruction, or to pursue "hybrid flexible" or "concurrent" approaches where some students are in the classroom and some are online, we need to understand that offering instruction through a technology-mediated tool does not, by itself, indicate that we are actually *teaching* students how to use technology. Taken with the broader concerns outlined by journalists like Bowles, ed tech critics like Watters, and others who we will meet later in the book, my guiding questions as I lead into this argument for teaching with principles of digital diligence are these:

What is it, really, that is happening with our children and teens
when they are using technology?

How, specifically, can we help them become more effective, efficient,
and, ideally, empathetic in the ways that they use these tools?

To understand how I arrived at these questions and the focal point for this book, the first chapter examines some of the broader conversations that have led these critics, scholars, educators, parents, politicians, journalists, and others to this moment, all as we consider the role of technology in our students' lives, both inside and outside of school.

As I have always tried to do with my work, I approach this task with humility. To the extent that I have tried to create for my colleagues the kinds of books that have a "shelf life," I know anything I write today has the potential to be out of date next year, let alone in the years to come. This book, *Mindful Teaching with Technology,* then, reaffirms the role of productive literacy practices in a technology-enriched English language arts (ELA) classroom, blended with specific ideas about mindful use of our devices and how we can help middle and high school students become better readers, writers, and thinkers.

To that end, I start with some premises to guide our teaching. We must do the following:

- Invite students to slow down, to savor language through reading, listening, and viewing, both on-screen and off
- Encourage students to express themselves, academically and socially, through writing, speaking, and visually representing their ideas, again in both print and digital spaces
- Engage students in substantive dialogue about what they are experiencing in and across these literacy/literate spaces and events

From these contentions, I define *digital diligence* as an alert, productive stance that individuals employ when using technology (apps, websites, software, and devices) for connected reading and digital writing, characterized by empathy, intention, and persistence.

Throughout the book, I demonstrate ways in which we can model, mentor, and move our students toward this stance in their own literate lives. Though some of the technologies may change, the principles will remain: intention and alertness, empathy and persistence, and an overarching sense of purpose that moves students toward the production of digital creations. These are the dispositions we want our students to have, and my hope is that this book provides some insights on how we can promote these stances.

As always, I welcome continued dialogue with K–12 colleagues, teacher educators, and others interested in these topics. You can reach me on Twitter (@hickstro) or email (hickstro@gmail.com).

Let's become more digitally diligent, together, in the months and years ahead.

Readers can use this QR code to access the book's companion website (hickstro.org/digitaldiligence).

Acknowledgments

The writing of a book is a journey, and much like other journeys it has ups and downs, fits and starts, and other joys and challenges packaged in interesting metaphors and euphemisms. This particular book has always seemed, for one reason or another, to push me toward the downward, fitful parts of the journey. However, as I make final edits to this series of acknowledgments in 2021, I am hopeful that there will be more starts and more joy, moving past a pandemic and putting this book into production. Part of this comes from my own life and work, with priorities in flux and this project always seeming to fall to the bottom of the list. Another part comes from me being a recovering perfectionist, and just trying to plow through the imperfections because, as I often tell my students, a project is "never done, just due." I am sure there are other reasons, too, and I am grateful to have had the time, energy, and ability to finally bring this book to fruition.

So, with the idea that this work does not feel done, yet is definitely due, I first thank the organizations and individuals that allowed me to integrate their tools and share screenshots throughout the book. I thank my editor, Craig Thomas, and the rest of the team at The Guilford Press, too, for guiding me through the final stages as we brought the book to life, including Monica Baum, Anna Brackett, Paul Gordon, Judith Grauman, Katherine Lieber, and Robert Sebastiano.

Many colleagues have asked about—and provided me with opportunities to deliver workshops and webinars related to—topics discussed in the book. I thank all of them for the chance to try out many of the lessons and ideas presented here, as well as for their feedback. One, in particular, has been especially helpful. She has been encouraging in many ways over the past few years by asking questions, listening to my lesson ideas, and—at a very critical moment when I needed some encouragement as well as collegial critique—stepping in to review a struggling draft of the book. For that, I thank Lauren Zucker, an English educator at Northern Highlands Regional High School in Allendale,

New Jersey. Three other colleagues stepped in to try out lessons and offer thoughtful feedback at critical moments too: Michael RobbGrieco, Director of Curriculum and Technology Integration at Windham Southwest Supervisory Union in Wilmington, Vermont; Andy Schoenborn, an English educator at Mt. Pleasant High School in Mt. Pleasant, Michigan; and Jill Runstrom, an English educator at Skyline High School in Ann Arbor, Michigan. As I noted above, many colleagues have given me a nudge here and there, yet the four of you gave me that extra push at moments I really needed it the most. And, in the spirit of collegiality, I thank those at the National Council of Teachers of English who have allowed me to quote extensively from their position statement on the "Definition of Literacy in a Digital Age" (2019b), especially Kurt Austin.

Finally, I thank my family and close friends, all of whom have encouraged me in their own ways. My wife, Sara, and our "fab five": McKenna, Lexi, Beau, Shane, and Cooper; my dad, Ron; my brother, Barry; and extended family and friends who have continued to support me. In particular, I thank my son Ty, to whom this book is dedicated. His ethos of diligence has been amazing to watch grow in the past few years through college and in his early professional life, and I look forward to seeing him embrace all life has to offer, including his new bride, Liz. You always know how to ask the difficult questions, Ty, and I appreciate that you love me enough to do that.

Contents

CHAPTER 1

The Case for Digital Diligence in English Language Arts Classrooms

We live in an era of distraction.

On this, we can all agree. Or, perhaps, at least we could agree if we might be able to stay focused long enough to have the conversation.

For any educator, from preschool through graduate school, the consequences of digital devices are present for our learners in every moment of every day. Students, even the most dedicated and attentive, can be preoccupied or sidetracked by the devices in their pockets and backpacks. The news media offers reports on the exponential uptick in the use of screen time. School policies on 1:1, "bring your own device" (BYOD), or other technology configurations can change, sometimes overnight, swinging from one extreme to another. One day, devices are allowed; the next day, or in the next classroom, those same devices are confiscated. These characterizations may be a bit extreme, yet the point is clear—schools can be consistently inconsistent places, and this applies especially so to our use of technology for teaching.

As we English language arts (ELA) teachers work conscientiously to help them become more attentive, substantive readers, writers, and thinkers, it feels as though we are fighting an uphill battle with our students, with their devices (and, oftentimes, with colleagues, parents, and our administration). Trying to figure out when, if, and how to use tech in our ELA instruction is a challenge in and of itself, outside of the actual content we want and need to teach. Then, given our broader, societal conversations about the use of digital devices, we see there are even more challenges ahead.

For instance, reports of increased anxiety, depression, and, terribly, suicides are linked to use of social media among teens (Twenge, 2017b). Silicon Valley employees have turned from their positions in high-tech companies to, instead, question the ethical foundations on which these companies are built (Harris, 2017). And all this happens in an era where smartphone use is, for all intents and purposes, nearly ubiquitous. For many people, in fact, their mobile device is their single entry point to the Internet (Jiang, 2018). While we continue to grow more dependent on our devices, the academic and public discussion around device usage constantly returns to the topic of distraction.

For instance, in her book *Reader, Come Home*, psychologist and reading researcher Maryanne Wolf (2018) has again raised a significant question about the role of reading in the minds of a constantly distracted population:

> The young reader can either develop all the multiple deep-reading processes that are currently embodied in the fully elaborated, expert reading brain; or the novice reading brain can become "short-circuited" in its development; or it can acquire whole new networks in different circuits. There will be profound differences in how we read and how we think, depending on which processes dominate the formation of the young child's reading circuit. (Loc 136, Kindle)

Echoes of this dilemma have been raised for a decade (and, as we will see, probably even longer than that), going back at least to a time where smartphones were just entering our lives. In another example of a cultural touchstone, journalist Nicholas Carr asked a question in 2008 that still resonates: "Is Google making us stupid?" (Carr, 2008). Since then, there have been warnings that we are raising the "dumbest generation" (Bauerlein, 2008), that we are spending time "alone together" (Turkle, 2011), and that we are, indeed, addicted to distraction (Pang, 2013). Concepts like "continuous partial attention" (2009) and "email apnea" (2008), both coined by technology writer Linda Stone, and a more general "addiction-like behavior" (Clay, 2018) that characterizes technology use, have entered our conversations. Even Carr took his initial question about Google and expanded on it to craft an entire book, *The Shallows: What the Internet Is Doing to Our Brains* (2010, 2020), which by its very title suggests a doomsday scenario for our already-fickle minds.

A brief exploration of how we got to this point is worthwhile, first with a definition of *mindfulness* and then a few more recent examples.

MINDFULNESS, DISTRACTION, AND THE (PERCEIVED) EFFECTS OF TECHNOLOGY

Especially as it relates to technology, we are all trying to figure out where to go next with the ways that we ourselves use—as well as how we teach our children to use—the devices that mediate our lives. What is it, exactly, that we are trying to accomplish with any given tool, in any given moment? What do we mean by mindfulness, and how do we go about achieving it, especially when it comes to using technology in meaningful ways?

As a place to start, I consider the idea of mindfulness. Though I am sure there are more erudite explanations in theological or philosophical texts, I borrow directly from the definition of mindfulness offered by *Mindful* (magazine and website, 2014):

> Mindfulness is the basic human ability to be fully present, aware of where we are and what we're doing, and not overly reactive or overwhelmed by what's going on around us.

Mindfulness, in this sense, is constantly compromised by all the other possibilities that present themselves to us, whether in a passage of medieval scripture (as described below), outside the window of a stuffy one-room schoolhouse in the 1800s, or in our classrooms (or Zoom video calls) of today. This "basic ability to be fully present" has always been a challenge for us, and it always will. The devices in our students' hands contribute to—but are not the sole cause of—our problem. As such, we need to stop blaming the devices themselves, or the students using them. Instead, we need to recognize these challenges while also aiming to overcome them as we always have—by learning to be better as individuals, as a society, and as educators working to support the students in our care.

It is worth noting that these concerns have gone back centuries, as history professor Jamie Kreiner notes in an article for *Aeon* (2019). She begins by describing a problem that we all face today in ancient terms—"medieval monks had a terrible time concentrating"—and documents the ways in which they employed renunciation and restraint, as well as strategies for building mental models. She concludes with a warning that resonates even today, "the problem of concentration is recursive. Any strategy for sidestepping distraction calls for strategies on sidestepping distraction." In this sense, though I am not a psychologist or neuroscientist, I would argue that the challenges of mindfulness that have plagued our human minds have only been amplified by the introduction of digital devices, not brought on by them.

This brings us back to the moment noted in the preface, the urge in the mid- to late 2010s that Silicon Valley itself has begun to embrace a revolution in "mindfulness." In early 2020, before the pandemic put a pause to such events, the annual Consumer Electronics Show occurred in Las Vegas, and a full battery (yes, pun intended) of new devices met the need for mindfulness. For instance, there were reports on a headband that monitors the electrical activity in one's brain and "uses neurofeedback therapy to show you a real-time display of your brain activity, with the goal of teaching you how to identify and change behaviors through different exercises" (DeNisco Rayome, 2020). This is but one example in an industry full of gadgets that monitor biofeedback and remind us when to stand and how far we have walked, among other tasks. Even now, it seems we are trying to find new ways to use tech to solve age-old problems that medieval monks struggled with as well.

Furthermore, we are in an age where the tech faithful have lost their faith. We find that former employees of Google, Facebook, Amazon, Apple, and others have begun movements for questioning the role of technology in our lives. Digital ethicist (and cofounder of the website and nonprofit The Center for Humane Technology) Tristan Harris (2017) forces us to consider deeper implications of the ways that algorithms drive our lives and how we can avoid the "digital attention crisis" engulfing our society:

> It's not just taking away our agency to spend our attention and live the lives that we want, it's changing the way that we have our conversations, it's changing our

democracy, and it's changing our ability to have the conversations and relationships we want with each other.

As noted above, terms like *continuous partial attention* (Stone, 2009)—or what has also been commodified as the *attention economy*—drive the dialogue about our screen time, not to mention our mental health and relationships with our partners, families, and friends. Couple that with the view expressed by Harris and others that, indeed, our entire democracy is disintegrating, and we are in for a load of trouble. Harris and many others from the technology industry who are raising these concerns were featured prominently in a 2020 documentary, *The Social Dilemma* (Orlowski, 2020), released to Netflix about two months before the presidential election, reminding us again of the power that our devices have to influence (or perhaps manipulate) our real-world actions. (Of note, this portion of the chapter was composed before January 6, 2021, and it is beyond the scope of this book to fully analyze the events leading up to, during, and after the storming of the U.S. Capitol.)

Journalists such as Manoush Zomorodi, too, are focused on an interrogation of our personal use of technology and the relationships that we have with our devices. In her book *Bored and Brilliant* (2017a), Zomorodi outlined a series of challenges that she conducted with listeners of her podcast, *Note to Self.* For 5 consecutive days in the summer of 2015, Zomorodi asked her listeners to engage in tasks that would help them redefine their relationship with their smartphones, ranging from the action of deleting the one app that caused the most distraction to another option that would have them avoid taking pictures and posting them to social media. The result, she argues, is that we simply need to put our phones away and let our minds wander. Her continued work with the *TED Radio Hour* and Mozilla's *In Real Life* podcast keep exploring such themes. In one sense, we can make the case that any rational user of technology could simply put down their phones to disconnect and to walk away (at least for a while).

However, we know it is never that simple.

In addition to the many challenges that rely on psychological principles for keeping people attached to their phones, many of the scholars and tech ethicists would also contend that having people put their devices away is, in fact, bad for business. The CEO of Netflix famously quipped about their biggest competitor being our need for sleep (Raphael, 2017), and certainly there are many similar examples that could be drawn from the history of technology and the Internet.

With conversations about Bowles's articles still fresh from October 2018, we then look to February 5, 2019, when Cal Newport's *Digital Minimalism: Choosing a Focused Life in a Noisy World* was released to rave reviews. Contrasting two extremes of (1) Luddism, where no technology should be used at all, with (2) the self-explanatory state of "mindless adoption," Newport advocated for "care and intention" (p. 193) to be used in our efforts to adopt new technologies. He argues for

a full-fledged philosophy of technology use, rooted in your deep values, that provides clear answers to the questions of what tools you should use and how you should use them and, equally important, enables you to confidently ignore everything else. (p. xvi)

Newport's book was at the top of the bestseller lists and, like many of the others cited above, offered us ways to consider what it means to live in an era of distraction, where we are caught in a constant tug of war for our own attention, fighting against devices that are meant to keep us from more meaningful tasks and relationships. (As a quick aside, it is important to note that the origins of the term *Luddite* suggests they "were neither opposed to technology nor inept at using it," according to *Smithsonian Magazine* [Conniff, 2011], and this misapplication of their namesake could become an interesting topic of inquiry for students.)

Still, we see this tug of war between what any individual can do (making conscious choices about when, why, and how to use technology) as compared to another narrative where technology is designed to keep us addicted with what's been called "the endless scroll," or the algorithmic suggestions for what to "watch next," and other kinds of automated suggestions for who or what to follow that might align with a person's interests, ultimately keeping one's eyeballs on a particular platform so more advertisements can be sold. More recently, this type of behavior has earned the moniker of "doom scrolling," especially during the pandemic, protests, and U.S. presidential election season of 2020, and refers both to the apocalyptic content of the scrolling itself and, I suspect, the idea that we feel a bit resigned to our own endless obsession to the devices on which we are scrolling.

These are not trivial matters. The rise of conspiracy theories, the threats to our privacy, and the ways in which many individuals have become radicalized by their experiences on the Internet are evident. As just one example of ongoing reporting on this matter, Kevin Roose of *The New York Times* began documenting the ways in which one young man became more and more infatuated with alt-right conspiracies through his 2019 article "The Making of a YouTube Radical" (Roose, 2019) and subsequent podcast series *Rabbit Hole* (Roose, 2020). Following the plight of Caleb Cain, Roose shares a precautionary take of what can happen to someone left with too much time on his hands and who is open to the influence of the algorithm. The effects on individuals, and society as a whole, are tangible.

Though, for every tech problem, there is a tech solution. In yet another seeming paradox, the technology companies themselves are offering countless apps and extensions that can help us manage our digital lives, such as the popular "Moment" or "Forest" apps that help us track our own device usage, as well as tools for parents to monitor—and pause—their children's Internet usage. For instance, Circle, a product from Disney that is described on their website as the "smart way for families to manage content and time online, on any device" (meetcircle.com), has been on the market for many years. In their release of iOS 12 in the fall of 2018, Apple, too, built in an app that would accomplish similar goals—Screentime, designed to "access real-time reports about how much time you spend on your iPhone, iPad, or iPod touch, and set limits for what you want to manage" (Apple Inc., 2019). These monitoring tools are but one way to address the problem, yet still do not always move our children toward self-regulated (as well as more critical or creative) digital behavior.

Thus, we are still struggling with ways to manage our own attention. And, in many ways, this is the essence of what it means to teach ELA; we are constantly pushing our students to read, write, and think with more intention, to interpret existing texts, and to design their own texts in thoughtful, productive ways. The devices they have in their hands can help them in these efforts, or they can continue to be situated in our conversations about educational technology as distractions. How we frame this situation through our words and actions matters, as demonstrated by the following brief example of a recent school visit I made.

FRAMING THE CONVERSATION: DEVICE USE AND DIGITAL DISTRACTION IN ONE AMERICAN SCHOOL

To begin, by no means is this single anecdote meant to be representative of what is happening in all schools, around the country, or around the world. Still, it is illustrative and demonstrates how important it is to frame the conversation about technology use with our students in productive (as compared to pejorative) ways.

To offer a specific example of these tensions, in a post I crafted for the *Educator Collaborative* blog in 2019 (T. Hicks, 2019b), I described a recent school visit in which I became quite intrigued, and then a bit infuriated, at the ways in which teachers, individually, and the school culture, as a whole, positioned students and their uses of mobile phones. From my blog post, I quote extensively to describe some of what I saw and share some images (see Figure 1.1) that I took while wandering the halls:

> At this particular high school, when I had a few moments to myself to walk up and down the academic wing, I began to notice (on door after door) signs that suggested to students that their technologies were not welcome. As I continued to walk around the school, some of the signs repeated themselves, and I began to wonder if various anti-phone campaigns had been launched at the school over many years, considering the multiple incarnations of the signs that were plastered onto classroom doors. Some of the signs featured a flip phone or images of a classic iPod, and I had to wonder if some of them had been in place for years—perhaps even more than a decade.
>
> I also became keenly aware that these signs took on different personalities, in a sense. The tone on the signs ranged from humorous to threatening, with very few words expressing any explicit rule or policy. One was in French, one in Spanish, and one even had a Seuss-like quality to it (though I'm unsure if that was intentional). What was most startling to me was the juxtaposition of one room that featured the classic Apple "Think Different" campaign posters on the walls and windows leading into the classroom and not one, but two copies of the "no phones" poster hung above the door. In this mid-size high school, these ten signs in the academic wing represented at least half of the doors that students would walk by on any given day. I was unable to see the library, the athletic wing, the arts wing, or other spaces of the school, but the images I did see caused me more than enough concern.

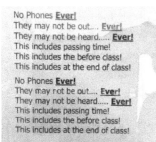

No Phones **Ever!**
They may not be out.... **Ever!**
They may not be heard..... **Ever!**
This includes passing time!
This includes the before class!
This includes at the end of class!

No Phones **Ever!**
They may not be out.... **Ever!**
They may not be heard..... **Ever!**
This includes passing time!
This includes the before class!
This includes at the end of class!

When you enter the classroom:
Your Cell Phones MUST be turned off and put away!
You are not allowed to have your phone out for ANY reason during class time.

NO SE PERMITEN ENTRAR CON TELÉFONOS MÓVILES

ATTENTION!
CELL PHONES
must be *turned off* and *put away* **BEFORE** entering my classroom.

FIGURE 1.1. A collection of mobile device policy signs (photos by the author).

Looking back at these images again, more than a year after summarizing them in the original blog post, I am still dismayed. With demands like "Cell phones must be turned off and put away before entering my classroom" and the simpler "No Phones Ever!" shouting at students, it is clear the teachers in these classrooms are positioning themselves as arbiters of power and that phones are disruptions to the natural order of things. This is but one series of snapshots, and I am not going to go into a full discursive analysis of what each of these messages mean as well as the inherent power dynamics that happen in American high schools. That is a sociological and psychological conversation far beyond the scope of my work, though I strongly encourage readers to explore these dynamics through the work of many educational critics, including John Taylor Gatto (2005, 2008), Alfie Kohn (1993, 2000), and others noted throughout this book.

Still, it all leads me to the following. We need to be safe, yes, but we also need to be smart. We want kids to know what the web is doing with their data, so they are not trapped in mindless consumption; at the same time, we want them to be creative, and to be so in an intentional manner. They need to be aware of the choices they are making and then consider the ways in which they are producing new knowledge for the world. And we need to be the ones who teach them this. Banning the devices accomplishes nothing, except putting us in an adversarial relationship, both with the phones themselves and with our students. Stated simply, the way we talk with (or talk at) our students about technology matters, and the warnings that dotted the doors in this school were ominous for many reasons.

This was the state of the conversation through 2018 and 2019, as I began working on this manuscript. Then, as we turned the corner into 2020, the entire world experienced a pandemic, one that shut down our schools—and our lives—in ways we had never experienced before, causing us to again confront the ways in which we were thinking about and using technology to deliver instruction to our students. The entire notion of what it meant to be a "digital teacher" shifted—as did much of the rest of what we consider to be normal, day-to-day activity in our world—in the spring of 2020. Without belaboring the point that most teachers were not prepared to be online instructors, coupled with the fact that "emergency remote teaching" (Hodges, Moore, Trust, & Bond, 2020) is not considered the same as more focused, well-designed, and (often) peer-reviewed courses delivered as part of online teaching, the overnight shift brought on by the COVID-19 pandemic was, perhaps, not the best way to demonstrate that online learning could be implemented, as it was happening in a contrived manner.

As we consider this context—and if it is not evident by now, the stance I hope educators will take—I now want to expand on the definition for *digital diligence* that I offered in the preface. It is an approach that ELA teachers can take in terms of their instructional design and delivery, as well as in the ways we invite our students to be both consumers and creators of digital texts. In order to make substantive change to our teaching practices—and to invite our students into more production-oriented uses of technology for critical thinking and creative expression—these shifts are needed.

ARTICULATING A DEFINITION OF DIGITAL DILIGENCE

So, how do we approach our own digital lives through a deliberate stance? Moreover, how do we help our students accomplish similar goals? Versions of these questions have been asked for years, as outlined above, and—for my entire teaching career—I have approached various responses about what it means to be intentional, focused, and productive with our uses of technology in my own work, first as a middle school ELA teacher and now as a teacher educator and researcher.

In a sense, writing this book is a retrospective for me about using technology, specifically technology to teach reading and writing. At the time I am completing this book, in the summer of 2021, I find that the past decade has afforded me the opportunity to author or coauthor numerous books, articles, and blog posts, as well as to provide dozens of professional learning presentations, workshops, and webinars. Also, it is somewhere in this frenzy between "distraction" and "mindfulness" that I've described above that we find ourselves, as ELA teachers, trying to figure out the best ways in which to introduce digital writing and connected reading tools into our curriculum, all while being ever-more conscious of our students' overall technology use and screen time.

As a parent, a teacher educator, and a researcher, these dilemmas and the context in which we find ourselves—and the inherent questions that this time, space, and series of concerns raise for us—resonate now more than ever. At times in the past, I have come down (sometimes forcefully) in opposition to the types of doomsday theories related to technology, some of which are outlined in the section above. At least one psychiatrist, Richard A. Friedman (2018), has also argued for a more nuanced approach. Parents, he believes,

> have bought into the idea that digital technology—smartphones, video games and the like—are neurobiologically and psychologically toxic. If you believe this, it seems intuitive that the generations growing up with these ubiquitous technologies are destined to suffer from psychological problems. But this dubious notion comes from a handful of studies with serious limitations.

He then offers insights into the ways that correlational studies of technology use have, through exposure and amplification in the media (and social media), led to a false narrative about "an epidemic of anxiety disorder rooted in a generation's overexposure to digital technology," betraying our actual biology and suggesting "an exaggerated idea about just how open to influence our brains really are." Again, I do not have the kinds of medical, scientific, or statistical training to know, for sure, whether these studies are (or are not) "exaggerated," yet I am always aware that we need to think about issues from a variety of perspectives, and Friedman's suggestion that, if we pathologize the devices, we will, in turn, pathologize our youth seems worthy of discussion.

Along these same lines, David Levy, a professor of information studies, has penned the book *Mindful Tech: How to Bring Balance to Our Digital Lives* (2017), arguing that

> So many of the discussions we are now having about the digital world tend to be based around simplistic dualisms. We ask whether texting is good or bad for us, or whether the Internet is making a smart or stupid. But when we can look at the richness of our own experience online, we have the chance to discover when and how texting is helpful and when it isn't, or when being online is productive and illuminating and when it isn't. (p. 12)

Levy's point here about "richness" is especially important. Just as we would ask our children and our students to look holistically at their lives, and to find balance across many relationships, activities, and challenges they could pursue, we need to position the different kinds of tasks that they might engage in (especially when using technology) among these broader life experiences. With this in mind, we can use—and teach our children to use—technology in ways that are productive, creative, and beneficial. Moreover, I believe there is little use in outright bans of devices in schools (and in the lives of youth outside of school), lest they find other ways of going online anyway (and might do so in deceitful ways). In short, how we mentor our youth to use technology matters.

Thus, knowing we do have professional obligations to teach students how to use technology (e.g., ELATE Commission on Digital Literacy in Teacher Education, 2018; National Council of Teachers of English, 2019b), my arguments are aligned with others who claim students should be media creators and not just consumers (Hobbs, 2017; Ito et al., 2009; Jenkins, 2009). I wonder (and model) throughout my many conversations and work with ELA educators how we might be able to help our students use tools in a mindful manner, where they have control over their own productive, ethical, and responsible device decisions. Moreover, when considering the many ways in which we can and must use technology to teach reading, writing, and other language arts skills, I am continually driven by the question of how we might renew our approach to doing so.

Yet, at the same time, I can't say I'm not beginning to doubt some of my long-held beliefs about the role of digital tools in our teaching and our students' lives, especially as I watch my own children engaged in remote learning here in 2020–2021. I acknowledge the very real concerns that have been raised through many of the sources I've cited in the section above. Moreover, watching my own teenagers—as well as reading and reviewing reports on teenagers from reputable sources such as Pew Research—suggests to me that *something* is indeed happening. As a nod to the report mentioned above, Pew's latest datasets, for instance, demonstrate that "54% of U.S. teens say they spend too much time on their cellphones" and that 36% of parents report similar feelings of their own (Jiang, 2018). Stories outlining the challenges of "remote learning," too, abound.

Using this book as an opportunity to deepen the conversation, I also want to rethink my own perspectives, sharing insight with other educators about ways to make their work life more productive and design lessons that would be useful for students in upper elementary, middle, and high school grades. And by *productive*, please know I am using this term in the sense that we need to be "production oriented," asking students to be creators of digital texts, as compared to the somewhat vague, tech-infused idea of *productivity*, in which we try to do lots of work, and to do so quickly. Production oriented work is often not fast work at all, and we need to allow our students time, space, and opportunity to play.

Moreover, the teaching of English language arts has evolved in the past few years to include many perspectives, especially those that honor culturally sustaining pedagogies and the inclusion of diverse texts and topics. It is beyond the scope of this book—as well as my own expertise—to cite extensively on these topics, though one important place to begin is with the work of Tricia Ebarvia, Lorena Germán, Dr. Kimberley N. Parker, and Julia E. Torres (2018), collectively known as the team who produces #Disrupt Texts, which is "a crowdsourced, grass roots effort by teachers for teachers to challenge the traditional canon in order to create a more inclusive, representative, and equitable language arts curriculum that our students deserve." Their work—and the work of countless other educators who identify as Black, Indigenous, and people of color (BIPOC) as well as educators who identify as lesbian, gay, bisexual, transgender, and queer/questioning (LGBTQ+)—needs to become a more consistent part of the conversation in all literacy instruction, and especially as we teach students how to engage in digital literacies.

In this sense, I see the idea of digital diligence in line with other lenses for teaching and learning that promote values such as attention and alertness, curiosity and perseverance, and, at the core of it all, inquiry-based practices that lead to deliberate action where we ask critical questions and provide creative responses. And, before moving into an overview of the book and subsequent chapters, I will provide just a bit more of my thinking about how I have come to this stance for teaching digital diligence, sharing some of the influences from professional organizations that have guided my current thinking about teaching and learning.

TEACHING AND LEARNING:
INFLUENCES ON ELA, DIGITAL LITERACY, AND MORE

Like many educators, I draw ideas from influences too numerous to name, ranging from casual conversations with colleagues that I have met at conferences to longtime friends, from books, journal articles, and workshop presentations, and from webinars, podcasts, and blog posts. Each of these resources in my professional life has been invaluable, and I appreciate the many ideas I encounter each day. For the many people who have influenced my work, let me pause to share a brief, yet heartfelt "thank you." There are more of you than could fit in a few pages of acknowledgments, and this feeble, wholesale statement of thanks will have to do for now.

As a way to ground the work presented here in the book, I do draw explicitly from three related pools of professional knowledge, and the underlying ethos of the organizations that have created the resources: the National Council of Teachers of English (NCTE), the International Society for Technology in Education (ISTE), and the National Association for Media Literacy Education (NAMLE). Also, though I don't go into detail about them, I draw from the six "social practices" that are encouraged by the National Writing Project as part of their "Teacher-Consultant Badge Framework" (2018), including the ideas that we "go public with our practice" and that we "lead" and "advocate." The approaches of digital diligence that I describe in this book are, in some ways, similar to other models of digital literacy and citizenship instruction yet are, in other ways, somewhat different. My hope is that by articulating these professional influences and sharing my own path toward this mode of thinking, other educators might be able to engage in similar kinds of professional learning too. Here, then, I focus on NCTE, ISTE, and NAMLE.

The NCTE and 21st-Century Literacies

The NCTE, founded in 1911, is an organization of approximately 25,000 educators representing all grade levels from elementary school through the university, broadly interested in the teaching of English language arts, including literature, composition, and related disciplines (NCTE, n.d.). NCTE has been my professional home since my senior year of college, when I joined as a preservice teacher, and I have been continuously engaged as a member ever since.

At the time of this writing, NCTE has compiled more than 20 different positions statements, resolutions, and research reports on "21st Century Literacies" (2019a). Beginning with 1970's "Resolution on Media Literacy" (1970) and stretching to 2018's "Beliefs for Integrating Technology into the English Language Arts Classroom" (ELATE Commission on Digital Literacy in Teacher Education, 2018), there are numerous examples of what students are expected to know and be able to do. The most recent document, NCTE's 2019 updated position statement on the "Definition of Literacy in a Digital Age" (2019b) aptly summarizes many of these overarching goals into nine concise points (see Figure 1.2). It will also serve as a touchstone throughout the topics explored later in the book.

In particular, my experience as a co-coordinator of the team that wrote "Beliefs for Integrating Technology into the English Language Arts Classroom" helped me to think about the complexities inherent in approaching ELA instruction in a holistic manner. Inherent in all these position statements and guiding documents are a broader conception of students as agents in their own literacy learning. The opening segment

---

NCTE's "Definition of Literacy in a Digital Age" makes it clear that the continued evolution of curriculum, assessment, and teaching practice itself is necessary.

Literacy has always been a collection of communicative and sociocultural practices shared among communities. As society and technology change, so does literacy. The world demands that a literate person possess and intentionally apply a wide range of skills, competencies, and dispositions. These literacies are interconnected, dynamic, and malleable. As in the past, they are inextricably linked with histories, narratives, life possibilities, and social trajectories of all individuals and groups. Active, successful participants in a global society must be able to do the following:

- Participate effectively and critically in a networked world
- Explore and engage critically, thoughtfully, and across a wide variety of inclusive texts and tools/modalities
- Consume, curate, and create actively across contexts
- Advocate for equitable access to and accessibility of texts, tools, and information
- Build and sustain intentional global and cross-cultural connections and relationships with others so to pose and solve problems collaboratively and strengthen independent thought
- Promote culturally sustaining communication and recognize the bias and privilege present in the interactions
- Examine the rights, responsibilities, and ethical implications of the use and creation of information
- Determine how and to what extent texts and tools amplify one's own and others' narratives as well as counter unproductive narratives
- Recognize and honor the multilingual literacy identities and culture experiences individuals bring to learning environments, and provide opportunities to promote, amplify, and encourage these differing variations of language (e.g., dialect, jargon, register)

FIGURE 1.2. Opening segment of the NCTE's (2019) "Definition of Literacy in a Digital Age." Used with permission of NCTE.

of NCTE's "Definition of Literacy in a Digital Age" (Figure 1.2) outlines these key points.

More than just passively reading a text or writing by rote formula, these expectations described across multiple NCTE documents encourage us to see students as designers, creators, and critics, able to use digital literacy skills and multimodal resources in authentic ways to meet goals both in and beyond the classroom. These intentional stances are in alignment with my definition of digital diligence and encourage educators to help their students to employ technology in ethical, productive, and responsible ways.

ISTE's Standards for Students and Educators

Having recently celebrated its 40th anniversary, ISTE serves approximately 100,000 members worldwide (ISTE, n.d.). Like NCTE, ISTE has created a variety of resources, including sets of standards for both educators and students. ISTE's 2016 revision of their standards for students encourages us to see them as active producers of digital products and contributors to a digital world (2016a).

Of the seven major standards and 28 substandards for students, many of them are useful in our exploration digital diligence; thus, it would be too much to list them all here. Instead, a brief explanation of how the revisions to the standards, drawn from the *ISTE Standards for Students: A Practical Guide for Learning with Technology* (ISTE, 2016b), demonstrates the intention with which the standards committee worked:

> In this new iteration of the standards, the focus is squarely on learning, not tools. Yes, students still need to be proficient in foundational technology skills, but that's not the end. It's the means to an end where the expectation is that students will use technology when appropriate to take charge of their own learning. (p. 1)

Throughout the ISTE standards, then, we see a conscientious effort to move students into roles where they are doing more than just consuming resources via technology, or using computers, devices, or websites for routine tasks. Instead, there is a focus on helping students generate their own ideas, communicate those ideas effectively in a variety of contexts, and embrace a collaborative spirit while doing so. All are available on the ISTE website, and I highlight just a few of the substandards that embody both the spirit and outcome of practicing digital diligence:

- "Students cultivate and manage their digital identity and reputation and are aware of the permanence of their actions in the digital world." (Digital Citizen, 2a)
- "Students plan and employ effective research strategies to locate information and other resources for their intellectual or creative pursuits." (Knowledge Constructor, 3a)
- "Students publish or present content that customizes the message and medium for their intended audiences." (Creative Communicator, 6d)

Also of note, the ISTE Standards for Educators (2017) encapsulate the dispositions we must embrace in order to fully enact the standards for students. Again, quoting them at length would be too much, so I highlight a few that are noteworthy in relation to literacy and encourage readers to explore them all on the ISTE website:

- "Model for colleagues the identification, exploration, evaluation, curation and adoption of new digital resources and tools for learning." (Leader, 2c)
- "Establish a learning culture that promotes curiosity and critical examination of online resources and fosters digital literacy and media fluency." (Citizen, 3b)
- "Model and nurture creativity and creative expression to communicate ideas, knowledge or connections." (Facilitator, 6d)

Combined with the NCTE definition of digital literacy, the ISTE standards provide educators with insight on how best to integrate technology into a model of collaborative, inquiry-based teaching and help their students critically evaluate media and technology too. Having recently completed the process to become an ISTE Certified Educator, I have become quite familiar with these ideas in the past 3 years. These themes align with my definition of digital diligence and provide more ideas for how we can actively promote these skills in our instruction.

NAMLE's Core Principles

Begun in 1998 as the Partnership for Media Education, evolving to the Alliance for a Media Literate America in 2001, and then becoming the National Association for Media Literacy Education in 2008 (NAMLE, n.d.), NAMLE now serves educators with a free membership and access to numerous resources. As part of their "Core Principles of Media Literacy Education" (2007), NAMLE embodies an inquiry-driven stance where students are encouraged to interrogate the messages they receive and to design their own messages in a critical, creative manner. Inviting students to be both media makers and conscientious consumers, NAMLE's proactive stance is woven throughout their core principles and the many resources they provide.

Of particular importance for the ideas behind my understanding of digital diligence, Principle 2 contends that "Media Literacy Education expands the concept of literacy to include all forms of media (i.e., reading and writing)," and Principle 6 "affirms that people use their individual skills, beliefs and experiences to construct their own meanings from media messages." As we teach our students to examine text, images, videos, maps, and other forms of media—as well as to create these types of documents—they must be aware of their own perspectives and how their own interpretations can be, during some moments, insightful, and at other times, limited. By bringing this sensibility to their own reading, listening, and viewing—as well as to the ways in which they write, speak, and visually represent their ideas—students can become more effective with their academic and personal use of media.

Like the NCTE stance on 21st-century literacies and the ISTE standards for students, NAMLE, too, embraces the idea that students should be critical consumers and creators of all media products. Though it may feel repetitive, I feel this point certainly deserves a reprise. As ELA educators, we must encourage our students to critically evaluate the technologies they use and the products that are delivered to them, all the while pushing them to create new work that demonstrates their skills at using these digital tools. This then models the kinds of mindful approaches that encapsulate the spirit of digital diligence.

OVERVIEW OF THE BOOK

As we turn toward the broad principles of digital diligence and the lessons that support this stance, I reiterate a concise definition:

> *Digital diligence* is an alert, productive stance that individuals employ
> when using technology (apps, websites, software, and devices) for
> connected reading and digital writing, characterized by empathy,
> intention, and persistence.

Throughout the book, I will work to provide ideas that can be adapted by educators and aimed toward an audience of middle and high school students. My hope is that, given any reader's own classroom context, there will be opportunities to adapt and extend the ideas presented here in many ways. Depending on the age and skill level of the students, as well as the time available to explore, I could imagine different topics being examined differently. The depth to which any individual educator may explore these ideas can be flexible, ranging from a simple introduction and awareness to several days of exploration. Here is an overview of what's ahead.

Chapter 2: Planning for Purposeful Arcs of Instruction

In Chapter 2, I will outline my thinking on what it means to teach in a *synchronous/asynchronous, real-time/anytime, both/and* world. (See the short Interlude after Chapter 1 for an introduction to these concepts.) What I mean by introducing the idea of a *purposeful arc of instruction* is something different than simply a lesson or unit plan. While there are some similarities, I want to avoid the use of *plan* as that implies a specific agenda for instruction with crystal clear learning objectives. And while having these in mind is important, the idea of an "arc of instruction" encompasses so much more than just planning what one will say and do when you are standing (or sitting) in front of students (in school, in a video call, or while planning for anytime online learning). This is about more than creating what I've started to call "digital dittos," or simply preparing an assignment sheet and posting it online. Purposeful arcs of instruction encompass several additional elements related to the ways that we reconceptualize time, topics of study, the teaching techniques we employ, and strategic uses of technology.

Then we move into Chapters 3 through 8, with topics for teaching digital diligence. As we think about the ways in which technology continues to affect our lives and our students' lives, these topics are ones we can explore as a way to introduce those dispositions of intentionality, persistence, and others. I outline a number of ideas I have explored with my own students (undergraduate, masters, and doctoral). Through my work with dozens of teachers in professional development and coaching contexts, I consider resources that could be useful for middle and high school students. We must think about all the ways in which we might work to become more aware of the history and impact of technology, as well as what we might want to do here in the present moment to better protect ourselves and our privacy as we move forward. These ideas for arcs of instruction are organized across six major themes, all of which I have explored in my writing, teaching, and professional development work in the past few years, and am pleased to be able to capture some of in these chapters.

Chapter 3: Protecting Privacy

We begin by exploring issues of privacy and why it is crucial in our "always on" world to still take measures that give us some control over our personal data. A recent series of articles from *The New York Times* (2019), "The Privacy Project," began in April 2019 with the idea that tech companies have been using our data in many ways over the years, especially since the advent of the smartphone, and while "the benefits of such advances have been apparent for years; the costs—in anonymity, even autonomy—are now becoming clearer." These benefits and costs are explored through a series of lessons that invite students to examine their own relationship with the web and use of various web-based tools. In doing so, they build a stance of digital diligence in which they are aware of the tradeoffs they are making and consciously choose to do so when the benefits do, indeed, outweigh the costs (or, at the very least, provide a reasonable tradeoff and make the use of such tools worthwhile).

Chapter 4: Maximizing Our Own Attention

The Internet is nothing if not a series of distractions. As noted throughout this introduction, humans have always faced the challenge of maintaining our focus, and the ways in which smartphones capitalize on our desire to be stimulated has, as described by the Center for Humane Technology (n.d.), given us technology tools that "are caught in a race to the bottom of the brain stem to extract human attention." We need to help students figure out how to use their own ingenuity (as well as some additional tech tools) to be focused when they need to be, and at other times to allow their minds to wander down the endless paths that the Internet offers, enjoying some of the serendipitous and wonderful things that can be found online. Working toward digital diligence requires us each to know our own strengths and weaknesses when it comes to using tech, and the topics in this section of the book help us make small moves in our daily lives that have the potential to keep us more focused.

Chapter 5: Popping Filter Bubbles and Breaking Algorithms

The algorithms that drive our lives are becoming increasingly problematic. Safiya Umoja Noble (2018), in her book *Algorithms of Oppression*, argues that "while we often think of terms such as 'big data' and 'algorithms' as being benign, neutral, or objective, they are anything but" (p. 1). Similarly, as described in his 2011 TED Talk and book of the same title, Eli Pariser (2011a, 2011b) notes that with increasing efficiency in platforms like Google and Facebook, we each live in a "filter bubble," or "your own personal, unique universe of information that you live in online." In order to move outside of these bubbles and to understand the algorithms at work in our lives, the lessons here will encourage students to see beyond what they might typically experience; moreover, I will share some ideas about how to engage in civil dialogue with others online as a part of digitally diligent practices.

Chapter 6: Understanding How Knowledge Gets Created and Circulated

Though this chapter could include a catchy title that draws in ideas of *alternative facts*, *post truth*, or the still-present term popularized in American politics *fake news*, I come at it from a different direction. Steering slightly to the side of those conversations and asking instead a question that philosophers, scientists, journalists, and others have been working on for millennia, I wonder: How do we know what we know? Or to put a slightly more modern twist on it, how do we understand the ways that different news organizations, entertainers, and social media influencers—as well as academics, officials, and other experts—create new knowledge? A scholar, senator, and ambassador, Daniel Patrick Moynihan (1927–2003), put it this way: "Everyone is entitled to his own opinion, but not to his own facts" (Moynihan, 2010). However, given our 24/7 news cycle, the question quickly moves from what we have discovered as "fact" (the who, what, when, and where) to an analysis of the why and how. Through these lessons, we ask these questions: What counts as evidence? For whom? In which context? Understanding the answers to these questions—and how to get the answers to these questions—is another aspect of building an intentional stance toward information literacy as one component of digital diligence.

Chapter 7: Extending Opportunities for Digital Writing

In addition to finding and consuming information, we must move students toward opportunities to share their own ideas. Based on a large portion of my work over the last decade, and in keeping with the spirit of digital diligence, this chapter explores openly available tools that students can use to become more critical and creative digital writers. While, yes, we can consider texting, word processing, and emailing to be core tools of digital writing (each with their own expectations related to formality of language, specificity of audience, and timeliness in terms of response), we also need to invite students to create multilayered digital compositions, rich with text as well as images, videos, maps, and hyperlinks to additional resources. Digital writing, as I described it with my coauthors in *Because Digital Writing Matters*, includes "*compositions created with, and oftentimes for reading and viewing on, a computer or other device that is connected to the Internet*" (National Writing Project, DeVoss, Eidman-Aadahl, & Hicks, 2010, p. 7; emphasis in original). The idea that we are creating texts that are meant to be consumed on-screen means we have many opportunities for helping students become more digitally diligent as authors, all the while embracing the needs of their readers, viewers, and listeners in the process of composing.

Chapter 8: Embracing Opportunities for Connected Reading

This chapter builds on my work related to reading with digital tools. We understand that reading on-screen is different than reading on the page, but exploring *exactly* what that means for our students is still up for discussion. Readers are increasingly being asked to engage in what technology journalist Clive Thompson, author of the book *Smarter Than You Think*, describes as "short take," "middle take," and "long take" forms of writing, varying their expectations and pace of reading from social media messages to blog posts and to extended, long-form journalism (Thompson, 2010, 2013). Working with students to explore these many types of reading environments—as well as different kinds of texts that can be accessed on their devices, such as ebooks and subscription databases—the goal here is to help students embrace what Kristen Hawley Turner and I have called *connected reading*, employing the mindful and social practices surrounding the use of digital texts (Turner & Hicks, 2015a, 2015b; Turner, Hicks, & Zucker, 2020). Turner, Zucker, and I have recently defined *connected reading* as

> a model of print and digital reading comprehension that conceptualizes readers' interactions with digital texts through encountering (the ways in which readers seek or receive digital texts), evaluating (the ways in which readers make judgments about the usefulness of digital texts), and engaging (the ways in which readers interact with and share digital texts). (Turner et al., 2020)

As with previous chapters, topics here provide ideas for how we might help our students use their devices for sustained, substantive engagement with texts, building their reading stamina and persistence.

Throughout each of these chapters, there will be examples of the many tools that are available for teaching our students to be mindful, to be digitally diligent. These will include tools for reading through purposeful annotation and interaction, as well as digital writing tools that use words, images, videos, data, links, maps, and other forms of media. With these tools, I will also consider the many ways in which students might be able to capture snapshots of their learning and reflect on that learning in intentional ways. As a reminder, I have a complete list of resources mentioned here available on the book's companion website—hickstro.org/digitaldiligence—and I welcome additional suggestions of tools to add to these lists. Please contact me with new items to add.

Chapter 9: Conclusion

Finally, Chapter 9 will bring our discussion of digital diligence to a close using a model for suggesting increases in particular digital literacy practices and a decrease in others. I draw the inspiration for this model from the fourth edition of Steve Zemelman, Harvey Daniels, and Arthur Hyde's book *Best Practice: Bringing Standards to Life in America's Classrooms* (2012). Using this model, I reiterate the key principles of digital diligence and offer some specific suggestions for how we can continue to innovate, even in an era of remote teaching and learning.

As we move into the next chapter of the book, "Planning for Purposeful Arcs of Instruction," I reiterate the point that, without a doubt, we live in an era of digital distraction. Numerous authors, media pundits, journalists, parents, academics, and others have spoken to the incredible challenges that we face as we prepare our students for the demands of an ever-evolving workforce and increasingly complex world. To ensure mindful practice—or what I call digital diligence—we as teachers of English language arts must move quickly to bring our pedagogy in line with the shifting expectations of society while, at the same time, adhering to the pedagogical principles that have, in the past, led our students to enhance their literacy skills, becoming critical and creative along the way.

My hope is that the ideas in the pages ahead lead us to adopt our own set of practices that bring digital diligence to our lives and, in turn, to the students we serve.

From *Synchronous* to *Real Time*; from *Asynchronous* to *Anytime*

For years, discussions of *online, blended,* and *hybrid* learning (all terms that have various meanings depending on the context in which the term is being used) have also included the terms *synchronous* and *asynchronous.* What any one educator means when saying *online, blended,* and *hybrid*—especially in an era that now has new terms such as *remote learning*—is confusing at best. As it happens, Cuban (2020a) offered an interesting footnote to one of his autumn 2020 blog posts about "remote instruction" by arguing that

> I use "remote instruction," "online instruction," and "distance instruction" rather than the noun "learning" simply because there is no body of evidence that "online learning," or similar descriptors does, indeed, benefit students.

To that end, we need to start coming to terms with, well, the terms we use to describe contemporary learning, moving beyond the words he describes above, and also words like *synchronous* and *asynchronous.*

Given that these descriptors for online learning emerged in conjunction with conversations about technology, these terms related to electronics and computers were added to describe learning events on computers. They may have been happening at the same time (synchronous) or happening as students interacted with content and activities provided by the instructor, building on a long history of correspondence courses (asynchronous). These terms, however, have always felt clunky and never really seem to capture the entirety of what happens as educators design experiences for learning when using technology in productive ways.

Instead, I have become fond of using the terms *anytime* and *real-time* learning, as introduced to me by a colleague and mentor, Renee Hobbs, in our preparation for the 2020 Summer Institute in Digital Literacy (digiuri.com). I find these terms easier to understand, conceptually, than the geekier terms we've used for so long. In addition, Hobbs has pushed my thinking on exactly what we really mean by *anytime* instruction. Part of this was a technical feature of the particular learning management system that we were using and the ways in which we developed workshops for our participants. While *real-time* instruction really did align with my existing understanding of what we would do in *synchronous* settings (while we were in a shared Zoom room to engage participants in active, collaborative learning), the ways in which we used the term *anytime* learning were different.

For instance, we are all familiar with the model where an instructor, especially in secondary and higher education, will prepare students for a lesson by asking them to read something ahead of time, will offer more insights on the content in class, and will then give some kind of homework assignment. In recent years, prerecording video lectures has become popular too, and we can ask students to watch those as a substitute for real-time instruction. This is happening more and more in K–12 with the model of "flipped learning," and especially in pandemic times as more and more teachers prepare screencasts. No surprise there, as these activities are all within the typical rhythm of instruction with which we are all familiar. Teach a lesson; have students do an assignment. It is comfortable and feels natural.

And for decades, the model of asynchronous learning fit this mold. Most of what the general public understands to be online learning, at least as I understand it, aligns with a model of asynchronous learning where it is self-paced and accessible at any given time. Thus, moving away from this entrenched model of asynchronous learning is difficult, because it also means—in some sense—that the learning is optional. Students may not *really* need to watch the video or do the reading. They can just fake their way through the learning and get on with the perfunctory assessments.

Thus, it was at a deeper level that Hobbs pushed me to think about what it is that we do when we typically move through what I call an "assign and assess" model. This is the classic model where a teacher presents something and then gives a task. Yes, there may be sharing preclass readings or activities, as well as postclass assignments that are to be turned in later, but there is little modeling, scaffolding, or collaboration. While certainly any lesson (or workshop) must have a beginning and an end—especially if it is constrained by a bell schedule in face-to-face settings—when we think about what it actually *is* we want students to do during online learning, we have some flexibility. To that end, and as a way to give adult participants in a professional development experience alternative ways to engage in the material (with some degree of choice and on their own timetable), Hobbs asked us to create *anytime* learning. With her collaborator and coauthor Julie Coiro, Hobbs outlines her extended definition of "digital learning anytime and real time," in their quick reference guide (Coiro & Hobbs, 2021).

This anytime learning was not meant to be something that our colleagues would be expected to do as they prepared for our real-time workshops (though it could be encouraged). Nor was the anytime learning meant to be homework for accountability and assessment after the real-time workshop (though, again, it could serve that purpose if necessary). Instead, the anytime materials that were provided were designed to be genuine, inquiry-driven enrichment activities. Yet, even that definition needs some explanation, after the negative connotation that "enrichment" took on in the spring of 2020. In contrast to the kinds of "enrichment activities" that educators were encouraged to offer their students in lieu of new content during the height of the pandemic and emergency remote teaching in the spring of 2020, what we typically think about when we think of enrichment is something extra that students could choose to do, or not. In this sense, enrichment was often equated with extra credit, with an option for some students to do it, should they choose, and no penalties for those who did not.

Anytime learning—as I considered it through conversations with Hobbs, Coiro, and the dozen other leaders in our summer institute—was designed to be purposeful as an inquiry-driven extension for our colleagues before, during, and/or after our real-time learning. In this sense, the anytime learning activities serve as a kind of glimpse into our own lesson planning and the thinking that has gone into an intentional instructional design. We would share additional information and insights with our learners, inviting them to explore more. In this sense, it is an option, and an enrichment, though we hope an enticing one. Rather than just being "seat time" or "homework" in another name, anytime learning was designed to be alluring and meant to spark curiosity. It really can—and should—be something that we use to prompt students' thinking, at any given time, in parallel to the learning that would happen during our real-time class sessions.

Moreover, anytime learning needs to truly be structured as an opportunity to do something at a time of one's choosing. That is, if we want students to read and be prepared for a class discussion on Monday, then they need to be informed in clear terms that they should read and prepare for discussion on Monday (and, moreover, be given the instructional support and learning tools to do so). This is homework. It is not an option, and it is meant to prepare students for learning or to reinforce ideas that have been presented.

However, if we really mean *anytime*—in the sense that students could engage in an activity before or after a real-time lesson, that they do not need to come having read a particular article or viewed a particular video before coming to class, and that they could, conceivably, gain as much value from it before or after the regular class session—then we need to make that clear. Anytime learning—in contrast to requirements or expectations around homework—is meant to be inviting. It is meant to help students extend their learning, though there is no demand that it absolutely must be done.

An example will show how I am structuring this kind of learning for a course in which I am teaching first-year undergraduates. The topic of the writing-intensive course "Our Digital Lives" provides students with opportunities to explore a number of ideas and activities that are infused with some requirements (homework) and explorations (anytime learning). That said, we can't explore everything, and I need to help my students stay focused while still helping them approach the topic in an inquiry-driven manner. I need to be clear about what they must do and what is optional.

Below is an example of a weekly announcement with expectations for real-time and anytime learning articulated. I do have specific expectations for real-time participation (a weekly Zoom meeting) and additional, required participation through an online discussion tool, Packback. These tasks fill what we would typically call "seat time," and then, for homework, students are also expected to do additional reading, viewing, and listening to other course materials. Then I offer my additional thinking that will move them toward anytime learning by providing them with more links and posing questions. Each week, these announcements are sent on Sundays, with our real-time sessions happening on Wednesday afternoons. Again, there is an expectation of required, additional learning through participation in a class discussion using Packback. Yet, I try to encourage anytime learning too, above and beyond what they are expected to do as an alternative to required seat time. With these brief segments, I highlight the instructional moves that I am making.

Announcement segment	Learning purpose

This week we will read and listen to the following:
• Read: Roose, K. (2019, June 8). The making of a YouTube radical. *The New York Times.*
  ○ This multimodal text documents the story of Caleb Cain, whom you will also hear about in Roose's podcast *Rabbit Hole,* and which we will listen to the first episode, "Wonderland" (April 16, 2020).
• Listen: Roose, K. (2020). *Rabbit Hole,* Episode 1. *The New York Times.*
  ○ The episode does contain some strong language, and if you prefer to just skim the transcript, you can do that instead. It serves as both the "content" that will fuel our class discussion this week and a model for how you might create a multimedia text for your later projects.
  ○ I encourage you to add *Rabbit Hole* to your podcast feed, as the entire series is powerful and explores additional situations where Internet users found themselves caught up in different experiences and platforms that they would have never anticipated.
• Read: Wikipedia. (2020). YouTube.
  ○ As you skim this entry, please do get a sense of the entire history of this popular service, and pay particular attention to Section 6.7 on the algorithmic design. We will be discussing this during our real-time class session.
  ○ There are nearly 600 additional references on this one Wikipedia entry. I encourage you explore at least two or three of them that might be compelling to you, as we share ongoing discussion.
	In preparation for our real-time meeting during the week, there is a mix of required learning, with the expectation that they will read the article and listen to the podcast to prepare for the real-time session. I clarify the purpose for the reading and listening task, both as content to discuss in our real-time session and as a model for what students might create later in the semester when they have choices for their own project.
	
	It is also an example of anytime learning, in the third subbullet point, as students could explore the entire series of *Rabbit Hole* podcasts, though the specific requirement of listening to the first episode is made clear.
	
	Moreover, they are asked to read the article about YouTube on Wikipedia and then invited to explore additional resources related to the topic from the many references on Wikipedia.

• As a CMU student, you have access to many resources! Be sure to activate your free account to *The New York Times,* a subscription available through CMU Libraries. You also have access to *The Wall Street Journal.*	This is anytime learning, with no expectation that students are required to sign up for either of these two digital subscriptions. Yet, by pointing out that they have free access to both a

	left-leaning and a right-leaning online newspaper, my hope is to encourage them to both take advantage of something that they are already paying for with their tuition dollars and stay more informed as news consumers.
Required participation (between midnight Sunday to midnight Saturday). Consider the ideas that Kevin Roose explores in his article and first episode of the podcast series, as well as the history of YouTube (and your own experience with it). Write an original question in our discussion forum on Packback, and respond to two classmates' questions. Feel free to build from the ideas presented in my questions below in the rest of the week's announcement.	This is required learning, an alternative to seat time. Though they can do this work at any point in the week, I do not consider this to be anytime learning, as students are participating in the discussion forum and posting in order to earn a grade.
Real-Time Participation on _____ [date]: • Join our seminar from 4:00 to 5:45 using Dr. Hicks's Zoom room.	And, this is the real-time learning component for the class. I do meet with students once a week, for a total of an hour and 45 minutes. During that time, we will engage in a discussion of the Roose article and podcast, with a "visible thinking routine" as a guide for small groups. Then we will engage in the filter bubble activity described in Topic 5.1, filling our time with purposeful instruction and collaboration.
This week, we look at the ways the Internet—and one particular site, YouTube—began to develop an algorithmic approach in the late 2000s and early 2010s, an approach that drives the modern web in ways that are both ingenious and insidious. • As you read Roose's article and listen to the podcast, what are your initial impressions of Caleb Cain? • In what ways is Cain's experience of using the Internet similar to or different from your own experience? • How have you experienced the sensation of "falling down the rabbit hole" when using technology? • Again, as you read and listen, what are your initial impressions of Guillaume Chaslot? • In what ways does Chaslot describe his initial goals for the algorithms, and his Google/YouTube team's goal to "increase the time people spend online, because it leads to more ads"? • If you want to learn even more about the Google Brain, one link from Roose's article will lead you to a deeper dive in this article from Casey Newton on *The Verge* and may raise even more questions for you.	In this segment, I am providing them with ideas for their required learning that requires them to write and post to Packback, pushing them toward more engaged anytime learning. On one level, I am simply providing them with some questions to guide their reading, which is required. Then, with the additional questions, I am also trying to get them to click on some of the links provided in the main text for the week, to more purposefully explore the topic at hand.

This is what works well for me with university undergraduates. My announcements for my online graduate students (whom I do meet with via videoconference, though not on a weekly basis) are a bit different than this. If I were teaching in the middle grades, or in high school, my expectations for regular announcements and expectations for real-time and anytime learning would, of course, be a bit different, too. Still, I would be clear to note when the real-time session would be occurring and what we would be doing, while also clearly delineating the required homework or assignments, as compared to anytime learning that students might choose to do on their own.

Rethinking both *what* we do in our instruction and *how* we do it is challenging, especially in a pandemic era. As before, we need to be clear on what we are asking students to do and how we can encourage them to learn from additional opportunities that we provide (but do not demand). Moreover, the *why* behind our teaching should remain consistent, with a clear focus on moving students into more substantive understandings of the subject area, a mastery of particular skills, and the habits of mind to move into life as confident readers, writers, and thinkers. With this in mind we consider the various kinds of activities that are well suited to take place in real-time instruction as well as required and invitational anytime learning, elaborating on a number of ideas and tools that can be useful for each through purposeful arcs of instruction.

CHAPTER 2

Planning for Purposeful Arcs of Instruction

During the pandemic that hit in the spring of 2020—and continued into the 2020–2021 academic year, as I complete this book—educators gave a great deal of thought to the ways that we typically design school-based experiences for learning (e.g., class periods and subjects, discrete lessons and units, assessments in the form of papers, projects, and tests). For decades, if not centuries, we have generally relied on a model of instruction that has students sitting in our classrooms for specific segments of time, moving through topics in a prescribed manner, performing a culminating task. Sometimes this is described as the "grammar of schooling" (Tyack & Cuban, 1995) and hints at the ways in which we design school not for curiosity but for compliance or complacency.

This model has been codified, in secondary and higher education, as the "credit hour" or "Carnegie unit." Without going into an extensive history of this system—or attempting to thoroughly analyze the benefits and drawbacks of it—I will summarize in another way. The rhythms of our school days and weeks, as well as marking periods, trimesters, and/or semesters, have all been paced by these systems. We internalize these markers—and the curriculum we think we can "cover" during these periods of time—and pace our instruction and interactions with students accordingly. We expect that students will do some things before they come to class, that they will do some things in class, and that they will do some things after class (in preparation for the next session).

There are a number of educational critics and historians who do a much better job of documenting and then picking apart these structures of schooling—how they began, why they persist, and what we can do to push back against them, especially in an age of increasing technology—including Larry Cuban (Cuban, 1986, 2001), John Taylor Gatto (Gatto, 2005, 2008), Alfie Kohn (A. Kohn, 1993), Joel Spring (Spring, 2012), Audrey Watters (Watters, 2020), and Yong Zhao (Zhao, 2009, 2012), among others. Cuban (2020a, 2020b), even in retirement, has been blogging regularly about what we might expect to see happen as schools shift to more and more remote instruction. And we have all been reminded of the ways that students who enter middle and high school can sometimes seem as if they no longer are curious, that they are going through the motions of schooling in order to simply get work done and move on to a next course in which, again, they will tread through the next set of materials, assignments, and assessments.

Without a deeper consideration of what students are being asked to do—and how we as teachers design effective instruction to get them to engage with materials that we are presenting to them—then, sadly, not much will change. Prep for class, come to class, do some homework after class. Eventually, turn in a paper or project, or take a test. Lather, rinse, repeat. These structures are so normalized that they feel natural. It is the rhythm of school, and technology largely supports this model without much in the way of offering our students any flexibility or autonomy. Again, many of the scholars noted above have documented the challenges present in the typical patterns of schooling, as it existed prior to 2020, and I encourage readers to explore those resources. Additionally, as it relates to the experiences of children who have historically been marginalized by traditional models of schooling, Cornelius Minor reminds us that there were systemic inequities in place and that, when the pandemic ends, we want those students to "go back to better" (Minor & Hicks, 2020), which includes a need for us to refocus our instructional practices on social justice and antiracist pedagogies.

Moreover, the typical model for instruction does not allow for substantive interactions and feedback. For instance, in her book *Balance with Blended Learning* (2020), English teacher and educational technology leader Catlin Tucker contends that there are many challenges with teaching in a traditional model, and a didactic approach to instruction does "not allow teachers the time or flexibility needed to give substantive feedback in the classroom" (p. 82). She provides a creative model for both responding to student needs and integrating technology through her "station rotation" model where she provides a variety of tasks and tools for students. And, as we will see below, she also provides a good taxonomy of how to think about reasons that she might use any particular type of technology tool to meet a teaching goal.

So, there is hope. Despite the need for "emergency remote teaching" (Hodges et al., 2020) that dominated the spring of 2020—and despite the idea that throughout the fall and winter we were simply moving traditional instruction online—there are many educators working to rethink both what was being taught and how it was being taught, all with new perspectives on the children and teens to whom this content was being taught. Different students react in different ways to the experience of working on a computer for much of the day, every day (and that the use of videoconferencing services like Zoom or Google Meet can offer opportunities for both creative innovation and entrenched instructional practices). So, I tried throughout 2020–2021 to move beyond conversations about the debates on teaching in *anytime* or *real-time* formats (or, for one final reminder, what has long been termed *asynchronous* or *synchronous* formats), or about limiting teacher-recorded video clips to a particular amount of time for a certain age level (like the oft-cited rule of thumb "one minute of video for one year of age"). In and of themselves, these debates seemed to me to be a bit off the mark.

To move into something more nuanced and meaningful—to genuinely reshape what it is that our students experience—will require us to move away from the typical ways in which we have been thinking about instruction, let alone what used to be labeled as *face-to-face*, *blended*, or *online* instruction. These distinctions—in an era where school can be canceled for a day or a week due to outbreaks, weather, or other factors—need to be critically examined. Teachers will still need to help students move through intentional activities and assignments, as well as to pursue their own inquiry. However, the structures we have had in place for decades are not likely to be as firmly set as they have been in the past. More important, teachers will need to provide flexible structures, model learning strategies, and inspire curiosity. They need to take advantage of the real-time interactions with students and maximize the ways in which anytime learning unfolds.

Given this context—and by working with dozens of educators across hundreds of hours of professional learning in 2020–2021—I began to think less about individual lessons or even single videoconference sessions and more about what I began to call *purposeful arcs of instruction*. Whether we are with students in face-to-face, blended, or fully online settings—or moving back and forth across these settings, or even teaching students concurrently across platforms—we need to think less about how we structure a single lesson or even a unit from a curricular/topical perspective and more about the moves we will make to get students wrestling with the materials and asking deeper questions—both anytime and real time—through required activities and assessments, and with encouragement for more self-paced, inquiry-driven learning. These arcs would have some similarities with what we typically see in a normal class period or unit of instruction, though they also have some differences, all of which we will explore next.

DEFINING A PURPOSEFUL ARC OF INSTRUCTION

Sometimes it feels as if we are stuck in a mode where we begin an activity and, one way or the other, we ensure it will fill a preset amount of time. By dialing these variables of instruction in slightly different directions, we can think about many ways to make our teaching more concentrated and meaningful. This all needs to happen within any given class session, whether face-to-face, in video class sessions, or fully online in a self-paced manner, as well as in service of the broader goals that we have. This shift in thinking about what makes instruction purposeful—as well as what makes it an arc over a set frame of time, moving beyond a typical class period—can help us. For instance, in a typical language arts course, we might see one class period where a bell ringer begins the hour, a lesson is presented, students have time to practice reading and writing skills, and then homework is assigned. This is a tidy model and what we are all used to.

Yet, teaching with digital diligence—and helping our students engage meaningfully with one another, as well as the content, across time and space—requires that we think about new ways for connecting with students at emotional and intellectual levels. This compels us to design assignments and activities that consistently push past the "remember" and "understand" stages in Bloom's taxonomy (Iowa State University

Center for Excellence in Learning and Teaching, n.d.), moving at least into the "apply" and "analyze" stages. Ideally, we would push into the "evaluate" and "create" stages over a succession of activities, especially ones in which students become producers of new content. In other words, big projects should not be saved until the end of an instructional arc. Instead, students will often be creating and sharing their work in progress, seeking feedback and making refinements.

Additionally, purposeful arcs of instructional require that students are allowed time for anytime learning that, in and of itself, is significant and inquiry driven. As noted above, this is more than just the typical kinds of homework that someone might be expected to do (read this, watch that, complete the worksheet or take the quiz). Instead, these are activities that are structured with intent, leading students toward a deeper understanding of the content while, when possible, engaging in activities that help them move to those higher levels in Bloom's taxonomy. To the extent they are able, students should be able to collaborate on these activities and have time for exploration of the topic in a manner that will help move them forward in their own understanding.

Purposeful arcs of instruction push students to try out new modes and media, both for reading and for writing, the dominant set of skills we aim to teach in ELA. Yes, we still want students to read books in print and to put pen to paper. That said, we need to acknowledge that they live mediated lives and to think about the ways they can represent what they are learning in different ways. Infographics. Podcasts. Blog posts. Wikipedia entries. Social media posts. These are all spaces in which our students can—and should—learn how to produce and publish. We want to have students use the tools in purposeful ways to express themselves and, at the same time, better understand the content they are learning.

By holding to these principles, we can create purposeful arcs of instruction that are aligned with the values of digital diligence, modeling an alert and productive stance for using digital tools, characterized by empathy, intention, and persistence. Within our control, then, are four factors: time, topic, technique, and technology. Exploring these variables is our next steps in adopting a stance of digital diligence, knowing how we can use them to shape the ebb and flow of our teaching.

THE VARIABLES IN AN ARC OF INSTRUCTION: TIME, TOPIC, TECHNIQUE, AND TECHNOLOGY

Though I am sure there are other scholars who have articulated these ideas in more distinct ways (perhaps with even more variables and in even more detail), for sake of simplicity, I will suggest here that we have four variables we can adjust in our instructional practice: the time, the topic, the teaching technique, and the technology we use. These "4Ts" allow us to think about nearly endless combinations of how we can adjust one or more of these variables in an effort to build relationships with and between students, introduce content and skills, inspire inquiry, and engage students in purposeful literacy practices.

Describing each in a bit more detail, we can consider the following:

- *Time:* How we might flex the duration of any given activity and expand (or contract) those activities within defined class sessions and across a series of real-time sessions and required work, as well as deliberately structured anytime learning activities.

- *Topic:* How any given topic can be explored at length or can be covered briefly. The extent to which we have students engage with any one topic hinges on many factors, including the curriculum and assessments determined by our schools; perceptions from colleagues, administrators, and parents; and our own interests as educators.

- *Teaching technique:* How we choose to structure any particular set of interactions with and among students in individual, small-group, or whole-class instruction. There are various ways that we can think about techniques for active, collaborative learning, as well as for individual reflection.

- *Technology:* How we choose to use any given tool in a manner that will allow students to engage more deeply with the topic or skills we are aiming to teach. Sometimes technologies are used to enhance the experience that students have learning specific content and skills; sometimes the technology allows us to perform a task in a more effective manner.

In order to better understand the ways these variables can be shifted, I will use Catlin Tucker's frames for designing meaningful online activity, both real time and anytime. Before doing so, a quick note on how we maximize the time that we have available during video class sessions. We need to realize that sometimes, in real-time learning sessions, we don't need to do all the talking. In fact, even though there might be awkward (or intended) silences, there are times that no one needs to be talking. Sometimes we can have students simply be in the same virtual space and work quietly (much as we would in school). With the expectation that they have already carved out time in their life for our class, at that moment they can use that time for reading, writing, or other reflection. As educators, we often feel such a need to "fill" space, especially in virtual rooms. However, we also know that just being in community with one another can be powerful too. So, I encourage educators to think about the moments of silence—time to read, to write, to think, or to let a question linger—and how to use them strategically.

BEYOND SYNCHRONICITY AND SEAT TIME: PLANNING FOR MEANINGFUL LEARNING IN REAL TIME AND AT ANYTIME

To describe different kinds of learning activities that are best suited for different modalities, Catlin Tucker (2020b) offers a list of activities that can be offered to students, both asynchronously and synchronously. In the next two sections, I will build from Tucker's list and consider a few tools that can support these instructional strategies, though I am going to return to the language first introduced in the Interlude above, shared by Renee Hobbs and Julie Coiro: real time and anytime (Coiro & Hobbs, 2021).

Moving beyond typical conceptions of seat time and homework—as well as the structures of didactic pedagogy—we can also offer our students opportunities for additional learning. In doing so, we provide our students with meaningful real-time interactions, as well as opportunities for anytime, additional learning, helping them gain deeper insights into a topic. If I want to engage students in the kinds of digitally diligent practices that I am describing in this book—an alert, productive stance toward the use of digital tools characterized by empathy, intention, and persistence—then I need to model that kind of thinking for them through the lessons that I build for them.

This boils down to three kinds of learning that I expect my students to engage in that would vary and reflect some expectations for typical "seat time" we would see happen if they were sitting in a classroom at a specific time.

- First, we have required learning in a typical classroom period or a video class session. There have always been—and will continue to be—times and places we can engage students with real-time learning. We must be able to take advantage of these precious minutes to fully engage students in a thoughtful exploration of a topic, lead interactive modeling, or engage in other instructional modes that encourage collaborating, questioning, and substantive thinking.

- In addition, there is still required homework, typically completed by individuals and submitted for evaluation. These tasks, ideally, are more than just simple questions answered at the end of a reading selection or by reviewing flashcards. Instead, they should be engaging and meaningful in the sense that they take advantage of technology and, to the extent that the content and products might demand, invite collaboration. This serves, in some ways, as a supplement to seat time and would genuinely extend learning in meaningful ways.

- Finally, there is anytime learning. This would be the supplemental learning, the kinds of learning that we would want students to follow through with because they are interested and engaged, not simply because they "have to." As I have tried to demonstrate through my own example with college undergraduates described above, this further kind of learning is one that we cannot demand of our learners, instead encouraging them to pursue their own inquiry by offering invitations.

With all this in mind, I will soon explore the ideas that Tucker proposed in her blog post in greater detail, suggesting ways we can use a variety of tech tools to plan for purposeful arcs of instruction. This is about more than just tools—it is about instructional scaffolding for students too. Certainly, there is an art to teaching students in face-to-face settings and moving students forward through a series of productive activities that lead them to deeper learning. Yet, in these settings, often we offer instructions and students can then ask—either by raising their hands or by raising their eyebrows—when they have questions. In these interactions, we provide them with clarification, and they are usually able to move along quickly with their work. However, when we do not see them face-to-face, we do not get that immediate feedback, and it is difficult to adjust our instruction on the fly in a video call, or by interpreting their thoughts and concerns via email or instant messages.

Thus, before creating real-time and anytime learning experiences (both required and optional) with students—and to reiterate the main goals of being digitally diligent in the ways we use technology tools—I encourage us to consider the kinds of assignments and activities we can design for students to help them become more (as follows):

- *Alert,* in the sense that we help them understand more about the websites they visit and the programs they use, as well as what those websites and programs know about them from the user data that they provide;

- *Productive,* in the sense that we encourage them to use digital tools to create digital products that are more robust than what they could typically do with paper and pencil, and that they interact with classmates and share their work with wider audiences beyond the classroom;

- *Empathetic,* in the sense that we move them toward finding a variety of perspectives, to listen actively, and to engage with others in ways that build and maintain positive relationships;

- *Intentional,* in the sense that we remind them to approach the use of their devices from a mindful perspective, recognizing the amount of time they are using the devices and the ways in which their device usage patterns affect their overall health and well-being; and

- *Persistent,* in the sense that we support them as they examine sources in more detail, explore alternative perspectives, and represent their ideas in complex, nuanced ways (as compared to superficial web searching and highly scripted projects).

Thus, in the sections below, I elaborate on Tucker's list of activities and suggest some specific ways in which they might be used for anytime learning, as either required or additional activities. As a reminder, various tools mentioned here are also found on the book's companion website (hickstro.org/digitaldiligence).

PLANNING FOR MEANINGFUL ARCS OF INSTRUCTION WITH ANYTIME (ASYNCHRONOUS) ACTIVITIES

As noted above, Catlin Tucker has provided many insights into her own classroom structures, relying heavily on a station rotation model for keeping students engaged in longer segments of real-time instruction during a block schedule-style class period. To do this, she designs some activities that are largely independent and could, conceivably, be accomplished outside of normal class time (though, to her credit, she also structures some well-thought collaborative exercises for her students during these particular station rotations).

In her August 2020 blog post, Tucker describes eight broad categories of asynchronous learning activities that she typically builds into these stations (and offers as homework) that can include the following (which I number here, for clarity, though they were not numbered or prioritized in her original blog post):

1. Reading and taking notes
2. Watching videos for both instruction and/or analysis
3. Listening to podcasts
4. Exploring teacher-curated resources
5. Engaging in online discussion
6. Practicing and reviewing
7. Researching and exploring
8. Reflecting and documenting learning

Each of these broad set of activities merits some additional exploration—as well as a description of tools that can be used to enact them—as learners work during real-time class sessions as well as through required, additional learning. Some lend themselves to a more structured, required approach that can be used for homework, whereas others lend themselves to more open-ended exploration, inviting authentic anytime learning. By exploring each, we can see different possibilities, and think about the tech tools that could be used to bring a more mindful approach to reading, writing, and engaging in other literacy practices.

1. Reading and Taking Notes

Actively engaging in the process of reading and note taking has been a fundamental skill for students since the invention of written language. We use writing as a tool to process what we have read, whether in a few quick notes in the margin of a text or through a deeper exploration of ideas where we form our own questions and response on a separate page (or screen). However, educators know we cannot just ask students to read without providing them some strategies for doing so, nor can we expect students to take notes without some models or frameworks to guide them. For any reading task, we want students to be continually mindful of their goals and to center their annotation and questioning strategies on those goals. For instance, note-taking strategies like Cornell Notes (two columns where a summary of the content is captured in the left column and an analysis and interrogation of the content is captured in the right column) or the "SQ3R" (survey, question, read, recite, and review) can be useful when performed with intention.

There are many lists of additional comprehension strategies that could be cited here, though some of the ideas from Beers and Probst's "notice and note" books with the "stances" and "signposts" (Beers & Probst, 2012, 2015) have gained traction in recent years. A web search for reading strategies will yield dozens of other ways to help students infer, question, and summarize, among other skills. There are many additional reading and note-taking strategies that can be employed, depending on the nature of the reading and the kinds of analysis a learner is hoping to apply to that text. In this spirit, we can use a number of tools to engage in annotation across digital spaces, framed with the idea that simply taking random notes, without purpose, is likely to become just a distraction to reading, if not just simply futile. We want our students to approach the task of reading with intention and a purposeful set of strategies.

For Reading

When reading ebooks, there are many built-in tools that allow us to resize and recolor the text, to quickly search through and navigate across the pages, and to find definitions of unfamiliar words. Tools like this are available as browser extensions as well and can help make the process of reading on-screen, particularly on the web, a more enjoyable and less distracting experience. For instance, tools to support clearer views are built into many browsers (Safari, Edge, Firefox, Opera), and extensions like Mercury Reader, Reader View, Just Read, or BeeLine Reader can be added to Chrome.

If students require additional support for reading and would prefer to have the text read aloud, there are other tools that can be helpful. One of the most popular tools, Read&Write, has a limited, "freemium" version that—when installed as a Google Chrome extension—will give users the option to have the contents of a webpage read aloud. Similarly, with access to Microsoft's suite of tools, their Immersive Reader offers similar functionality, including the clearer views of text noted above and the read-aloud functions like Read&Write.

For Annotation

There are different types of annotation tools, such as Hypothes.is, that allow annotation of existing webpages as a "layer" on top of the page. As a web-based tool, Hypothes.is provides an open-source option to "enable sentence-level note taking or critique on top of classroom reading, news, blogs, scientific articles, books, terms of service, ballot initiatives, legislation and more" (Hypothes.is, n.d.). Similarly, there are tools like Kami and Edji that allow for collaborative annotation, yet they are used specifically for shared PDFs. Also, there are tools like NowComment for importing materials into a new document that can then be shared and annotated.

From another perspective, there are programs such as OneNote and Evernote that allow users to import and annotate a variety of formats, including text, images, and PDFs. While the free versions of these tools are limited, many schools have subscriptions to Office 365 and, with that, have access to OneNote. With these kinds of tools, students can create—and share—ongoing "notebooks" of materials where annotation can continue to happen seamlessly across devices. These annotations can take the form of typed text, handwritten text (with a stylus), and audio comments.

2. Watching Videos for Both Instruction and/or Analysis

Much like reading and taking notes, we can ask students to watch videos as a way to be exposed to new information, gain insight on materials with which they are already familiar, or to analyze and critique these materials as part of disciplinary inquiry. For instance, a TED Talk curated through TED-Ed or a video from Crash Course could serve as an introduction to a topic, or students could watch scenes from a feature film or documentary to engage in analysis and critique. With an abundance of freely available content—and the ability to easily create one's own video content—there is no lack of material available.

At one level, we can have students watch video content with the intention of basic levels of interactivity. Tools like EdPuzzle and PlayPosit allow educators to layer on quiz questions to existing videos (or videos that an educator can create). These quizzes can provide students with immediate feedback and, if the settings are adjusted appropriately, can force students to rewatch a segment of a video if the answer is incorrect. In this sense, these kinds of interactive elements do provide students with entry-level engagement on video content.

To encourage even more effective viewing, annotation, and interaction with video, we can invite students to use tools such as NowComment, Vialogues, and Video Ant to engage in threaded discussions on video content. Each of these tools allows a user to pick a point on the video timeline and insert a marginal comment. Much like what we would expect to see with comments showing up alongside a word-processed document, these comments on the video have a specific marker that shows where the comment was inserted, and the threaded discussion appears in a pane to the side. Students can then carry on a dialogue in which they share their analysis, critique, and questions.

From another angle, individual students could clip and annotate a video using a Chrome extension like Reclipped, or a separate web service like Timelinely. These tools allow users to put comments on a particular video, either privately or publicly, and then to share that annotated video. They can then share these videos with classmates, as well as the teacher, for further conversation. For all these viewings tasks, we again want to provide students with critical perspectives that they can bring. For general strategies about viewing and interpreting other messages, we can draw from the work of Renee Hobbs (Hobbs, 2006, 2011) to examine the news media and advertising, and for specifics related to the study of film, John Golden (Golden, 2001, 2006) provides useful strategies for us to consider with both cinematic and documentary productions.

3. Listening to Podcasts

In addition to viewing videos, we can also ask students to listen to existing content in the form of podcasts, as Tucker suggests, as well as audiobooks. Of course, the goal for moving to an aural format is not that it is simply a convenient substitute they can listen to (in lieu of paying close attention to the words on the page). Instead, we want students to think about both the words being spoken (read) and the ways in which they are being spoken. For instance, when a narrator invokes various voices to bring characters to life, we can discuss these choices with students and have them think about the ways that the narrator's tone and pacing contributes to character development. Both the National Public Radio (NPR, 2018) and *The New York Times* (J. Hicks, Winnick, & Gonchar, 2018) have each produced an entire guide for students to create podcasts, with many resources that are useful for listening to podcasts too.

With podcasts, given that there are usually many people being interviewed as part of the production, and sometimes additional audio footage—not to mention music and sound effects—all of this is layered into the final composition. Inviting students to listen with a critical ear can help them think about these rhetorical moves and their overall effectiveness. Some are as simple as a person talking by themselves and posting the recording, though many—both amateur and professional—are of higher production value. For instance, the first season of the podcast *Serial*, which documented a murder mystery of a teenage girl, was a hit production that caught the ear of many English teachers in 2014, reported by Sarah Koenig (2014).

With more and more podcasts being produced all the time, there are many other series that could be equally as compelling. For podcasts, there are some tools that allow users to access premium content, and one, Listenwise, is designed specifically for students. Founded by a former producer for NPR, Listenwise structures the listening experience with interactive transcripts and lessons (similar to the way that Lexile-level changing websites works for articles).

For audiobooks, there are, of course, subscription services like Audible. Yet, it is worth noting that many local and state libraries have robust online lending libraries, including audiobooks. The Libby app, for instance, has become a useful way to discover audiobooks available in one's local library collection, and to begin listening immediately. Recently, I learned about Libro.fm, a service that promotes independent bookstores and invites educators to get early access to contemporary audiobooks. There is also LibriVox, a site dedicated to making audio versions of all literature available in the public domain. More of these tools are explored in detail in Chapter 8.

4. Exploring Teacher-Curated Resources

As a way for us to keep track of our wanderings on the web, there are many tools that can help us make note of resources, including using bookmarks within our browser, or copying and pasting information into a separate document. This is helpful for us, as individuals, as a way to document and then easily retrieve the resources we find most useful. Additionally, there are a number of browser extensions that can help us manage—and even share—lists of links with other users. These curated lists of materials—sometimes described as *learning playlists*—have the potential to help students engage in more inquiry-driven work. By providing context and guiding learners, these collections can be useful, though we need to stay on top of them so they do not become unruly assemblages of links without context, even for the most diligent among us.

To assist us with this challenge, many browser extensions abound, including cloud-based options like Diigo, Papaly, and many more. Also, some browsers allow users to sync their bookmarks from desktop to laptop to mobile devices using their own cloud services (like Apple's Safari and iCloud integration). Moreover, there are other ways to curate and share that can be both easy to distribute and more visually appealing, in a Pinterest-like manner. Two in particular that have become popular among educators are Padlet and Wakelet.

Padlet, originally called WallWisher, is an online corkboard-style tool that allows users to quickly share sticky-note-style posts on a flexibly formatted wall. Each post can include content that ranges from text—added by the user—to hyperlinks and images, as well as embedded videos and images, voice or video recordings, a drawing, or even a location on a Google Map. In addition to allowing for easy collaboration by having users click a "plus button" to make their own post, Padlet's many wall formats include the classic "wall" look (like bricks that stack in order), as well as options like an open canvas, a stream that runs top to bottom, a grid, and a shelf. There are also options for adding content as points on a map and a timeline. In short, there are countless ways to curate content in a Padlet wall (and to invite students to share and respond to that content too).

Another service for curating and sharing materials (as well as inviting collaborators to do so) is Wakelet. With the ability to make a single resource, or a collection of resources that are tied together, Wakelet provides users with the option to annotate their materials and bring together links, images, videos, and more. As a clear, concise way to categorize materials, individually or as a group, Wakelet can be useful for organizing content so students can move through it in a sequential manner. These resources are then accessible by a hyperlink that can be shared with students and can also be accessed in the Wakelet mobile app. Returning here to the broader themes of creating meaningful anytime learning, we again need to keep in mind that asking students to peruse a curated list of resource could be part of a required homework task, or it could be part of an encouraging, inviting space that students would choose to explore on their own.

Another potential tool to help ensure that these curated lists actually become meaningful lessons comes in the form of HyperDocs. Described as "a transformative, interactive Google Doc replacing the worksheet method of delivering instruction" (Hyper-Docs, n.d.), HyperDocs were developed by Lisa Highfill, Kelly Hilton, and Sarah Landis (Highfill et al., 2016). With the goal that students move through a series of steps that lead them into more substantive learning, HyperDocs are typically built in Google Docs or Slides and distributed to students through a learning management system (LMS), as a "viewable" document for copying, or pushed out as a "forced copy." Then students work on the HyperDoc, moving through the tasks and exploring the curated resources, sometimes on their own and sometimes in collaboration with others. Well-designed HyperDoc lessons also encourage students to explore and create with other digital tools. Again, the idea here is that teachers create a curated list of resources that students can then use to learn more about a topic in a flexible, inquiry-driven manner.

5. Engaging in Online Discussion

Another of Tucker's points for asynchronous interaction is in the oft-maligned online discussion forum. In thinking about the many tools for online discussion, most LMSs have built-in discussion board tools that allow users to post their own ideas and respond in a threaded manner. Most LMSs have discussion forums with "WYSIWYG" (or "what you see is what you get") editing tools that allow for formatting like bold and italics, lists, hyperlinks, and even embedded media. However, it is likely that most teachers do not require—or even encourage—students to use these additional digital writing tools to make their discussion forum posts more nuanced and complex.

For instance, having students create and share their response can be extended by asking them to include a video or visual from a reputable source. Teaching them how to cite that material in a typical MLA or APA format, or to even put a hyperlink in the document leading out to a resource they are using to support their own claims, we extend what it is that we are asking students to actually *do* with a discussion board. This is more than just a quick post and reply; instead, it can be an opportunity for engaging students in substantive digital writing. By simply making use of the WYSIWYG editing tools available in the discussion forums, we can invite them to be more productive with their writing and thinking.

Another possibility for ongoing, anytime discussion can come through "back-channel" conversations. Tools for these kinds of conversations are typically ones that can be used for a chat-style interaction. While there are certainly options for using chat functions within videoconference systems like Zoom, WebEx, or Google Meet, there are websites and applications that are built for these kinds of interactions. For instance, tools like YoTeach, Backchannel Chat, and MIT's Unhangout allow educators to create persistent chat spaces, ones that will not disappear at the end of a web conference call. Other apps like Voxer, GroupMe, Signal, WhatsApp, and Slack allow for these conversations to be shared easily on mobile devices, as well as via the web.

In short, class discussions do not need to happen only in typical discussion forums and for limited periods of time; instead, they can be robust, ongoing dialogues. Some instructors use these types of discussions as completely casual chats, without any specific expectations or demands for participation. They could also be informal, ongoing conversations that help students stay connected across class sessions. Other instructors may choose to document student participation in these forums as a part of course assessment, though we must balance these with opportunities for informal, ongoing dialogue too.

Also, it is worth noting that we can certainly use these chats during synchronous instruction. As we are providing instructions, we might encourage students to ask questions in the ongoing, persistent chat, so we can address them aloud and even post a response in the chat. Similarly, we might pause instruction and ask them to jot some ideas or questions about the content in the ongoing chat. And, though I can't recall who first introduced the idea to me in a video conference call, the idea of a "chat waterfall" is a strategy where students type their response in the chat room but hold off on hitting "enter" to post it for a few moments, allowing everyone to type in their response and then sharing them all at once. In short, discussions can happen both in class and beyond, even—and perhaps especially—during real-time instruction.

6. Practicing and Reviewing

Practice and review are typically tasks that can rely on "skill and drill" style studying: quizzes, flashcards, matching, fill in the blank, and other similar tasks. In most cases, these types of tasks stay at the lower levels of Bloom's taxonomy such as remembering and understanding, though a well-crafted multiple-choice question could, on its own, potentially push students' thinking into application, analysis, or evaluation. Also, when provided with a compelling, complex question, multiple-choice questions can be formulated in a manner that invites students to offer a response and compare their ideas and opinions on a single idea to those of others in the class. There are a number of formative assessment tools, including Formative (sometimes referred to as GoFormative, due to the site's URL), Socrative, Kahoot, GimKit, and Quzizz, all of which can be used to move beyond simple recall.

Similarly, educators can build lessons in Nearpod or Pear Deck, tools that allow questions to be layered into slideshows. In doing so, these companies have encouraged us to think about how we might bring some interactivity to a traditional slideshow-based lecture. With tools like Nearpod or Pear Deck, an educator can build a multiple-choice question, a continuum or "slider" style question, a space where students can draw or type a response, and many other functions. These tools were built to engage students in real-time presentations, though recent adaptations have allowed educators to now create student-facing versions of the lessons that can be taken at a student's own pace.

Again, while many of these tools generally stay closer to the lower levels of Bloom's taxonomy, there are ways to encourage higher-order thinking with multiple-choice questions, often by allowing additional time for students to really explore them. Rather than constructing a question that could be easily answered in a few seconds and tests a students' "understanding" level of Bloom's taxonomy, we can create questions that force students to slow down, reason through the alternatives, and choose an appropriate answer. For more on constructing good multiple-choice questions that, in turn, can be created in one of the online tools noted above, the Vanderbilt University Center for Teaching has a succinct article on "Writing Good Multiple Choice Test Questions," which contends that multiple-choice questions have many strengths when assessing student learning (Brame, 2012). "The key to taking advantage of these strengths," the article goes on to argue, "is construction of good multiple-choice items."

For instance, in a typical quiz, we might ask, "Which of the following is not a literary device?" If we were to ask a question like this, it would not really assess much in terms of what students actually know about the application of literary devices, and it is framed in the negative, which can be confusing. In contrast, if we were to provide a brief passage from a literary text we had been reading, and then ask students to identify both a segment that was an example of a literary device and the kind of literary device that segment exemplified, we could more accurately assess what they know. Constructing these kinds of questions takes time and requires that educators themselves continue to think critically and carefully about the materials they are teaching, as well as skillful ways to engage student in questions on those subjects. This is challenging, yet good for us as we continue to think and rethink our content. Relying only on flashcard-style games and interactive slide decks with multiple-choice questions is not enough. We need to conscientiously craft these quizzes in a manner that will push our students' thinking further, and truly take advantage of the opportunity to share these quizzes online in both anytime and real-time learning.

7. Researching and Exploring

Especially pertinent for additional learning, we know that inviting students to research and explore topics on their own can be a meaningful experience. However, we also need to teach students effective strategies for engaging in the process of research and keeping track of what they have discovered. Just as there are many tools for searching, there are also many tools for keeping track of those explorations in addition to the bookmarking tools noted above.

Of course, foremost in search information and strategy, Google's own Search Education resources are robust and include activities for individuals to engage in "power searching" as well as lesson plans at the beginning, intermediate, and advanced levels (Google in Education, n.d.). The lessons include options for choosing appropriate search terms, interpreting the search results, and evaluating source credibility. While slightly dated (as the lesson still references the ISTE National Educational Technology Standards for students, pre-2016), the lessons and activities are still applicable. As another option, the "Power Searching with Google" course has been recently updated on Code Spaces (Code Spaces, 2020).

An additional, recent set of resources for critical online reasoning and search strategies can be found with the Stanford History Education Group's (SHEG) Civic Online Reasoning materials (SHEG, n.d.), developed from the research of Sam Wineburg and his team (Wineburg & McGrew, 2017). With lessons on "click restraint," "lateral reading," and discerning sponsored content from other search results, among dozens of others, the materials offered here provide teachers and students with additional critical perspectives on search strategies they may not get from search companies themselves. Another pair of resources that align with the SHEG curriculum is Mike Caulfield's openly available ebook *Web Literacy for Student Fact-Checkers* (Caulfield, 2017b), which contains similar strategies and builds on the SHEG work, and the series of videos from Crash Course, hosted by John Green, entitled "Navigating Digital Information." All of these resources warrant further attention and could, in and of themselves, become a series of lessons.

As students navigate through their searches, they should also use web-based tools to document what they have found. It has never been enough to say that "I found it on Google" and call that an adequate citation. There are, instead, many tools we can help our students learn how to use in order to keep track of where they have been. Even when returning to scan through our search histories, we are not always likely to find a specific source that we were once looking at. In order to be digitally diligent, and to keep track of our sources, we can capitalize on tools like the ones mentioned above, including Diigo and Papaly for bookmarking as well as Padlet and Wakelet for more visual curation.

Another tool for curation, Mozilla's Pocket can also be useful. It was previously named "Read It Later" before a rebranding to the less obvious and more metaphorical name, suggesting the idea of putting a reading into one's pocket for safekeeping. With an app for mobile devices as well as extensions that work within web browsers, Pocket can help one curate materials and (even when off-line) go back to read them at a later time. Teaching our students to curate—that is, adding a summary or comment on a key quote, not just bookmarking—is yet another digitally diligent skill that will carry onward from ELA courses. Understanding how to use these tools, we can help students grow from being someone who is simply surfing and stumbling across the web to being a strategic searcher and curator (Turner et al., 2020; Turner & Hicks, 2015a, 2015b).

In order to maximize those curated collections in an academic sense, we also need to teach students how to turn a bookmarked or curated website into a full, academic citation. There are many tools that help convert online materials into more formal MLA, APA, Chicago, or other styles of academic citations. However, many of these services are laden with advertisements or based on a subscription model (and students can no longer access them once out of school). Additionally, while they may seem like a viable alternative, tools that are built into word processors—including the citation feature that has existed in Word for some time and a similar function that was introduced in Google Docs in 2020—do not provide users with flexible options for accessing and transferring their citations into other spaces. To that end, I strongly discourage use of those tools for citation management, as they are not persistent and transferrable.

Instead, I encourage teachers and students to make use of two free, openly available tools from the Corporation for Digital Scholarship: their standalone program Zotero and their online bibliography generator ZoteroBib. As described on their home page, "Zotero is a free, easy-to-use tool to help you collect, organize, cite, and share research" (Corporation for Digital Scholarship, n.d.-b) and has been in continual development since 2006. Additionally, it is open source and does not collect private information from users. With a browser extension installed, users can find articles, books, videos, podcasts, and other sources online, and quickly click a button to save the metadata from the web-based source into a new entry for their Zotero library. They can also save notes with each Zotero entry, and this is a space where I will often copy and paste quotes from the reading so I can search for—and then cite—key ideas later on. Granted, the use of the full Zotero program works best with Windows or Mac machines, as it is a standalone program that runs on those devices (though not Chromebooks). Still, there is a web-based integration with Google Docs and Zotero.org that could be worth exploration, especially for students in high school who are pursuing longer research projects.

As an alternative, in 2018, the Zotero team introduced a web-based tool that could serve as an quick way to create citations and would compete with many of the ad-driven or subscription-based tools that are popular in schools. This tool, Zotero Bibliography, or ZoteroBib, is completely web based (Stillman, 2018). Students can capture a URL, a DOI, an ISBN, or some other data about a source and try to have ZoteroBib search for it, or they can create new entries from scratch. With numerous options for entering bibliographic information in the form of articles, books, podcasts, films, and more, the ZoteroBib interface provides helpful reminders for students about the kinds of bibliographic information they should be looking for from their sources. Once complete, there are easy options for copying/pasting the bibliography or exporting it as a rich text file (RTF) so students can easily put their alphabetized list of sources in their research paper as a final set of references.

The entire process of examining and exploring one line of inquiry through a web search quickly becomes a multifaceted, nuanced, and often complex milieu of overlapping tasks. Again, it is not as simple for students as saying they found sources from a web search; instead, this citation process is about encouraging them to move into lateral reading and deeper inquiry, documenting their sources along the way. This, in and of itself, is an act of digital diligence, demanding that students use a variety of skills in a deliberate and sustained manner.

8. Reflecting and Documenting Learning

With devices in our pockets that now serve as cameras, audio recorders, and scanners, the opportunities to document and reflect upon one's learning are nearly endless. For instance, I have watched my own children many times during remote learning pull out their phones and snap a picture of a worksheet to upload and share with their teachers. However, this is a very low-level cognitive task as we consider levels of Bloom's taxonomy and what we might want our students to be able to do when engaged in metacognition and reflection. With tools like Flipgrid and Seesaw—which allow students to easily snap pictures, record videos, and even record screencasts to share their work—teachers are able to build in activities on a regular basis for engaging in this kind of metacognitive behavior.

Rather than just making a scan of a worksheet, a student could be asked to take a picture of a piece of writing that they created by hand in their journal—or a screencast of a piece of writing on the screen—and share it within a Flipgrid discussion. In addition to providing peer review to others, students could also receive timely, targeted feedback from their teacher in order to make revisions to the piece. Once the piece is completed, the teacher could offer some reflective prompts that the students could then use to record a brief video reflection. We can also invite students to practice and review by sharing their own thinking through screencast recordings where they demonstrate a specific skill. These kinds of formative measures of learning would be appropriate at many stages in a lesson cycle.

Another way to reflect on learning could be through website-based portfolios. With options for creating individual webpages using Adobe Spark or entire sites using Google Sites, Weebly, Wix, or Canva, students could generate an ongoing collection of materials—as well as written or recorded reflections on those materials—in the form of a digital portfolio. Recently, I have begun to see student portfolios in the form of slide decks, and with free templates from sites like SlidesCarnival, SlidesMania, and Slidesgo, these options are becoming more dynamic as well. The goal for documenting learning in a portfolio, however—no matter what tool is chosen—must remain focused on substantive growth, not merely showcasing the very best work. When we invite students to share artifacts of their learning and to reflect on that learning in text, speech, or image, we want to ensure they are using the opportunity as a genuine exploration of where they have been and where they want to go, as well as to have an artifact that provides a moment for celebration (T. Hicks & Schoenborn, 2020).

With any of these anytime activities, we must provide instructional scaffolding and support—sometimes even real-time support as students are in the process of working on these activities—all as a way to encourage meaningful learning. These are not just alternatives to traditional "drill and skill" homework assignments, nor are they large projects that are tossed at students without much direction. Instead, all of these activities we provide for them in anytime learning must be designed intentionally, just as we would those that occur during real-time learning. We can move students into conversation with their peers and producing work for a broader audience. By bringing the same mindset in our instructional design to both sets of activities, we can ensure that students have a consistent experience in our courses, especially as they move across face-to-face, hybrid, and fully online modalities.

PLANNING FOR MEANINGFUL ARCS OF INSTRUCTION WITH REAL-TIME (SYNCHRONOUS) ACTIVITIES

As we have adapted to the new language and mindsets of pandemic pedagogy, one term seems to be almost strange in our need to redefine it: class time. For hundreds of years, "class time" happened when students gathered in a physical space with a teacher. Of course, this has shifted quite a bit over the years with individual tutorials, correspondence courses, and, in the past two decades, online learning. And, as noted above, there are opportunities to make these kinds of anytime learning quite robust. Still, our notions of what constitutes "class time" has largely centered on the idea of one group of people sitting in desks or at tables while another one stands in front of them. This has happened—and likely will continue to happen—in a variety of contexts, for decades to come, though the pandemic of 2020–2021 has accelerated the ways in which we think about how, exactly, class time can happen. Beyond the *how* of real-time learning, we also need to think more carefully about the *why*.

In this section, we consider what happens when we gather students in a shared space, even if some are in school, some are at home, and all may be mediated by a videoconference room with a chat box on the side. Variously called *concurrent* or *hybrid flexible* (sometimes abbreviated as "hyflex") classrooms (Ladd, 2020), the idea has been around for quite some time. I recall in the early 1990s when I was in high school, students could take Japanese language courses by going to a particular computer lab in the school building and watching a teacher from another building be televised on the main screen while they worked on their lessons. In college, one of the lecture courses I took was broadcast on campus television concurrently, and I only ever went to an actual classroom on the days of the exams. Also, this kind of simultaneous participation in a live class session stands in contrast to many models of online learning that are offered *only* as asynchronous experiences. For instance, in Michigan, our state's main virtual learning provider prides itself on noting that all of its courses are asynchronous, and a 2011 press release from the governor at the time touted the goal of "Anytime, Any Place, Any Way, Any Pace" learning (Wurfel, 2011), meaning that learning would be decidedly asynchronous. So, this set of trends and expectations leaning against synchronicity in online learning is not new. For many, learning online has been lonely.

What is new, however, is that the ability for students to connect to the classroom, in real time, has become much simpler. While, yes, there is still a digital divide in which many students are struggling to have adequate access to devices and high-speed Internet, one of the net results of the COVID-19 pandemic is that many districts have worked industriously to put devices (and, if needed, hotspots) in the hands of most students across the country. Disparities still exist, yet I would argue that we are as close to ubiquitous access in the K–12 world as we have ever been. With that, we can now have a teacher present in the classroom with some students while additional students are participating via videoconferencing (Zoom, WebEx, Google Meet, or another similar tool). These sessions, for better or worse, are sometimes being recorded too (which can be seen as an intrusive form of surveillance on teachers or as a way in which to help students who may have been absent or needed extra help the opportunity to watch the recording later). Whether the teacher is in a classroom—or broadcasting from home—the point is clear: We can gather students together in real time, online, and we need to use those precious minutes in purposeful ways.

This mainstreaming of the real-time, video-based learning phenomenon that is going on now—which had been happening in isolated pockets and in different ways for decades—is one additional component that we must keep in mind as we consider what it means to offer real-time instruction. It is quite likely that, even after the pandemic subsides, many students may choose not to return to the classroom. As one eighth-grade student, Veronique Mintz, summed up in an opinion piece for *The New York Times* in the spring of 2020, she did not miss any number of disruptions:

> Talking out of turn. Destroying classroom materials. Disrespecting teachers. Blurting out answers during tests. Students pushing, kicking, hitting one another and even rolling on the ground. This is what happens in my school every single day.
> You may think I'm joking, but I swear I'm not. (Mintz, 2020)

So, whatever "class time" might continue to look like in the foreseeable future, to offer a string of clichés that might best sum up the state of students "Zooming in" rather than sitting there in person, we can say that the cat is out of the bag, the genie is out of the bottle, and the horse has left the barn. In other words, teachers are going to need to think critically, creatively, and carefully about instructional design for every live class session they offer, as these classes could include students sitting in front of them in their rooms as well as joining from afar. Even more so than before, we need to structure real-time learning in productive ways.

Returning to Tucker (2020) again, she provides a list of learning activities that could happen during a class session (which includes a continuation of the numbering from earlier, meant for clarity and, like before, not necessarily to indicate any priority):

9. Building community and relationships
10. Leading interactive sessions by providing instructional modeling
11. Differentiating instruction for small groups
12. Personalizing instruction and providing individual coaching
13. Guiding practice and specific applications
14. Facilitating conversation
15. Fostering collaboration
16. Providing real-time feedback on work in progress

In a manner similar to the segment above on asynchronous tools, each of these activities also merits additional exploration. Notably, the explanations offered here do not focus on tools—in contrast to the prominence they're given in the segments above about anytime learning, which requires using a tool, even at a very basic level, to engage students. When we think about real-time work, we are very much concerned with the *activity* over any specific *tool*. While tools are important—effectively managing Zoom or Google Meet, for instance, is a specific skill set that educators need to master—once we have students in a shared physical or virtual space, we will want to consider what we do with our limited time. The ways in which we design effective activities, as Tucker notes—to do everything from building relationships to modeling our thinking and providing real-time feedback—become a complete set of skills that takes a great deal of work in face-to-face settings, as well as online ones.

Part of the criticism of online learning, especially when students are required to "sit and get" by participating in real-time class sessions, can be summarized in a phrase like "Zoom fatigue." And, yes, sitting in front of a screen for long stretches of time can be exhausting for our eyes, bodies, and minds. Yet, talking about Zoom fatigue misses the point. At risk of disparaging my K–12 and higher education colleagues (or dismissing the idea that Zoom fatigue is not becoming more and more recognized as a specific, medical diagnosis), I think we need to face a harsh reality, one that has been laid bare in the time of pandemic pedagogy: The simple fact is that many educators do not fully engage students in meaningful learning activities when working together in real time. By resorting to lecture-based instruction and an "initiate–respond–evaluate" model of calling on students to pretend to participate and feign understanding through simple kinds of questioning (Fisher & Frey, 2010; Mehan, 1979, 1985), we have ingrained decades of bad habits into our pedagogy. Having learned by "the apprenticeship of observation"

(Lortie, 2002), many of us are stuck in modes of teaching that do not translate well into online spaces.

However, I don't want to dwell on these negatives for too long. There is hope for engagement in remote learning, as literacy experts Fisher and Frey (Fisher, Frey, & Hattie, 2020), among many other educators in books, blogs, podcasts, webinars, and more, have all made a case. As they summarized in an op-ed for *The New York Times* in the early fall of 2020, Adam Grant and Allison Sweet Grant suggest there are ways to engage students online, summarized in three principles: "mystery, exploration, and meaning." Other educators have described effective ways to engage in successful videoconference classes; for instance, English professor Elizabeth Stone (2020) described her experiences during the spring 2020 phase of emergency remote teaching as a success. "In the end, my efforts to build community worked," she contends, "and my Zoom class turned into one of the most gratifying teaching experiences I've ever had."

Having said all this, I also recognize that different schools and districts have different policies when it comes to setting up and monitoring class sessions (and especially breakout rooms) for students using videoconference tools. For instance, on one end of the continuum I have heard from some K–12 colleagues that under no circumstances are students to be put into any videoconference breakout room (though I have not been able to substantiate those initial reports). Others are allowed to use breakout rooms as part of instruction, so long as the educator is moving between rooms in a timely and consistent manner (as suggested in a guiding document from the School and College Legal Services of California, 2020). To reframe this conversation, I also rely on the insights of Maha Bali, who speaks directly to her readers and contends that "I am assuming having camera on is mainly a proxy for engagement, but you need to consider other ways of gauging and maintaining engagement" (2020). My hope is that some of the ideas below offer these alternatives.

So, I realize there is variation, yet I still encourage educators to attempt using small- and large-group videoconference sessions in different ways to encourage collaboration, build community, and invite students to share their understanding of course content with one another. In short, we need to offer students meaningful experiences in our real-time, virtual class sessions. This should have always been the case, long ago killing off the lecture as the dominant mode of instruction in both face-to-face and online instruction. Yet, as with most things we have experienced in pandemic times, we see the need for engaging in meaningful experiences becoming even more important now as we engage in more video-based lessons.

Building off of Tucker's eight suggestions, let me elaborate more below, again reminding us of a simple truth about the time we spend with students. When we say "I don't have time to . . ." because of curricular constraints, testing, pressure from our colleagues or administrators, or other forces, what we are saying is that "I don't choose to spend time on . . ." As we consider the needs of our students, especially those joining at a distance, we need to choose to spend time on instructional moves that matter while also supporting them each as individuals and as a classroom community. Digging more deeply into Tucker's general suggestions, we now consider some ways in which technology might be able to help us accomplish these goals.

9. Building Community and Relationships

During these moments we have with our learners, we will want to take advantage of the time we have with them to help them learn about our ELA content, as well as to learn more about one another (T. Hicks, Murchie, Neyer, Schoenborn, & Schwartz, 2020). There are many activities that can lead to community building and stronger relationships among students, some of which include whole-class activities and others that could be shared in smaller-group breakout sessions. For instance, with a student group that I advise at my university, one took the time-tested activity—Stand Up, Sit Down—and adapted it for having "camera on, camera off" in a video call. I will forgo a deep exploration of the many kinds of icebreakers that can be adapted to online spaces, as a web search will yield dozens of results. For instance, one source that offers dozens of free icebreakers (as well as many available for a fee), is Playmeo (n.d.). There are some interesting adaptations of traditional icebreakers available from Stanford's dSchool (n.d.), Game Storming (Gamestorming, n.d.), and Training for Change (Training for Change, n.d.) sites too. Many of these, as well, could be adapted for videoconference calls.

As relationships develop, one of the additional challenges that will emerge is maintaining them, over time, and across various activities and projects. In the physical classroom, we have methods such as seating charts to remind us of who sat next to whom last time when we reconfigure space (if we use seating charts), or we have popsicle sticks in a cup, each with a student name we can call upon when the stick is drawn. Though I am not a fan of certain apps and web-based tools that track and reward (or punish) student behavior, I think there is a place for some technology to help us mix things up from time to time and to ensure we are bringing more voices into the classroom conversation.

For instance, Flippity, a web-based app that builds on data from Google Sheets and was created by a technology integration specialist, Steve Fortna (@stevefortna), provides educators with free templates for creating a number of classroom resources, including a Random Name Picker. With options to select an individual students' name with a "spinner" or "lineup" mode, as well as tools for creating various group and team combinations, a random generator tool like Flippity can be helpful in the task of calling on students during videoconference calls and helping them connect with peers, as well as ensuring we have created random teams for breakout rooms.

Helping students move into breakout rooms has been a challenge across many videoconferencing apps but continues to become more functional as time goes on. At the time of this writing, Zoom had recently integrated an option within breakout rooms to allow participants to self-select a particular room (Montgomery, 2020), which was a highly requested feature. Of course, teachers can still assign students to rooms too. Also, at the time of this writing, Microsoft Teams, Google Meet, WebEx, and other platforms were also working on breakout room options. In whatever way educators design and implement breakout rooms, before students even go to those shared spaces, we must be sure to help them by creating purposeful tasks and encouraging conversation and collaboration, which I will elaborate on more below in the "Facilitating Conversation" and "Fostering Collaboration" segments, 14 and 15 below.

10. Leading Interactive Sessions by Providing Instructional Modeling

In the past few years, there have been a few tools that have been popularized for creating interactive sessions. As noted earlier, Nearpod and Pear Deck are two tools that, as one describes itself, can be "the fastest way to transform presentations into classroom conversations" (Pear Deck, n.d.). With options for building in a variety of question types including multiple choice, a sliding scale, brief written responses, and more, each of these tools can be used to lead interactive sessions. In and of themselves, these tools that add interactivity are nice, yet they do not necessarily ensure that instructional modeling is taking place. In fact, it is somewhat likely that the goal of adding interactivity might, inadvertently, keep us from providing the kinds of more intentional instructional modeling we would want to really encourage.

Another way to provide modeling during real-time activity, at risk of sounding obvious, is to actually *do* the modeling. In a framework they describe as the "Model–Practice–Reflect" instructional cycle, Steve Graham and his colleagues (2016) argue in their publication for the What Works Clearinghouse, "Teaching Secondary Students to Write Effectively," that this process where writers "observe a strategy in use, practice the strategy on their own, and evaluate their writing and use of the strategy" (p. 6) is the most effective way to help them understand what good writing is and how the best writers work. In other words, we, as the expert readers and writers in our literacy classrooms, need to emulate for students the ways they can approach texts by using think-alouds while reading, or by composing a thesis statement of our own.

By modeling our own literacy practices for students, we are providing them with insights into our own thinking as disciplinary experts and demonstrating protocols for approaching similar tasks on their own. As possibly the most common example seen in an ELA classroom, most of us can relate to the idea that we would do some brainstorming with our students as we think about topics for a personal narrative or persuasive essay. Similarly, we might generate a list of questions we want to explore as we prepare for a research project. In contrast to direct instruction (aka "lecturing") about content or talking in generalities about our writing process, the act of modeling requires us to demonstrate our own thinking. To the extent that we share our thinking with students and demonstrate how we would move through a process by asking them to watch (and, ideally, contribute some ideas along the way), modeling serves as a way to encourage interactivity and to help them envision a process they might then use on their own.

During a live, synchronous video session, this modeling can take place in a number of ways, many of which could then be shared with students in screenshots or other documents. For instance, we could model the process of writing a thesis, periodically and strategically using the "track changes" feature to show our revisions. Similarly, we could model the process for annotating a reading passage by taking a picture of a text and using whiteboard tools to comment on it (or importing the text into a document and using the commenting features). As this modeling unfolds, in real time, our goal would be to use the technology tools available to us in a videoconference—including the chat room, polling, opportunities for students to "raise hands," or other tools for providing reactions—to make sure our modeling process is clear and students can apply the ideas into their own work. Recordings could be made of these sessions, taking the most useful instructional segments and sharing them with students later on too. Finally, many educators were able to gain access to document cameras during remote learning, and free apps like Charlie Chapman's Overviewer were released to provide teachers with easy ways to convert their smartphone into a document camera.

11. Differentiating Instruction for Small Groups

Though it is beyond the scope of this book to offer a full-fledged description of the differences between terms like *universal design for learning* (UDL) and *differentiation,* one useful analogy is offered by Katie Novak (2017). She compares the two models with hosting a dinner party. The idea behind differentiation, she contends, is for the host to create a different meal specifically for each guest, at the host's discretion. In contrast, the idea behind UDL is that the host provides a buffet with options for all guests with various dietary preferences and needs, allowing them to choose what they want to eat. In the sense that Tucker refers here to "differentiating instruction for small groups," I am assuming she is, indeed, referring to the teacher taking the lead in a specific, timely, and targeted small-group session. In addition, and in parallel, the section below on personalizing instruction speaks to those principles of UDL that are good for all lesson design (Center for Applied Special Technology, n.d.).

Thus, as teachers are thinking about how to maximize real-time class sessions and take advantage of small-group breakout rooms for differentiated instruction, there are a few ways to frame that invitation. This is challenging, of course, during the midst of a video call, so some preparation and instructional decision making needs to occur ahead of time, as well as on the fly. Before the class session, the teacher should review students' recent work through a formative assessment and make some general predictions about which students will likely need to be moved into different breakout rooms based on their skills and needs. In the early part of a video class session, ideally, the instructor would want students to be given the choice as to which group they would join (though, sometimes, we know we need to nudge students into particular groups) and have a mechanism for students to choose. For instance, they could share their preferences in a Google Form (to keep responses private), type their preferences into a GDoc, or change their names in the video call settings to put a room number at the beginning of their name.

Once they have moved into the breakout rooms with specific tasks, the instructor would likely move into the room with students who have self-identified as needing support, or who the instructor has determined needs the most support. Establishing a goal for what the group needs and moving quickly into some direct, specific instruction, the group can move forward quickly. The group should still be accountable for documenting their discussion and work. For more ideas about how to differentiate the tasks in which small groups might participate, I encourage you to view a blog post I wrote in preparation for the 2020–2021 academic year, "Designing Breakout Rooms for Maximum Engagement" (2020). In that post, I contend there are both technical and pedagogical steps to set up breakout rooms and that "before even considering small group work, especially in virtual settings, we need to have clear structures in place, both for the entire class session and for what happens in breakout rooms," and I offer a number of suggestions for doing so with visible thinking routines (Ritchhart, Church, & Morrison, 2011) and protocols (McDonald, Mohr, Dichter, & McDonald, 2013), which will be discussed in more detail later in the book.

12. Personalizing Instruction and Providing Individual Coaching

There have been many discussions about the differences between algorithmic, adaptive, "personalized" learning systems and their levels of effectiveness with different kinds of learners. For instance, in some of the more grandiose visions of what such a system might do for students, we can hear echoes of an educational utopia. One such document, produced by senior scholars at a multinational educational publisher, proclaims we will be able to generate data from students that "would be constantly tracked and used to update profiles that follow each student across classrooms, grades, and schools, helping facilitate more customized learning experiences for each" (Herold, 2014). From this perspective, a personalized learning system can step in to support the work that students are doing and to adapt to the level of proficiency at which they have been accomplishing their goals. For certain kinds of learning tasks, the idea of a computerized tutor has a certain appeal.

However, this level of personalization raises a number of concerns and is in contrast to more humane, generative, and localized forms of assessment (Gergen & Dixon-Román, 2014). In this sense, we can look at ways that educators are motivating students to engage in inquiry through "personal digital inquiry" (Coiro, Dobler, & Pelekis, 2019) and by "inspiring students to take action" though effective uses of digital tools (Ziemke & Muhtaris, 2019). These more personal (though not algorithmically personalized) methods continue to emerge and deserve our attention as we think about what it means to really customize instruction for each of our learners. These inquiry-driven, action-oriented models of instruction remind us that—even though we are using digital tools—we are still connecting with our students and encouraging them through individual reading and writing conferences, practices that have been proven effective and long advocated for by practitioners of the reading and writing workshop and that can be enhanced with technology (e.g., K. Gallagher & Kittle, 2018; T. Hicks & Schoenborn, 2020; Reed & Hicks, 2015).

Just as in our face-to-face teaching, in order to productively plan for individual coaching, there are two moments in which this can happen: as a quick aside during whole-class instruction or by setting up a time to meet with an individual student outside of normal class times. During a videoconference session, we can always break out into a room with an individual student to offer some swift support. Depending on the video app being used, this process will differ, though the goal for a conference remains the same as always: encouraging a student, in the moment, to become a better reader or writer who identifies their own questions and goals, leaning on us for timely support.

Knowing that time for individual appointments with students is limited given the overall instructional duties to which we are bound, it likely is not possible to meet with each student for a sustained 10- to 15-minute conference even once a week. And the extent to which these conferences are "required" as compared to "encouraged" will also depend on one's overall number of students in any given term, as well as the complexity of navigating the school calendar. Still, to schedule a longer appointment, based on the availability in our face-to-face or virtual teaching schedules, we might look to tools like Calendly, YouCanBookMe, or Meeting Scheduler for Gmail. Microsoft, too, has recently released a Bookings app that integrates with Outlook. While none of these tools are flawless, especially when using the free versions, they do help to automate the process.

As a follow-up to any individual conference, we might also be able to offer voice or video feedback to students as a form of asynchronous conferring. Having first seen Jim Burke share this idea at a local English conference, the idea that we could quickly provide voice feedback by recording a piece on our phones was revolutionary for me at the time (though, in the 1990s, I had heard of some college professors who would record their feedback on audiocassettes). Burke (2012) is still an advocate for formative feedback (pp. 296–299). Bringing us to contemporary times, we can see that tools for this kind of feedback could include an ongoing dialogue using Flipgrid, tools that can be connected to Google Docs such as Kaizena or Mote, separate recorders like Vocaroo, or screencasting tools like Screencastify, Screencast-o-matic, or Loom. By following up on a quick conference and providing students with additional, direct support using an audio or video tool, you can reinforce the skills in a timely, targeted manner. In some ways, this could extend the individual conference, as the teacher asks students to respond to the suggestions and record their own audio/video response.

13. Guiding Practice and Specific Applications

Building on the mantra of "to, with, and by" as a means for instructional scaffolding, what Tucker seems to be suggesting by "guiding practice" and "specific application" is that we can coach students through instructional tasks and invite them to learn how to use applications in productive ways. Guiding practice, in the classroom, involves a great deal of movement around the classroom space, checking in with students and ensuring they are both on task with their attention and on target with their development of skills.

Also, teaching students the specific applications to accomplish instructional goals is often accompanied by lots of individual tech troubleshooting, with a reliance on classmates to provide help to one another as well. In virtual spaces, both of these tasks are somewhat more complicated, yet still quite possible.

For guiding practice, it is no doubt difficult to quickly look across 20 or more screens. And while there are software programs that allow teachers to quickly peek into students' own screens, these are costly (and, some would argue, an invasion of privacy). Other tools like Nearpod, Pear Deck, Whiteboard.fi, and Whiteboard.chat can allow us to see across the specific workspaces of multiple students, if we wanted to employ those tools. Similarly, we can invite students into shared spaces and tools, at least for a limited time, before moving back into their own individual projects or documents. For instance, as students are all working on a thesis statement or a transition into a quote, they could copy and paste their current drafts of their writing into a shared Google Doc. Then, through that shared doc and screen sharing, we could pull up examples of what students are writing and provide real-time feedback, as well as invite feedback from other classmates. A similar process could be used to examine a text for close reading, or to engage in other forms of guided practice for listening and speaking tasks.

As we help students with these specific skills, we will also want to consider how they will apply those skills (in the sense of Bloom's taxonomy) as well as to consider the specific applications (software, apps, websites, or devices) they will use to engage in such practice. For instance, in teaching students to create and manage citations to the many sources they might use for research, we can teach them both about different citation formats (MLA, APA, Chicago, etc.) and how to use a particular tool for organizing those citations, such as ZoteroBib, mentioned above. When doing this during a videoconference call, it could be worthwhile to record that portion of the class session, as students can return to that video to review the steps in using the application at a later time. Similarly, if we were to teach students how to use a mind mapping tool like WiseMapping (or to adapt a graphic organizer built in a Google Drawing or slide deck), we would also want to be teaching them about the skills of organizing information in different ways (such as a problem/solution format, in chronological order, or in order of priority).

With all the instructional moves that go into creating opportunities for guided practice followed by the use of specific applications (and, at the same time, moving students higher up on Bloom's taxonomy), we need to be mindful of the concept of "chunking." Described by the Facing History and Ourselves team (n.d.) as a process where an "activity involves breaking down a difficult text into more manageable pieces and having students rewrite these 'chunks' in their own words," we can also think about chunking as an instructional move especially relevant in virtual instruction. Students could be in a receptive mode of reading a text, viewing a video, or listening to a podcast (and we want them to process that information in smaller chunks), or they could be in a productive mode where they are composing an essay, creating a video, or developing another multimodal product. Having them share that work—while getting feedback from their classmates and instructor—can be a powerful process. To that end, using our real-time instruction to engage in this kind of work is especially meaningful.

14. Facilitating Conversation

Even with models for facilitating classroom dialogue such as the Socratic circle (Copeland, 2005) or an online adaptation of the "literature circle" that my colleague Jeremy Hyler and I adapted from Harvey Daniels (Daniels, 2002; Hyler & Hicks, 2014), we know that getting students to engage in purposeful conversation in our classrooms can be a challenge. We must help them prepare for, participate in, and debrief from conversations. Simply telling students to jump in and start talking is insufficient. If we want students to engage in substantive conversations, we must give them clear instructions and meaningful structures for participation.

This is even more challenging when we note that some students may not want to—or are simply unable to—engage in synchronous web conferencing with a webcam on and being able to provide full attention to the screen. This is a point that bears repeating, based on conversations I have been having with fellow university faculty and K–12 colleagues. I again share a succinct insight from a recent blog post by scholar and educator Maha Bali (2020), one that captures the spirit of what we really need to focus on: "I am assuming having camera on is mainly a proxy for engagement, but you need to consider other ways of gauging and maintaining engagement." This has seemed to be an underlying theme in my conversations with colleagues in the move to emergency remote teaching. The fact that a student is there, with a webcam on—as I can attest to with my own children having to participate in real-time remote learning during this 2020–2021 academic year—does not equate to them actively using their brains and paying attention in a substantive manner.

Facilitating conversation—in real-time settings—is a distinct skill. As noted earlier, the "initiate–respond–evaluate" model of interaction does not adequately engage students, nor assess their understanding of content. In order to have students participate in substantive dialogue and to move them into deeper inquiry, we need to consider different models for setting up the dialogue. Of course, there are some basic ground rules for dialogue that can be set (e.g., everyone takes a turn; different people serve as facilitator, timekeeper, or in other roles), yet these are just the logistics. What really matters is what people are going to talk about, thus making the purpose of the real-time communication—and the need to be together in a shared virtual space at a particular time—worthwhile.

To that end, we can bring models of face-to-face dialogue into virtual settings and adapt them appropriately. For instance, the National School Reform Faculty (NSRF, 2020), the group known for their work with "Critical Friends," and the School Reform Initiative (n.d.), both have dozens of available protocols. While there are some behind a subscription paywall with NSRF, the free ones are all more than adequate to explore and build into meaningful discussions. Some of the protocols are meant more as ice breakers, while some are designed to push into deeper, more substantive conversation. All are aimed at promoting equitable participation, active listening, and a sense of group cohesion. Without going into extensive detail here, I can share that some of the protocols I find most effective for use with students and teachers have been Affinity Mapping

(Peterson-Veatch, 2017), Save the Last Word for Me (Averette, 2017), the Charette Protocol (Juarez, Thompson-Grove, & Feicke, 2017), and the Jigsaw Description (School Reform Initiative, adapted from Spencer Kagan, 2017), among others.

Another effective conversation tool is the Question Formulation Technique (QFT) developed by the Right Question Institute (2019). Described as a method to "stimulate three types of thinking: divergent thinking, convergent thinking, and metacognitive thinking," the QFT can be used in flexible ways to help students generate questions about a single, focused question. Moving through these steps—in which participants produce as many questions as possible in an initial brainstorming and then label them; reformulate their questions from open-ended or closed questions to improve them; and, finally, prioritize questions as a group—the QFT encourages a vast array of questions to be developed in a short period of time. Participants are then encouraged to step back from that process and reflect on what they have learned and how they might carry their questions forward. This process, in short, serves as a springboard for further conversation and inquiry.

With any of these protocols taking place in an online video conversation, we want to ensure that students are documenting what they have discussed. Once the protocol for an effective conversation has been determined, we can then think about the most applicable tool for helping a group capture their thinking during class discussion. This could be as simple as asking them to have a note keeper jot the group's ideas in a shared GDoc, Jamboard, Padlet wall, or other space. Or it could involve a more elaborate process in which the teacher designs a more formal template for students to complete. For one example of this, see the book's companion website—hickstro.org/digitaldiligence—for a link to an activity I adapted from one of the visible thinking routines, the "4 Cs," where students must make connections to the text, challenge the text, draw out key concepts from the text, and understand the changes that the text aims to impart (Harvard Project Zero, 2019c).

As the real-time class session comes to a close, and we ask students to consider how they might carry their ideas further, we can turn to other tools. As noted in the asynchronous activities above, a number of options for text-, image-, and video-based conversations can be found through resources like NowComment, Hypothes.is, Vialogues, Video ANT, and Kami. Extending the conversation in these ways, we can remind students that their original dialogue can continue even after we are done with our shared time together. And as noted in the previous chapter, being able to extend these conversations in a purposeful arc of instruction will continue to be a useful instructional move as we connect students across time and space.

15. Fostering Collaboration

To build on the ideas presented above in "Facilitating Conversation," we can also consider some structures for intentional collaboration. There are many educators that have articulated their own perspectives on the differences between *cooperative* and *collaborative* learning, so I will not go into extensive detail here. By collaboration, I will simply note that I am suggesting structures and activities in which students must move beyond engagement in a task at a superficial level, often in ways that they might have successfully completed on their own and without interaction. For instance, asking students to "have a discussion" is not nearly sufficient. Instead, we need to provide groups, just as we would individuals, with scaffolding in the opportunities to push their thinking together, rather than alone. In this sense, I have begun speaking more and more to the idea that we want to encourage our students to engage in genuinely collaborative work, not just conveniently cooperative activities.

One such set of resources to inspire collaboration (which, like the protocols mentioned above, could be used for individual work too) is the Visible Thinking Routines developed by Ron Ritchhart and colleagues from Harvard's Project Zero, mentioned above. Described in their book *Making Thinking Visible: How to Promote Engagement, Understanding, and Independence for All Learners* (Ritchhart et al., 2011), and with dozens of protocols available on their Thinking Routines Toolbox website (Harvard Graduate School of Education Project Zero, n.d.), these routines are meant to help students articulate their ideas and questions. Though the term *visible* seems to suggest that the routines lend themselves to drawing (and, in that sense, many could), they are also useful as thoughtful question stems that can lead into writing. Moreover, there are many tools that can be used to enact the visible thinking routines, ranging from a Google Doc or Google Slides deck to other tools like Padlet, Google's Jamboard, or other whiteboarding tools.

For instance, with the "See, Think, and Wonder" routine (Harvard Project Zero, 2019b)—in which students are invited to look at an image, a chart, a map, or other visual and then to describe what they see, in detail, as well as to push deeper into their thinking about the artifact and by asking questions about it—adaptations for use in GDocs, Google Slides, Padlet, or Jamboard could all be appropriate. Students could each have access to a collaborative space, in which they document their own "see, think, and wonder" responses and add comments to the ideas posted by others. Similarly, the "I Used to Think . . . Now I Think . . ." routine (Harvard Project Zero, 2019a) encourages students to articulate specific points of difference and overlap between their previous and current ways of thinking about a topic. This could lend itself well to a t-chart, a table with columns, or even a Venn diagram that, again, they could share with others and invite further conversation. These are fairly straightforward applications of the thinking routines and would be useful for beginning conversations that could turn into deeper collaborations.

Though they are likely to be outside the scope of most real-time class sessions, tips for managing projects and staying connected could be useful. For instance, to help students engage in collaborations over a sustained period of time, some tools could be helpful as they begin project planning and a division of tasks. At one level, simply adding students to a shared GDoc and having them use the "@" reply in comments to tag others will bring up the option to "Assign to." In this way, students can self-assign (or be assigned by their peers) certain tasks in a list in GDocs. A shared Google Keep note could serve a similar function, and of course there are other project management tools that students could use too, such as Trello, Asana, or Microsoft Teams.

Sustained collaboration might require, too, the use of "backchannel" communication, such as group chats, through some of the tools mentioned above. Depending on the age level of students and the school's acceptable use policy, this kind of communication might be frowned upon, or not allowed at all. That said, most students are likely engaged in some backchannel conversations with their classmates through various chat-based apps, whether we want to admit it or not. Of course, they may be using any number of social media tools, including Snapchat, Instagram, Facebook, WhatsApp, Signal, GroupMe, Slack, Microsoft Teams, or others. In considering the ways that we continue to ask them to engage in meaningful collaboration, it might be worth having some conversation with them around the use of these tools and the ways to ensure they are participating in genuine, dialogic interactions that align with broader goals and skills for collaboration, including active listening, effective verbal and nonverbal communication, empathy, negotiation, and managing team expectations.

16. Providing Real-Time Feedback on Work in Progress

First, it must be acknowledged that providing timely, specific, and goal-oriented feedback to students is a challenge in any context, especially during whole-class instruction and even more so in a videoconference call. That said, there can be times when inviting one student to share work—and to then provide feedback—can be instructive for all students. For instance, in the early stages of drafting an essay, if one student is willing to share her draft, the instructor can respond, offering encouraging comments on segments of the essay that are strong, as well as providing suggestions for revisions, additions, or deletions on segments that are not as strong. Providing this kind of feedback on one student's work—as a model to other students for how they might shape their own writing—can be powerful. Using many of the tools and general strategies outlined above, we can have students share their work in a common GDoc, or even on a collaborative whiteboard.

Another strategy would be to simply provide time and space in a videoconference call for students to get work done by moving them to individual breakout rooms and circulating to support them. In some ways, this seems antithetical to maximizing our limited amounts of time in videoconference call. Yet, much like we provide time for independent reading and writing in our regular classroom schedules, we can also provide this time through individual breakouts in a videoconference call. In this quiet space, students are perhaps less likely to be distracted by the classroom chat or other students (though, of course, we still recognize that they may have other distractions that could pull them off track). Then, by hopping from individual to individual, the teacher can do quick, private check-ins.

Some of these check-ins may be simple, with a brief acknowledgment that all is well. In this sense, it would be valuable to use the real-time opportunity during the video call to acknowledge the student, rekindling the personal connection that can sometimes be lost through extended sessions of instruction over a webcam. Some other check-ins may lead to a brief conference, like the ones described above in the "Personalizing Instruction and Providing Individual Coaching" section, leading to an invitation to an individual conference outside of whole-class time. No matter what the outcome of the meeting, simply reestablishing a connection is important as one step in the continual process of building and maintaining relationships.

Tucker has also written extensively about the use of a "station rotation" model in her blended high school English classroom. Even in an era of social distancing and remote teaching, she continues to innovate the station rotation model, with a June 2020 blog post describing "Station Rotation in an Era of Social Distancing" (C. Tucker, 2020a). While continuing to have students move through various activities that include teacher-led stations, as well as various online and off-line activities, she contends that students would stay seated in the same location, and she "would love to see teachers think about desk formations that would allow for social distancing without relegating students to rows." She also provides a GDoc template for setting up one day's worth of lessons as students move through teacher-led, as well as off-line, small-group work, and online, largely individual work.

As I close this section that has elaborated on Tucker's suggestions for both asynchronous, anytime learning and synchronous, real-time learning, I would be remiss if I did not point out the dozens of posts related to these topics on her blog, as well as through her recent books, including her most recent title, *Balance with Blended Learning: Partner with Your Students to Reimagine Learning and Reclaim Your Life* (2020). Published at the end of February 2020, she presciently argued for a model of learning in which "instead of thinking of our relationship with students as hierarchical, we should think of ourselves as partners working with our students to customize learning to best meet their needs" (p. 16). As with many truisms during an era of remote teaching and learning, these words echo even louder now than they did when they were released right before pandemic times, and they can guide us when thinking about the design of real-time and anytime learning.

SETTING THE STAGE FOR PURPOSEFUL ARCS OF INSTRUCTION

As I close this chapter and prepare to dig deeper into topics for teaching digital diligence, I offer a few final suggestions as we all seek additional professional mentors. Much of what I have offered in this chapter is predicated on the idea that we are structuring meaningful reading and writing workshop opportunities in our classroom (as noted throughout this chapter) and that assignment design is purposeful. All of the books mentioned above are worth having on our professional bookshelves. And, by creating a list below, I know that I will inadvertently exclude dozens, if not hundreds of other resources. Still, I share a few that I have come to find useful in the past couple of years.

For reading instruction, and additional resources to provide insights on how to support adolescents as they select meaningful books that resonate with topics in their lives, the educators from #DisruptTexts have developed many blog posts on their website and through a new collection of resources with Penguin Random House. Also, Carol Jago's

The Book in Question (2018) is useful for moving adolescents toward independent reading. For writing instruction, specifically assignment design, I recommend Jim Burke's *The Six Academic Writing Assignments* (Burke, 2018) and Traci Gardner's *Designing Writing Assignments* (2011). To consider even more for integrating digital writing tools, I would humbly suggest some of my own work (T. Hicks, 2013; Turner & Hicks, 2016), as well as Michele Haiken's *New Realms for Writing* (2019). Finally, for a solid framework on which to build one's instructional approach when using technology, I suggest exploring Liz Kolb's "engage, enhance, and extend" model in the Triple E (Kolb, 2017, 2020). And, as we consider ways to engage and support BIPOC and LGBTQ+ youth, an ever-growing group of scholars and educators are contributing titles to our professional catalogs, including recent titles from Dana Johansen and Sonja Cherry-Paul (2016), Carla Espana and Luz Yadira Herrera (2020), and Blackburn, Clark, and Schey's collection, *Stepping Up!* (2018).

These are just a few suggestions, of course, as I continue to learn and grow my professional library. I welcome your thoughts about them—and other recommendations—through continued dialogue via email or social media.

No matter when or where a lesson occurs, the intentional steps that we take before, during, and after a real-time lesson—all the while providing substantive guidance for required homework and invitational, inquiry-driven anytime learning—matter. By planning for purposeful arcs of instruction that can move across time and space, we will improve our own skills related to mindful use of technology in our ELA classroom, all the while preparing our students to engage even more deeply in the topics presented in the chapters ahead. Tucker's 16 ideas for asynchronous and synchronous learning—and the elaborations above—provide us with what we need to dig deeper into the principles and practices of digital diligence.

The Rationale for Focusing on Google Chrome

For any book of this sort, as technologies continue to shift and change, an author will have to make some concessions. There are always questions of how much to cover, as well as the likelihood that any particular tool will be around by the time a reader picks up this book. I've heard this referred to as the "shelf life" of a book, and I know I have faced that with some of my previous work. I look back fondly at screenshots and descriptions of Wikispaces and Google Reader, knowing at the time—and even more so now—that some technologies simply will not last.

Thus, before moving into the chapters ahead where I dig into a number of topics that will, by their very nature, be connected with particular tools, I offer a brief interlude here. In particular, I want to articulate how I framed the choice of technologies used in the topics described in this next section of the book, namely, the use of Google Chrome as a primary tool, as well as how to use its vast collection of extensions from the Chrome Web Store. I will say right up front that there are legitimate concerns that can be raised about the use of Google tools in K–12 settings, including issues with individual privacy and system security (Alim, Cardozo, Gebhart, Gullo, & Kalia, 2017). These concerns need to be addressed by IT professionals, school attorneys, and others who are well versed in such matters. Like many other browsers, it has come under increased scrutiny and has released many new features to help protect privacy (Whittaker, 2019).

Whether teaching in a 1:1 school where limits are strictly set and controlled by centralized IT services, or whether students are asked to "bring your own device" (BYOD), there are always tiny tweaks, changes, or exceptions to what might work in any given moment. For one particular student, on any particular device, an extension or a website may work fine. Even if they are both using school-issued machines, another student in the same classroom may struggle due to a slightly different setting, a wonky Wi-Fi connection, or—let's face it—user error. There is no way to account for every single problem that might bubble up, so I will not even try. The best solution I have heard is that some schools have a designated student "tech team" (or, playing on the idea of technology experts, "tech-sperts") that can be at the ready for (relatively) simple tech solutions. Relying on our students for tech support can empower them and lessen our own stress levels.

At a deeper level, in writing a book about teaching English language arts in an era of increasing tech use—and among renewed calls for mindful attention when using such tools—we (and our students) must be able to explore our own device's settings to make adjustments, as well as discover new tools for persevering in multiple digital environments. As a writer and educator, I simply cannot anticipate everything a reader might encounter with a personal or school-specific device when one begins engaging in the topics ahead. I know this is difficult for us, as teachers, to fully accept this reality; we want all students to have the best experience possible, and that requires a certain level of control over our classroom community, student behavior, and, of course, the technologies being used.

Still, decisions must be made about how best to represent the ideas I am sharing here in the book, so I am making some assumptions and offering options for Google Chrome. In addition to personal experience by talking with dozens of teachers over the past decade about what they have available in their schools (more and more, it is Chromebooks), I focus on Chrome because outside sources confirm this is the case too. Futuresource Consulting, based in the United Kingdom, continues to report that Chrome is taking hold in U.S. markets (reported in Geekwire by Catalano, 2017), with Windows more prominent worldwide (though, of course, Google Chrome can be installed on Windows machines). iOS still carries some of the market for school purchases and is, of course, still the operating system that powers about a quarter of the world's mobile devices (StatCounter, 2019).

For purposes of writing a book for other educators, I am just beginning with the simple truth that many of us use Chrome. To that end—and because there is no way for me to cover all the nuances of different web browsers as well as the apps and extensions for any given topic in the chapters ahead—I focus on Chrome. My goal for each topic is to introduce a concept about digital diligence, one that can be enabled through a variety of similar tech tools. As a reminder, I provide links to everything mentioned in the pages ahead on the book's companion website (hickstro.org/digitaldiligence).

So, while I am creating the examples with Google Chrome in mind, as readers of this book and digitally diligent educators, please know that nearly all of the types of extensions (with similar kinds) of functionality can be found across various web browsers. A quick rundown of where to search for these extensions, as well as a few alternative browsers, include the following (with active links on the book's companion site). Inevitably, I have not included all possible browsers here, but I do include the major ones:

- Mozilla's Firefox (with their Add-Ons directory)
- Microsoft's Edge (with the Edge Store)
- Apple's Safari (with the Safari Store)

- Opera Software's Opera Browser (with Opera Add-Ons)
- MoboTap Inc's Dolphin (for Android and iOS)

Finally, since I know teachers are big fans of "free," I do try to share as many no-cost and openly available resources as possible. There are, however, some things worth paying for, and when appropriate, I will point out apps, subscriptions, and other tools I feel bring value to the ELA classroom. In short, when considering what students can do with desktop or laptop devices, I am defaulting to sharing examples with Google Chrome and a number of add-ons available from the Chrome Web Store. The web store can be accessed from a link in Google Chrome when the following address is loaded in the URL omnibar: chrome://apps/, or through a search for Chrome Web Store; it can also be accessed from the link on the book's companion page. With that, I am trying to cover the bases for most readers of this book, though some exceptions are sure to be present when considering all the options that are available in any particular classroom, school, or community.

I end this interlude with a direct appeal here to you, as the reader. If you are unable to install apps from the web store without administrative or IT approval, this provides you with an opportunity to have a conversation with others in your school district who are in those roles, working with them to ensure you and your students have access to a robust set of tools within the Chrome ecosystem. This is an advocacy stance we need to take, as ELA teachers who want to prepare our students to be digitally diligent.

CHAPTER 3

Protecting Privacy

Consciously choosing what we share, how much, and with whom
(publicly or privately) requires persistence; students need to know why
and how privacy matters.

Though the Internet has been part of our students' lives since before they were born,
it has been my experience that they don't fully understand exactly what the World
Wide Web (just one part of the Internet) really is, how precisely it works, and what has
changed about it over the years. And while they have probably heard about their "digital
footprint," and even considered some of the many places where their digital feet may
have stepped, sometimes we all take our anonymity and privacy for granted. In what
spaces have our students walked across the web, and how can we help them make more
intentional choices in the future?

As ELA teachers, these issues are of particular importance to us and the ways in
which we invite our students to engage in inquiry, move toward deeper and more sustained reading, and, ultimately, express themselves through digital writing. What they
do on the web is tracked and, in turn, leads to additional predictive algorithms that
will anticipate what they might do next. Helping students to see themselves the way
that the web itself sees them is a way to bring new lenses to their literate lives, lives that
are increasingly unfolding online. The three topics in this chapter will help them as
they come to understand what the web knows about them; they can then make more
informed choices about their current and future web-based activities, both consuming
and creating.

Beginning with Topic 3.1, "The Web and Me," we examine the ways in which our
search histories are likely to guide our search futures, as well as ways to maintain some

control over that data. Then, in Topic 3.2, "(Re)Setting Privacy and Disabling Distraction," we consider some simple changes that can be made to our web browser and mobile device settings in order to, again, retain some control over our data. Finally, in Topic 3.3, "(Re)Searching Our Search Engines," we begin to think about the ways in which search engines work and how using a variety of search tools and techniques can yield different—and sometimes surprising—results.

Though not cited explicitly, some of the resources that have informed my thinking in this chapter—with links on the companion website: hickstro.org/digitaldiligence—include those from *The New York Times*'s "Privacy Project" and Mozilla's partnership with Tactical Tech and their projects, including the "Data Detox Kit," "Exposing the Invisible," "The Glass Room," and "Our Data Our Selves." In addition, the Center for Humane Technology offers a number of resources for families and educators. As with all kinds of tech-related resources, there certainly are more, and I will work to keep the book's companion website updated.

TOPIC 3.1. THE WEB AND ME

To help them become digitally diligent, we need students to understand how their search histories inform what they are likely to see on the web, as well as how to see what web companies know about their tendencies and preferences.

Overview

More than ever before, our desktop web browsers and mobile devices are the primary, if not the sole, portals for our communication. For students learning to live and work on any number of individual and shared projects—as well as conducting other personal business online, such as banking, booking medical appointments, and researching sensitive topics—they must understand how browsers, apps, and the associated tracking systems, like cookies, work. Moreover, as companies and services like Amazon, Apple, Google, Microsoft, and Mozilla sync information across devices, students need to understand what is shared and with whom. With the ideas in this topic, students can explore aspects of privacy on the web, including how to protect their passwords and personal information, as well as what their web history says about them.

As we search the web, we leave footprints in our browsing history. While looking at a long list of links in our own search history (or searching through that search history itself) can give us some insights, it is difficult to fully appreciate where we have spent our time online and just how often—as well as how long—we have been there. Just as Eli Pariser noted over a decade ago in his TED Talk (Pariser, 2011a), our search history is not neutral, because the search engines themselves, especially Google, takes note of "everything from what kind of computer you're on to what kind of browser you're using to where you're located—that it uses to personally tailor your query results." Seeing where we have been could help us make better choices about where we are going . . . and what additional tools we might need to help us get there.

One tool that can be used is the web-based application Web Historian, which is developed by Ericka Menchen-Trevino (n.d.), a professor at American University, and is available as an extension for Google Chrome. In her description of the tool, she notes that "Web Historian . . . helps you visualize the web browsing history [so] . . . you can see what you've been looking for online and how you navigate through the web using interactive visuals." Web Historian does not store your data or track you, and it runs in your browser; so, once you close the application, the visualizations are gone. Students might be encouraged to take snapshots of the Web Historian visualizations, so they can save them and reflect on what they see.

Because Web Historian provides four views of your search history, students could use it in a variety of ways before, during, or after a research project. For instance, before students begin a project, they could run Web Historian to get a sense of their past searching patterns and to consider what they might need to do to broaden their search strategies. Web Historian could also be used in the midst (or at the end) of a research project, providing them with an opportunity to evaluate the sites that they used most often and reflect on whether they moved beyond their typical search patterns. Finally, with the *heatmap* of their most active web usage times, students can think about their overall use of search and how that fits into a typical day, week, and month of web use.

Teaching Points

This tool, unlike many others that can work with different browsers, requires that the Web Historian extension be installed in—and that the user's search history also be in—Google Chrome. I will only make this point one final time here, hearkening back to the Interlude on Google Chrome, otherwise I would need to echo it over and over; if readers are unable to install extensions without permission from the school or district's IT staff, this is a conversation that should be had immediately. Teachers and students should be able to have access to particular extensions when they need it, whether that comes through individual ability to install those extensions or for the IT professionals to push them out in a timely manner.

Web Historian, as noted above, relies on Google's search history. If the user has not been using Google as a primary tool for search, there are instructions for importing one's search history to Chrome from other browsers (linked on the book's companion site). Again, in keeping with the broader conversation about privacy and security, the Web Historian FAQ page notes that it does not store users' data or share it with other organizations. Web Historian offers four different views of your search history, each worth exploring in detail: web visits, search terms, network, and time heatmap, each of which provides insights on one's searching habits. Invite students to install—and run—the Web Historian add-on; then consider the follow opportunities for students to extend their thinking.

As Students View the "Web Visits" Section

This view (see Figure 3.1.1) provides users with a "bubble map" of their most recent web visits and can be adjusted to show many weeks' worth of search history, or a specific range. Students could look at their patterns from a month ago and compare to now, and they could toggle between "All Visits" and "Daily Habits." There are various other settings, such as changing the bubble colors, that can be toggled too to gain more insights on web visits. Figure 3.1.1 provides a glimpse of the bubble map of my own recent search history in Web Historian.

It is worth noting that students can "hide" various domains. For instance, because Google Docs is constantly refreshing, if students are using this tool consistently, then it may take up an outsized space on the bubble map. A quick right click on that bubble will yield the option to "permanently delete," which will yield a pop-up asking: "Do you want to PERMANENTLY remove ALL visits to URLs from _____ from your local browser history?" where the blank space here would be shown as the domain in question. This option would realign the bubble map yet, as noted in the warning, would remove those search results from the history. Depending on how the user feels about the consequences of this action, that particular site can be removed, or not. In the figures below, for instance, readers will see the dominant role that Google Docs plays in my search history, and I can confirm that I use this site often, sometimes for many hours each day.

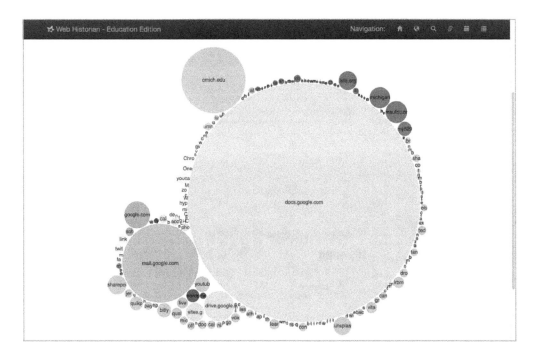

FIGURE 3.1.1. A screenshot of the "Web Visits" section of a Web Historian analysis. Used with permission of Ericka Menchen-Trevino.

As Students View the "Search Terms" Section

This view (see Figure 3.1.2) provides users with a word cloud of recent search terms and, like the web visits, can be adjusted to show different timelines. By clicking on an individual word, a user can then pull up a data table to see all the sites that have been clicked to, using that particular word. Even hovering one's mouse over the word gives some insight on sites that have been visited based on the term, without opening up the full data table. Again, as one clicks on those terms, a right click will yield this option: "Do you want to PERMANENTLY remove all URLs with the search term '_____' from your local browser history?" In doing so, if the user is OK with the outcomes of this deletion, that particular term could be removed.

As Students View the "Network" Section

This view (see Figure 3.1.3) provides users with a network map of connections where, according to the Web Historian site, "a link [appears] between two websites if you visited one website before the other." Seeing how one's web search patterns move from one site to another is important, as it shows the ways in which information is connected and how we found it. It is sometimes easier to visualize the network map for just one or two days, using the slider at the top of the page. Asking students to follow any single "path" on the network map could lead to a compelling example of how one search can lead into many

FIGURE 3.1.2. A screenshot of the "Search Terms" section of a Web Historian analysis. Used with permission of Ericka Menchen-Trevino.

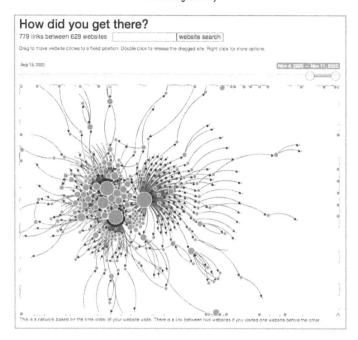

FIGURE 3.1.3. A screenshot of the "Network" section of a Web Historian analysis. Used with permission of Ericka Menchen-Trevino.

different directions. Also, URLs that have been typed in directly then appear as outliers in the map, and it is interesting to consider why we might choose to go to a URL directly as compared to arriving at that URL from another source or search.

As Students View the "Time Heatmap" Section

This view (see Figure 3.1.4) provides users with a grid of search history for 1 week, or across 12 weeks of search history. By viewing the heatmap from week to week, one can see patterns of general web usage on particular days of the week and times of the day. Considering this kind of data—and thinking about our own work pattern—it could be useful to have students identify their heaviest and lightest usage points during the week, what they are typically doings online during those times (at school or at home; in one class where they use their devices often compared to another class where they do not), and how that usage pattern connects to their overall productivity and focus.

When considering the teaching points above, there are numerous connections to the position statements and standards documents by the professional organizations as outlined in Chapter 1. Here—and at this point in subsequent chapters—I offer just a few connections to the NCTE's "Definition of Literacy in a Digital Age" as a way to begin thinking about extensions and adaptations from this topic that educators can make in their own classrooms. There are, certainly, connections that could be made to specific standards proposed by NCTE (NCTE & International Reading Association,

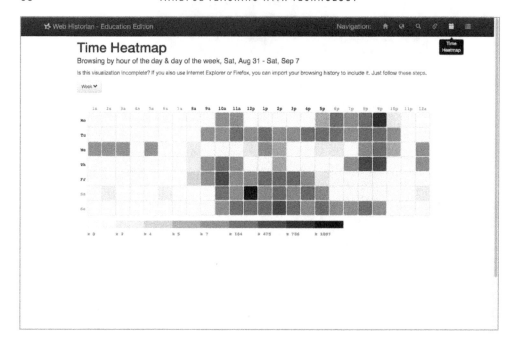

FIGURE 3.1.4. A screenshot of the "Time Heatmap" section of a Web Historian analysis. Used with permission of Ericka Menchen-Trevino.

2012), as well as ISTE and NAMLE standards. Also, depending on the products we might invite our students to create, various frameworks for multimodal projects could be considered too (Burnett, Frazee, Hanggi, & Madden, 2014; National Writing Project Multimodal Assessment Project Group, 2013). To maintain some focus and consistency, I will instead focus on NCTE's definition of literacy in a digital age (also noted in Chapter 1), offering a few connections here (and at this point in subsequent topics).

For instance, with the topics presented in "The Web and Me," the goal for students to "consume, curate, and create actively across contexts" can be realized as we encourage students to use Web Historian to evaluate their own utilization patterns through the search visualizations. Moreover, they can look at the ways in which they clicked from one resource to another, exploring these connections and understanding how they moved from one online space to the next. Similarly, as they take this information that has been presented in Web Historian and reflect upon it, they can then analyze these new views of their own online work that have been provided and make their own thinking about these new insights visible through screenshots, annotation, and written (or oral) reflection. They can also compare and contrast their own search histories with those of their peers, engaging in even more conversation about their own web searching habits and how they might change those habits in the future. In this process, they can ask about the ways in which they "build and utilize a network of groups and individuals that reflect varying views as they analyze, create, and remix texts" as well as "find relevant and reliable sources that meet their needs" (NCTE, 2019b).

Guiding Questions

When working with students and exploring this topic, consider the following questions when designing lessons, assignments, and assessments.

- When, how, and why do you use the web?
- What apps and websites do you visit most often? What devices do you use?
- What can you learn about yourself from your web browsing and device habits?
- When viewing your search history—across multiple visualizations offered by Web Historian—what do you notice about the sites you visit most? What about the sites you visit less frequently?
- With your web visits, where are you spending the most time? In what ways does the web visit map align with (or diverge from) what you thought you were doing with your time online?
- Are there some specific times of day or days of the week where your "heatmap" shows that you are online more than others? What are you typically doing at those points of a normal week?
- Considering your word cloud of search terms and the network map, what do you notice about how you begin your searches and where, ultimately, you end up?

TOPIC 3.2. (RE)SETTING PRIVACY AND DISABLING DISTRACTION: AD BLOCKING, TRACKING, AND INCOGNITO MODES

To help them become digitally diligent, we need students to see the ways in which they are being tracked on the web, as well as the control they have over the ways that different trackers can—or cannot—be used to follow their activities.

Overview

Building on the ideas presented in Topic 3.1, "The Web and Me," this topic delves even deeper into an understanding of how web browsers work, looking closely at issues of tracking and search history. While we are able to review our data and delete our histories, in the world of web browsing, an ounce of prevention is worth well more than any cure. Using tools developed to stop tracking and ensure privacy, students begin to see many of the reasons that simply saying "I have nothing to hide" is not a good approach to building our digital presence.

In the context of their daily literacy practices, it may be a bit difficult to explain to students exactly why they should be concerned about these issues. Indeed, for many adults, managing our privacy settings and ensuring we are using the web in appropriate ways—allowing certain sites to access a full range of our data, with other sites having limited access or none at all—is a challenge. Because we want students to fully understand their rights and responsibilities as technology users, and to participate in a variety of online communities in effective ways, it is imperative that they understand how their data is being used by the websites they frequent most often.

Moreover, to appeal to adolescent learners who are working through questions about their own personalities, preferences, and peculiarities, these issues of privacy can be particularly useful. My own teenage children, for instance, talk about using incognito mode in their web browsers to maintain privacy, yet they do not fully understand the limitations of what incognito mode can (and cannot do). For instance, a recent *Consumer Reports* article highlights a quirk of incognito mode by describing how the cookies left in one's web browser from a search for a birthday present could spoil the surprise for later when their partner starts using Facebook and an ad for the surprise shows up (Deleon, 2018). Though the browsing history is not there, the cookies are. This is just one concrete example of how tracking technology can affect our lives, albeit a relatively innocuous one.

Teaching Points

For anyone who has spent any amount of time online, we know that advertisements are unavoidable. That said, they are not inevitable. With a combination of some tech tools—ad blockers and reader-view mode—as well as some "click restraint," we can keep some, even if not all, of the distraction at bay. To begin the discussion of when and how to install and use these tools, we can talk with students about the science of human attention. With the additional texts linked on the book's companion website under this topic, there are a number of resources related to attention and the Internet. Before having students explore and begin using the ad-blocking and reader-view extensions, it would be worthwhile to talk about the general nature of human attention, with or without technology. For centuries, humans have been in a battle between daydreaming and boredom on the one hand and efforts toward focus, meditation, and other tricks to stay on task on the other. How has the Internet exacerbated these existing conditions? In what ways can we, as tech users, bring some agency back to our digital lives?

There are many ad blockers available, with AdBlock, AdBlock Plus, and uBlock Origin among the most popular. A search for these websites (or on the browser's extensions) will quickly lead you to them. Personally, I use AdBlock, though I think each works about equally as well. While there are some ethical considerations on using ad-blocking software (noted in the next paragraph), the overall browsing experience can become more effective, efficient, and engaging. Also, if students are using an Android or iOS device as their primary tool, they can explore the Dolphin web browser, mentioned in the previous Interlude, as an alternative to other browsers, with easy ad-blocking settings to adjust without additional extensions required.

While most of us can agree that avoiding ads is generally a good thing, there are some downsides to blocking everything. First, because many smaller organizations rely on revenue from ads to keep their sites open and available, they will often ask users to turn off ad-blocking software, or to "white list" their site so appropriate and limited ads can get through. In fact, both AdBlock and AdBlock Plus are part of a broader consortium, the Acceptable Ads Committee, and do suggest that users are judicious with white-listing some websites and services. As shown in the AdBlock interface in Figure 3.2.1—captured as screenshot from my own browser on a popular news website—on this single page, 20 ads have been blocked (and, I am pleased to see, more than 70,000 ads have been blocked in the many years I have been using AdBlock, saving me hours of scrolling and frustration). To that end, I periodically contribute to them via PayPal, as their service is well worth a small donation now and again when it can block dozens of ads for me each day.

Once ad blocking has been explored, a second layer of analysis can be gained through resources provided by the Electronic Frontier Foundation (EFF). First, we can ask students to run the Cover Your Tracks tool and install Privacy Badger. Cover Your Tracks (recently renamed from the original version, Panopticlick) is a website that "will analyze how well your browser and add-ons protect you against online tracking techniques" (Electronic Freedom Foundation, n.d.). By running a quick test of the web browser, it can determine many elements about your browser's ability to block tracking ads and invisible trackers, as well as "fingerprinting," or identifying the characteristics of your browser, such as the plug-ins, time zone, screen size, and use of an ad blocker (or not). These fingerprint data are what your browser serves to companies for targeted ads. Once Cover Your Track's analysis is complete, we can ask students to view further information from the EFF about "acceptable ads," "do not track," and "fingerprinting."

To gain ongoing insights into what data websites are gathering from us, Privacy Badger is an extension that blocks trackers from across the web, providing users with a summary of key tracking statistics from websites, including Amazon, Google's Double Click, Facebook, and Twitter, among others. When landing on any given website, Privacy Badger will start counting trackers, and with a click, a user can open up a dashboard indicating "red" (related to the domain), "yellow" (related to the cookies), and "green" (related to sites that users have given explicit permission to track) levels of concern for the tracking tools enabled on that site (as seen in Figure 3.2.2). We might also have students turn on Privacy Badger and invite them to begin to browse the web as they normally would for 5–10 minutes and note the various trackers and ad services that it identifies with some sites they visit.

FIGURE 3.2.1. A screenshot of the AdBlock interface.

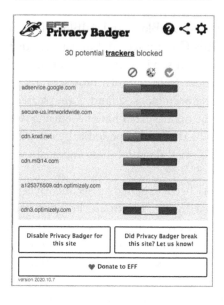

FIGURE 3.2.2. A screenshot of the Privacy Badger interface.

Next, HTTPS Everywhere is another tool from the EFF. When browsing the web, most pages load through standard "hypertext transfer protocol," or "http." Users are sometimes directed to an "http" secure site, the "https" version. In order to always use the secure site, as described on their website, "many sites on the web offer some limited support for encryption over HTTPS, but make it difficult to use. . . . The HTTPS Everywhere extension fixes these problems by using clever technology to rewrite requests to these sites to HTTPS." Thus, it will always redirect your browser to the encrypted, safer version of any website. This is a helpful tool to determine if any given website does, indeed, have a secure URL. If it does not employ HTTPS, this does not inherently mean the website is malicious; yet, without a secure connection, it is important for users to be more mindful of interacting with that site.

As students explore issues related to privacy and security, they might assume that using their web browser's "incognito" mode will protect them. This is a misconception that bears some investigation, as a tech reporter for the United Kingdom's *Independent* notes. "While incognito mode stops Chrome from saving your browsing activities, they could still remain visible to others," meaning that the websites that are being visited may still be using trackers (Sulleyman, 2017). Even though the search history for that session wasn't recorded, trackers from sites like Facebook and Google are still at work. According to an article in *Wired,* "Although cookies and tracking data are deleted when your private session finishes, they can still be used while the session is active, linking your activities between various accounts and profiles" (Nield, 2020), much like the example of Facebook serving up ads from cookies, mentioned above. In short, a user's browsing history may not be evident, but the tracking was still happening in the background.

Returning to NCTE's "Definition of Literacy in a Digital Age," a connection to the questions under the "Examine the rights, responsibilities, and ethical implications of the use and creation of information" section is particularly useful for this topic. While they themselves are not necessarily in the position of being considered a hacker engaged in hostile activity, students can consider how these topics point out issues related to the potential for being spied upon and the need to "practice the safe and legal use of technology." Moreover, in understanding exactly what kinds of data the websites they are visiting are actually collecting from them, students begin to understand the need to both "attend to the terms of service and/or terms of use of digital software and tools" and "read, review, and understand the terms of service/use that they agree to as they utilize these tools" (NCTE, 2019b). By gaining insight on what various companies are tracking as users visit their sites—as well as the cookies that continue to track them across other sites—students will be able to discuss their own rights and responsibilities, as well as what they trade off when using these services.

Guiding Questions

When working with students and exploring this topic, consider the following questions when designing lessons, assignments, and assessments:

Opening Questions

- What does "privacy" mean to you?
- What do you already know about (your) privacy on the web?
- What do you know about how is your data shared?
- What kinds of privacy are you willing to give up in order to use technology (or to make technology more useful for you)?
  - Your likeness in a photo or video?
  - Your email address?
  - Your location?
  - Your browsing history?
  - Your relationships with other people in your social network?
- What can you do to take control of your own data?

As Students Try Out Ad Blockers

- The ad blockers will indicate a tally of blocked ads on any given site, which can also be accessed by clicking on the ad block icon.
  - What kinds of sites or specific URLs have the most ads?
  - What kinds of sites or specific URLs have the least?

○ Which ones will prompt you by showing a pop-up window, or otherwise hiding content, and suggesting you "disable your ad blocker"?

○ Why might this be the case?

• The ad blockers also offer users the option to "pause" blocking on a page, or to stop running on an entire web site.

○ When, how, and why might you choose to pause or completely stop ad blocking on a page/site?

• As they continue to use an ad blocker, invite students to answer the following questions:

○ What is the cumulative total of ads that are blocked after one day? One week? One month?

○ What do you notice about your overall web browsing experience, with the ad blocker enabled?

○ How might this connect to the idea of "click restraint" and helping you make more intentional browsing and reading decisions?

Further Questions

• How might you adjust your browser settings (the tool) so, in turn, you adjust your actual browsing habits (the actions)?

• Are there times when you would want to view a website in its full form, with ads, in order to analyze it using the questions of critical media literacy?

• When concluding discussions of the topic, we might ask students to document their thinking about what they have discovered. They might use sentence starters like these:

○ When I first visited [website], I noticed . . .

○ When I looked at it again with the ad blocker on, I noticed . . .

○ After turning on Privacy Badger, I could see that . . .

○ After turning on HTTPS Everywhere, I notice . . .

○ As a result of using these privacy and security tools on this site, in the future I will . . .

TOPIC 3.3. (RE)SEARCHING OUR SEARCH ENGINES

To help them become digitally diligent, we need students to compare the ways in which various search engines return their results to a user, noting the ways that certain services will customize results in ways that the company may suggest are highly personalized and useful yet will also hide other results, potentially leading to a biased perspective on a topic.

Overview

We use search engines (or perhaps one particular search engine) over and over, across devices, to access the information we need and to navigate our worlds (both virtually and, increasingly, physically). Understanding the advantages and disadvantages of different search engines is crucial as we consider which ones to use, as well as strategic ways in which we can use them. Exploring multiple search engines is an important way to gain insights into how they work, and in doing so this topic encourages students to better understand the one tool they are most likely to use: Google.

Search engines are not neutral tools. As authors and speakers like Eli Pariser (2011a, 2011b) and Safiya Umoja Noble (2018) make clear, recognizing the ways that search engines work is crucial as we teach our students to be critical, conscientious users of the web. Moreover, the ways in which search engines use our data to make predictive searches—for ourselves and for others who search for similar terms—means that one user's experience of "being online" may be drastically different than another person's experience. Pariser's ideas will be explored more in Topic 5.1, so I focus here on Noble's work.

In her book *Algorithms of Oppression: How Search Engines Reinforce Racism* (2018), Noble documents her own experience as an African American woman of searching for information about "black girls" and the disturbing results that Google displayed. Her journey began in the fall of 2010, at the time as a marketer of multicultural products. When doing some searching for products to share with her stepdaughter and nieces, she describes how she was "overtaken by the results" (p. 3) as her first search for the keywords of "black girls" led her to a porn site.

From this initial shockwave, she refocused her academic career and has built a compelling series of arguments around the idea that "a corporate logic of either willful neglect or a profit imperative that makes money from racism and sexism" (p. 5) is baked into the ways that Google works. One of her contentions can be summarized in her belief "that Google functions in the interests of its most influential paid advertisers or through an intersection of popular and commercial interests" (p. 36). In short, Google does not work to help us find what we are looking for in an egalitarian, utopian version of the web; it serves us up content that will lead to their own profit.

Google, of course, is the default for the majority of all searches. Given that the action of "googling" has become a verb, the search engine itself has redefined the ways in which nearly all of us interface with the web. To that end, we need to explore not only the "advanced search" features of the tool but also the ways in which the search itself functions. Whether or not students ultimately choose to switch off some of these options that contextualize searches (such as "autocomplete" for web searches or adding location) or the way that results appear (by opening in a new tab)—or move to an entirely different search engine—they must analyze the ways in which results are delivered to them and make informed decisions about when, how, and why to click into those results.

With this topic, students will explore deeper aspects of what Google knows about their own search history, altering their settings and exploring the ways in which these tweaks and changes can affect their search experience. Students will then compare the results with other search engines. Three of Google's features—(1) autocomplete for predictive search, (2) regional or location-based settings, and (3) automatic opening of search results in a new tab—could also be explored as a way to provide foundational knowledge and to reiterate themes about digital diligence.

Teaching Points

Without a doubt, search engines have revolutionized the ways in which we think about information: what it is, how to find it, and what we can do with that information once we do find it. As noted above, we use a search engine's name, Google, and turn it into a verb, "googling." This shift in our language demonstrates the ways in which search engines are an integral part of our daily lives and how much we rely on them. Yet, there are more search engines than just Google. And sometimes we may want students to begin online inquiry not with a search engine but with a more robust database or collection of materials curated by experts.

While there are still the big three search engines that comprise the vast majority of the search engine marketplace (Google, Yahoo, and Bing), a number of lesser-known search engines can give students insights into topics that can also be useful. Begin by inviting students to explore Google Search and Advanced Search. Examining the affordances and constraints of Google Search is an important goal for students as they continue to think about the ways they use the web. Google's own Search Education resources can be useful for exploring lesson plans and activities, as well as practicing one's own advanced search skills through "power search" and their "A Google a Day" challenges. These resources provide a good place to begin teaching students about the ways that search engines work.

From there, they can explore other search engines. Two, in particular, are helpful to show a variety of search experiences. First, DuckDuckGo, which calls itself "an Internet privacy company" (DuckDuckGo, n.d.), is a search engine that will not track you and has, more recently, devoted itself to a broader movement about online privacy. Second, described as a "metasearch," Dogpile examines multiple search engines and then "decides which are most relevant to your search, eliminates duplicates and reveals them to you" (Dogpile, n.d.). There are many other search engine options, and Wikipedia has a comprehensive list. Links to all of these resources are available on the book's companion site: hickstro.org/digitaldiligence.

To begin an inquiry from another perspective, moving away from typical search engines could be useful too. Examining topics from sources that show multiple perspectives can be illuminating for students. Depending on which ones are accessible at school or through the state's online library, subscription databases like EBSCO's Points of View Reference Center and Gale's Opposing Viewpoints in Context can be good places to begin. Also, for perspectives on a variety of topics, the openly available ProCon, All-Sides, and Kialo EDU websites each offer students additional talking points and links to even more resources, demonstrating this variety of perspectives. These will be explored more in topics in Chapter 5.

Asking students to compare and contrast what they find through their initial web searches with what they discover through other engines—and through portals that show multiple perspectives—can help them understand their topics in more complex and nuanced ways. As with other topics, there are additional resources on the book's companion website that will further explain how search engines work and can be used as part of a text set to introduce the concept to students. As they read and view these resources—and continue to use various search engines—the overarching questions as they view results of a search term across multiple engines, drawn from Harvard Project Zero's visible thinking routine (2019b), could be summed up like this: What do you see, think, and wonder? When comparing and contrasting results, even more conversations can emerge.

NCTE's "Definition of Literacy in a Digital Age" provides us with more questions to consider as we move this topic into lesson planning. For instance, under the "Consume" subheading in the "Consume, curate, and create actively across contexts" section of the statement, NCTE asks a number of questions relevant to a discussion about search engines. For instance, they ask if "learners review a variety of sources to evaluate information as they consider bias and perspective in sources?" as well as if "learners examine the credibility and relevancy of sources they consume" (NCTE, 2019b). In order to move into these deeper levels of perceiving differences, students must first be able to access this variety of sources. Knowing more about their search engines—and the ways in which these engines deliver results—is a foundational step if we want our students to be able to make these kinds of judgments.

Guiding Questions

When working with students and exploring this topic, consider the following questions when designing lessons, assignments, and assessments:

Opening Questions

- What search engine(s) do you use primarily? Why?
- Based on your browsing history, device usage, and locations, what does your search engine know about you? How can you tell?
- How does "search" work? What are the methods at work when we use search engines? What happens behind the screen when we type a term or query into a search engine?
- How is "search" a literacy practice? What are the ways in which we write search queries, and how do these queries affect, ultimately, what we find?
- When the search engine "autocompletes" a search query for us, what are we, as readers and writers, giving up in the process?

As Students Try Out Various Search Engines with the Same Search Term(s), Invite Them to Consider the Following

- After ads and sponsored content or recent news, what are the top five sites in the search?

- Review the ads. What are the top three ads in the search? How do they align with the regular search results?

- What, if any, images show up on the main search page? What images are dominant when switching to the "image search" option?

- Where, if at all, does a Wikipedia entry show up in the search results?
  - Why might this be the case that it appears in this slot?

- Thinking about the results of the search term across multiple search engines, what do you notice, think, and wonder about the results?
  - How might a combination of searches across multiple engines enhance a user's research experience?

CHAPTER 4

Maximizing Our Own Attention

Our attention, as any advertiser will tell us, is our most valuable asset; there are tools and strategies we can use to stay focused, minimize distraction, and increase productivity.

Knowing the Internet has become inextricably tied to nearly everyone's daily life in some manner or another, we need to understand what it is, how it works, and how it has been designed, intentionally, to capture—and, as some would argue, keep a stranglehold on—our attention. As noted in Chapter 1, there are many negative consequences that can radiate from too much technology use. The American Psychiatric Association's (2013) fifth edition of the *Diagnostic and Statistical Manual of Mental Disorders* (DSM-5) describes an "Internet gaming disorder," which has also been compared to (though not equated with) a broader condition of a behavioral addiction related to using the Internet: "Internet addiction disorder." While I am a doctor (of philosophy), I need to make it clear here that I am certainly not a physician, nor a mental health professional, so I leave further discussions related to whether overactive technology use is an actual medical "condition" up to others who can offer more informed insights about the causes—and long-term mental health effects—of addiction to technology (Griffiths, 2016; Twenge, 2017a, 2017b).

Still, as ELA teachers, the issue is right in front of us. The ways that we ask students to engage with their devices matters. Moreover, we know from our own experiences that these devices are full of distractions, offering us opportunities to participate in leisure and stay informed about general topics, though also sometimes preventing us from pursuing sustained inquiry or produce new content. In order to employ our devices in ways that lead to more literate ends, how can we help our students learn how to maximize their own attention? Or, to draw a phrase from the NCTE (2019b) definition, how do we help our students "make decisions in information-rich environments" when there are endless decisions to be made?

Beginning with Topic 4.1, "Clearing the Clutter," an exploration of some commonly available, though often unused, tools—including reader-view options, as well as tools for wrangling web browser tabs—can help students think about how to focus their attention across browsing sessions. Following that, in Topic 4.2, "Feeding Our Own Interests," I offer some thoughts on how we can help students create their own curated—and, in some cases, self-updating—list of interest-driven materials for further inquiry and exploration. Last, in Topic 4.3, "Self-Monitoring Our Screen Time," a further exploration of how we might teach students to be self-regulating is presented (though, I admit, we are all still likely to struggle with screen time, even with some of these technological solutions applied).

Like Chapter 3, though not cited explicitly, my thinking on these topics has been drawn from many sources, linked on the book's companion website: hickstro.org/digitaldiligence. In particular, the Center for Humane Technology's podcast series *Your Undivided Attention* has provided a great deal of information about how the addictive nature of the Internet was developed. Also, as noted earlier in the book, Manoush Zomorodi's "bored and brilliant" challenges were a useful turning point, in 2015, for me and hundreds of other listeners of her *Note to Self* podcast. Finally, as we think about ways to harness technology in the service of teaching students to be more mindful, Common Sense Education has gathered a collection of tools in their "Top Tools for Building Mindfulness in the Classroom" collection. As always, this list of influences continues to grow, and I will work to keep the book's companion website updated.

TOPIC 4.1. CLEARING THE CLUTTER

To help them become digitally diligent, we need students to understand
their own needs as readers and viewers who are constantly working
to make sense of an Internet that is competing for their attention,
employing tools that can make the experience more manageable.

Overview

Anyone who spends time online knows that the default manner for content providers to earn money is to serve up ads on their websites. While this does make a great deal of the content we are able to view online free (and not stuck behind a "paywall," or a password-protected space that requires a user to subscribe to that content in order to gain premium access), the simple fact is that it can be distracting. Content providers also design their headlines and opening sentences—along with appealing visuals—to make us want to click. As Internet activist Sally Kohn suggests in her TED Talk, because of rising incivility and the ways in which media makers try to influence us, we need to get beyond the "tyranny of the loud" and "we've got to stop clicking on the lowest-common-denominator, bottom-feeding linkbait" (S. Kohn, 2014). As with nearly every other action that we need to take in order to become more digitally diligent, we sometimes need a little bit of help to keep us from our own worst instincts.

Some of this begins with the ways we read, quite literally. From left to right, top to bottom, reading in English requires us to move our eyes in certain patterns. Hearkening back to a scholar introduced in the first pages of this book, we consider the argument that Maryanne Wolf articulates in *Reader, Come Home: The Reading Brain in a Digital World* (2018). Like other scholars who have studied the actual patterns of reading, Wolf reminds us that extensive research about reading shows that most of us, when reading on paper, tend to run our eyes across the text in a *Z* pattern. This means we generally track from left to right and then zig back to the left as we move to the next line of paragraph. We then go all the way to the right before moving to the next line. Without ads and other types of clutter to distract us, we (generally) engage fully in each line and move strategically to the next.

With website viewing, however, researchers have used eye-tracking software to note that we use an *F* pattern. What this means, according to the Nielsen Norman Group, which documented the pattern in 2006, is that readers may skim and scan pages in an effort to be efficient, or because they are bored (Pernice, 2017). Unlike the *Z* pattern, where our eyes move all the way to the end of a line before moving down to the next, the *F* pattern shows that readers will generally read to the end of a line at the beginning of an online article and—as they continue down the page—the amount of text they consume, in a thorough manner, begins to fade. Looking at smaller and smaller segments of text as they scroll down, readers are not even skimming the entire text and may, by the time they reach the end of an article, be barely attending to anything other than the first words on a line of text. Put another way, these studies that employ eye-tracking software confirm that many readers are not as fully engaged in their reading as they could be.

Some scholars, like Wolf, continue to argue that there is little to no reason for students to read on-screen if, indeed, we want them to be fully present and use immersive reading practices (e.g., Baron, 2015). Others, including, me, suggest that we need to explicitly teach students how to interact with digital texts in purposeful ways. This involves two processes. At one level, we want to help students make their on-screen reading emulate, at least sometimes, what they would typically experience when reading a more traditional print text. That is what we will explore in this chapter. The other level, which will be the focus in Chapter 8, is the idea that we invite students to read and respond to texts by maximizing the digital tools they have available to them. More on that later. For now, the goal of this topic is, as noted in the title, to clear the clutter. In addition to blocking ads (as outlined in Topic 3.2), there are two other kinds of tools that can help students stay attentive when reading: reader-view tools and tab organizers.

Teaching Points

In an initial web search, as we are trying to gather as much information as possible about a particular topic, we will likely be using lateral reading and moving through many sites to gather information. Pausing for just a moment on each site to annotate important information and save the URL for future use can be a good way to summarize and synthesize what we are doing as we move through our research. No matter what tool is chosen, to begin a conversation about the utility of these tools, it could be worth talking with students about what happens for them when they are browsing the Internet. Perhaps it would be useful to model a "think-aloud" related to browsing habits, showing students how to open multiple tabs when searching for and evaluating information from various websites.

Reader-View Tools

With reader-view tools, most web browsers have these features for helping hide the distractions, if we know how to use them. The advantage of a "reader view" is that additional banners, sidebars, and advertisements are removed (if ad block hasn't already), making the reading experience clear and simple. Additionally, these tools often allow the user to adjust font size, text and background color schemes, and other settings for easier reading. Microsoft's Edge, Mozilla's Firefox, and Apple's Safari all have reader-view functions built in. A quick web search or look at the software's help guide will demonstrate how to use them, and Figures 4.1.1 and 4.1.2 captures screenshots of what an article might look like on a popular news site home page in Safari without ad-blocking

FIGURE 4.1.1. Blurred screenshot of an article on a major news site.

FIGURE 4.1.2. Blurred screenshot of an article on a major news site with Reader View enabled.

or reader-view enabled and the distinctly different view when reader view is enabled. Please note: The images have been intentionally blurred due to copyright restrictions.

As is the case with Chrome, even if the browser doesn't have built-in features for clearing the clutter, there are extensions that can help too. Searching the Chrome Web Store for "reader view" or "readerview" yields a number of options. Ones that might show up include Clearly Reader, EasyReader, Reader View, or Just Read. Some of these extensions offer more options than others, so trying out two or three of them might be a good option as students make their initial decisions about which one might work best.

As a side note, it could be worth talking a bit about why there is no "default" for ad blocking in any browser and why, specifically with Google Chrome, there is no reader view. On one level, it is easy to understand the reasons that Google—a service largely driven by in-line and banner-style ads—would want to keep their browser from having a reader view as a default. Yet, they allow them in the web store. What motivations do the software designers and advertisers at Google have for not including this as a default option? Why, then, do they allow developers to create extensions for this purpose? These could be questions to pose in an informal manner, or as the start of a larger inquiry.

Tab Suspenders and Organizers

In addition to reader-view tools that help us manage our experience on a single tab, another category of tools can help us focus on the work at hand once we open more and more tabs in our work session: tab suspenders and organizers. If we are asking students to purposefully use lateral reading (Wineburg & McGrew, 2017), we also want to help them make sure their efforts at fact-checking and finding additional sources will not go to waste. Keeping track of sources is an important part of being digitally diligent, and these tools can be useful for keeping us structured.

These tab suspenders and organizers are useful both for keeping us ready to find the information we need and because—as more and more tabs are opened—the computer's available memory, or RAM, will decrease. There are programs you could use to actually demonstrate this reduction in RAM—through Activity Monitor in Mac OS, through Task Manager in Windows, as well as various apps that can be installed on smartphones and tablets—if that kind of real-time illustration of CPU usage seems useful for your students. Even a quick overview of what happens in a normal web browsing session can be useful for students to understand what is happening on their devices when they are browsing the web (Horowitz, 2016; TechStacker, 2018).

To that end, tools to pause tabs such as Tab Hibernate, Tiny Suspender, and Tab Suspender can all be helpful for pausing inactive tabs, both reducing the drain on RAM and "greying out" inactive tabs once a certain period of time has elapsed. For instance, I use Tab Suspender and have it set to pause inactive tabs after five minutes. There are also options to ensure that tabs where you have ongoing work—such as inputting data into a form—are not suspended. Once a user clicks on a suspended tab, it can reload automatically, or after another click reactivates it. Finally, users can indicate "white-list" sites that will never be suspended. Given the many options for customizing one's tab suspension preferences, these extensions can be configured in ways that best suit an individual user's needs.

In that same spirit, we want students to understand that curating the information they find online is important so they can document their web-based sources and return to trusted ones. Having multiple browsing sessions saved in different windows can be helpful. One set of tabs can be related to one school subject, like ELA, and another set of tabs related to math, science, or social studies. Additionally, having a set of tabs open related to a passion project, entertainment, news, or other trending topics can be helpful too. Thus, when students move from one window (with a number of tabs related to one topic) to another, they are not losing time in task switching, trying to find the specific tab they might be looking for among dozens in one window.

Just as there are with the tab suspenders, there are many tools for managing tabs and, by extension, the bookmarks that we might save in our browsers, or through web-based services like Diigo and Papaly. Again, there are multiple tools that serve similar purposes, so it is partially a matter of preference as we help students identify what will work best for them, especially as they move from their personal devices to school devices. Some look like a more linear list of bookmarks. Others have a more visual interface, with columns, tiles, and color coding to help users make sense of their various open tabs and lists of bookmarks.

In addition to Diigo and Papaly, described earlier, I have also included links to Netvibes, Pearltrees, Raindrop.io, Tagpacker, and Wakelet on this book's companion website. In our current context—where an individual user is moving across mobile devices, as well as laptop and desktop computers—many browsers allow users to sync their bookmarks, or "favorites," across devices. Chrome, Firefox, Safari, Edge, and Opera allow for this, when user accounts are enabled, and additional services like EverSync, Atavi, TeamSync, and xBrowserSync are options too (Writtenhouse, 2019). Additionally, "visual bookmarking" tools like Speed Dial, Symbaloo, and Start.me offer an aesthetically pleasing interface for managing and viewing one's bookmarks and launch pages. Another tool, Pocket—described as a tool to "curate your own space filled with everything you can't wait to learn" and as a way to "read or listen without distraction, on any device" (Pocket, n.d.)—was acquired by Mozilla in 2017 and is now a component of the Firefox browser, and has extensions for all other major web browsers. Moreover, with the ability to sync bookmarks across devices, students may find that Google Chrome's own bookmark management tool is sufficient.

As in previous chapters, taking a moment to return to NCTE's "Definition of Literacy in a Digital Age" exhibits the ways in which these efforts to clear the clutter can also align with the goals we have to support our digitally diligent learners. Because of the variety of tools available, this topic demonstrates the distinct need for our students to "select, evaluate, and use digital tools and resources that match the work they are doing" (under the "Participate effectively and critically in a networked world" subheading) and "collect, aggregate, and share content to develop their voice/identity/expertise on a topic" (under the "Consume, curate, and create actively across contexts" subheading). Further, this could lead to efforts where they "evaluate content they find online before sharing with others" (also under the under the "Consume, curate, and create . . ." subheading; NCTE, 2019b). In all these efforts, we will then continue to encourage them to expand their view of what it means to fully document the sources they find online and provide attribution to their sources.

Guiding Questions

When working with students and exploring this topic, consider the following questions when designing lessons, assignments, and assessments:

Opening Questions

- How do you browse the web? Are you more likely to browse with multiple tabs open? If so, how do you interact with multiple tabs?
- By default, are your browser/search engine settings already in place so links open in new tabs?
  - If your settings are such that clicking on links does not open new tabs, are there times that you use contextual menus by right-clicking (on a computer) or holding down a link (on a touchscreen) to "open in a new tab"?

As Students Try Out Reader View

- To what extend do you feel you are usually acting with intention and focus when reading on the web?
  - How long would it take to read a typical article on a website, without reader view enabled?
- While it is, of course, impossible for students to track their own eye-movement patterns, we could encourage them to think about eye fixations and movement (whether in a *Z* or *F* pattern).
  - How long would it take to read a typical article when reader view is enabled? (Again, encourage them to think about the *Z* and *F* patterns.)
- With many reader views, there will often be an "estimate" for the amount of time it will take a user to read a particular article.
  - Discuss this estimate with students and consider how we vary our reading rates, depending on topic and purpose.
  - When and how might these estimates be useful for readers to consider?
  - When and how might we choose to ignore these estimates?
- Even in reader view, links and many images are still available.
  - As we think about the ways we read web-based texts, what additional strategies will we still need to employ, such as click restraint and lateral reading (opening in new tabs)?

As Students Try Out Tab Suspenders

- If we want to have students delve deeply into CPU usage statistics before installing a tab suspender, we can ask them to open Activity Monitor (in Mac) or Task Manager (in Windows) and keep an eye on their usage statistics as they browse.
  - Ask them to try suspending tabs and look at what happens to the overall CPU statistics.
  - There are also Chrome Extensions, such as Clean All, Clean Master, and History and Cache Cleaner, among others, that could be useful for an exercise like this.
- Once the tab suspender extension is activated, have students look at the particular settings that are available.
  - For instance, most tab suspenders allow for students to manually suspend tabs immediately and to "never suspend" a particular URL or entire domain.
  - Additional settings allow users to decide how quickly to suspend tabs (with ranges from a few seconds to a week or longer) and other conditions under which tabs should never be suspended (for instance, when playing audio or video, even in the background).
  - Explore all these settings as a way to think about when, how, and why certain websites could or should be suspended.
- As students become more adept at suspending and organizing tabs, ask them to consider how these tools have changed their overall browsing habits.
  - In what ways are your browsing habits more efficient now than before?
  - In what ways might this accumulation of tabs/windows perhaps cause even more "FOMO" (fear of missing out)?

As Students Try Out Tab Organizers

- Invite students to think about the various reasons they use the web and encourage them to be specific.
  - For instance, even if they say they are using the web for random browsing and entertainment, it is likely they might be following a certain celebrity or social media personality at one time, while at another time they might be streaming music or video clips.
    - In what ways do students describe their own web use?
    - Who and what do they follow?
    - Where do these initial encounters lead them?
    - How do the tabs open in their web browser affect them as readers?
  - While these purposes may sometimes overlap, how might students try to discern the different ways they use the web in order to create different windows with sets of tabs?

- Once students have set up at least two, preferably three or four, different windows with a few tabs in each, have them turn on the filtering/organizing extension.
  - Many of these extensions will then condense all the open tabs into a single window. In that view, students can then use a number of tools to organize their information, including renaming groups of tabs, merging different windows together, and sharing the lists of tabs with a URL or QR code.
  - How might students collaborating on projects together share their tabbed browsing sessions with one another to help further their work together?
- Like anything else in our lives that requires (at least occasional) decluttering and reorganization, how might they review what they have saved, over time, and reprioritize tabs that have been closed yet still exist in the tab manager and could be opened again quickly?
  - Are there sites that were visited/used in the past that could, again, be useful in current projects, or in line with current interests?

TOPIC 4.2. FEEDING OUR OWN INTERESTS

To help them become digitally diligent, we need students to select and organize high-interest materials that will be delivered to them through an app or web-based delivery tool, as well as to curate and annotate those materials for future use.

Overview

Since the beginning of written communication, and the accumulation of countless texts—from parchments to manuscripts and bound books and, in our current moment, social media posts—we have always been trying to take those many, many texts and organize them. Library sciences and cataloging systems are one manifestation of our work to coordinate these texts; similarly, we try to manage and make sense of the World Wide Web too. In the early days of the public web in the late 1990s and early 2000s, browsers came equipped with the option to "bookmark" an item and to even sort those bookmarks into other usable lists (as noted in Topic 4.1).

With the advent of "Web 2.0," a number of services for *social bookmarking*, a cloud-based service to store and share bookmarks, emerged with services like Furl, Delicious, and CiteULike (all three are currently defunct). These systems popularized terms such as *tagging* (the use of tags to organize a single bookmarked site across multiple categories) and *folksonomy* (in contrast to a formal taxonomy, a folksonomy is a user-generated hierarchy based on the tags that users assign). Though a bit dated, Clay Shirky's 2005 TED Talk, "Institutions vs. Collaboration," is actually a unique snapshot of the Web 2.0 zeitgeist. He discusses the use of tagging with one of the original social photo-sharing sites, Flickr (Shirky, 2005), and he captures the spirit that such social, collaborative practices could engender.

Still, it is challenging to even know exactly how to start organizing our own information in nested folders of bookmarks. The ways in which any one of us accomplishes this goal is, by the very nature of the task, slightly different than the way another might do so. In addition, we want students to engage in bookmarking in a purposeful manner, and most browser-based bookmarking does not allow for any tagging or annotation. As a quick side note, and in connection with the tools, described in Topic 4.1, using an RSS reader does allow the user to keep an organized list of materials, though typically does not save a copy of the website for later reading. So, having some way to tag and/or annotate is both a technical and a literacy skill that is worth teaching in combination with the skills outlined here.

This leads us to an examination of RSS (defined as either "rich site summary" or "really simple syndication"), which has been around since the earliest days of the graphical interface of the World Wide Web. RSS, and the more recently developed Atom, are both ways of syndicating—or pushing out web content—to users in the form of social media posts, podcasts, blog or article entries, and other forms of news feeds. Regardless of the technical specifications (and as we know from current updates in our in-boxes and via smartphone notifications), these syndicated feeds are a ubiquitous part of online life. As one summary, Wikipedia's entry on "web syndication" captures the importance of the syndication function succinctly: "Today, millions of online publishers, including newspapers, commercial websites, and blogs, distribute their news headlines, product offers, and blog postings in news feeds" (Wikipedia, 2020c).

Taking control of these feeds—and using them to stay on top of our own interests, passions, and inquiries—is another matter. In *The Digital Writing Workshop,* I introduced the idea of using RSS tools to help students manage one's online reading life (T. Hicks, 2009). Since that time, I have often talked about the idea of "sustained silent reading," or SSR, with RSS. This is more than just random scrolling through social media. Helping students identify the sources from which they can gain useful, entertaining, and provocative articles is a critical part of our role as ELA teachers, and depending on the settings that are enabled by default, or what we have clicked to approve in the past, any number of notifications may fill our screens, some of which seem pertinent and others that distract us. Moreover, we need to develop a balanced news diet, looking at what Eli Pariser calls "information vegetables" and "information dessert" (Pariser, 2011a). Moving beyond simple searches and what our news apps send us, this topic invites students to learn more about news feeds and how to make them more manageable.

Teaching Points

Whether you know it or not, much of what you read on the Internet or via smartphone apps has its roots in one simple technology: RSS. While there is some variety in how technology standards change (there are newer syndication tools like Atom and others), the main idea is that new content from websites—including text, images, video, and audio—can be "syndicated" or pushed out to a variety of other websites and applications. These tools then "aggregate" that content and we can subscribe to websites and blogs that share content (as we used to, and still sometimes do, subscribe to physical magazines and newspapers). Figure 4.2.1 shows the logo that indicates that a feed is available on a website.

Despite the end of Google Reader in 2013, there are still numerous tools that can be used to aggregate content, including Feedly, Inoreader, CommaFeed, FeedReader, and Feedbro (Chrome extension), all linked from the book's companion website. Because Feedly is both a web-based service that one can access through a browser and an app available for mobile devices (and offers a great deal of functionality even with the limited, freemium features), it is one of the most useful tools for reading RSS feeds. Another tool, Flipboard, functions as a kind of interactive magazine, and Mozilla's Pocket (noted earlier) can serve similar purposes. For this topic, it is probably best to focus students on efforts to find RSS icons and to add those feeds to a reader app, as I originally described in a lesson from *Connected Reading* (Turner & Hicks, 2015b), adapted here.

For instance, with Feedly, a user will be presented with their Feedly home page and it will invite them to search for sites to add. As one example, I search for CNN first. Feedly quickly finds the main feed for CNN.com and presents me with the option to add it to my reader by clicking a "+" sign, as shown in Figure 4.2.2. After this, I will see the feed for CNN appear on the screen with all the latest stories. To add it to my Feedly home page, I click the green button that says "+ add to my feedly." In this manner, I can continue to search for other topics and sources of interest and then add them to my Feedly account. It is worth taking time and helping students choose multiple sources of interest, including a number of reputable news organizations; individual bloggers; social media accounts of a celebrity, an athlete, an artist, or another person of interest; and other topics related to their academic and personal passions.

Sometimes, websites will clearly share links to these feeds. They may show the orange symbol right on their site. Clicking on it will take users to a new page that may look like gibberish, but it is actually the computer code for the RSS feed. By copying that URL and taking it back to Feedly, one can add to their subscriptions there too. Other times, it won't be quite as easy to find an orange icon. Sometimes, one can search for RSS feeds with tools like Instant RSS Search, RSS Micro, and RSS.app. Further, users

FIGURE 4.2.1. RSS logo. *Source:* Wikipedia (public domain).

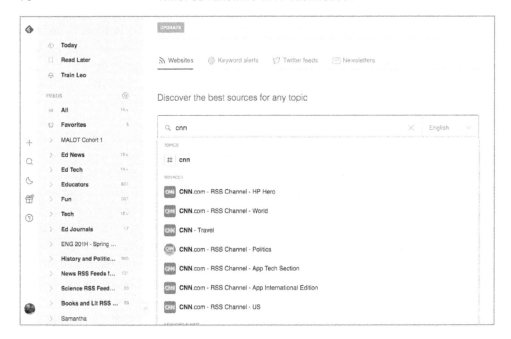

FIGURE 4.2.2. Screenshot of Feedly with CNN search.

may not be able to find just the right RSS feed for what they're hoping to read. In this case, they can create their own RSS feed using Google Alerts. In Google Alerts, a user types in a search term and it will then generate the option of receiving updates as an email or via "feed."

No matter how users begin to search for feeds and organize their ongoing reading spaces, there are a number of connections to the NCTE "Definition of Literacy in a Digital Age." When students only stay focused on their own social media feeds, they can quickly become stuck in their own "filter bubble" (as described by Pariser), or "echo chamber." By actively seeking out and gaining new updates from multiple news sources, they are forced to see different perspectives. By experiencing a variety of texts and media forms through one connection, they have an opportunity to "explore and engage critically, thoughtfully, and across a wide variety of inclusive texts and tools/modalities." Also, by following a variety of sources—and engaging in sustained inquiry, with their classmates, over time—students can begin to "determine how and to what extent texts and tools amplify one's own and others' narratives as well as counter unproductive narratives." Again, with critical approaches to their news feeds, we can also push learners to "analyze information for authorial intent, positioning, and how language, visuals, and audio are being used" (NCTE, 2019b).

To go even deeper, the list of questions within the "explore and engage critically, thoughtfully, and across a wide variety of inclusive texts and tools/modalities" subsection of the definition asks a number of important questions as students begin "making choices and using texts and tools in ways that match purpose." A few of the NCTE questions that are especially pertinent as we ask them to set up their feeds include the following:

- "Do learners seek out texts that consider multiple perspectives and broaden their understanding of the world?"
- "Do learners critically analyze a variety of information and ideas from a variety of sources?"
- "Do learners strive to see limitations and overlaps between multiple streams of information?" (NCTE, 2019b)

In combination with some of the topics and activities I will suggest in Chapter 5, these syndication tools/feed readers are underutilized options for helping our students begin to read more widely and gain various perspectives.

Guiding Questions

When working with students and exploring this topic, consider the following questions when designing lessons, assignments, and assessments:

Opening Questions

- What information is typically delivered to you through news alerts that you have set on your mobile device? Do you remember making a conscious decision to receive these notifications? Do you know how to silence or terminate these notifications?
- To what extent have you tried to customize the information that gets delivered to you?
- What other information might be useful to have delivered to you, and in what format (mobile notification, email, social media, etc.)?

As Students Try Out the RSS/Syndication Reading Tools

- How do you feel about the reading interface of the app/website that you have chosen? How does the layout and design compare to what you normally read on the web or through social media apps?
- In what ways is the process of reading on the app/website (skimming and scrolling, as well as delving more deeply into sustained reading) similar to—and different from—the ways that you normally read online?
- What do you notice about the frequency of updates from various sources? What does this tell you about them as content creators?
- As you see information coming from different sources, all of which might focus on the same topic, what do you notice about how this information is presented?
- How might you continue to use a tool like this in the future in addition to other social media outlets like Snapchat, Instagram, TikTok, and other tools?

TOPIC 4.3. SELF-MONITORING OUR SCREEN TIME

To help them become digitally diligent, we need students to recognize
when, why, how, and how much they are engaged in screen time,
justifying their uses of technology in various ways given different
personal and academic goals.

Overview

As highlighted in the opening of this book, recent stories in the mass media, discussions among medical professionals, and hand-wringing among parents suggest that we are in the midst of a screen-time crisis. Understanding the current research on screen time and device usage—as well as how to use tools to discover our own usage patterns—can help our students make informed decisions about when, why, and how they use their devices. More than just setting limits, this topic encourages students to instead consider setting goals and think about the balance between consuming content and creating it. As *Washington Post* reporter Reed Albergotti reported in late 2019, this is a challenge that extends into the relationships that we have with youth, noting that "the problem has bedeviled parents who have struggled to strike a balance between allowing smartphone access for school work and basic social interactions and protecting their children from the pitfalls of the mobile world."

For instance, even before Apple introduced its Screentime app in 2018 as a way to help parents and caregivers set limits on their children's iOS devices, there were other parental control apps and subscription services. Google had offered a "Digital Wellbeing" self-quiz with tips for finding ways to disconnect from technology and remain more focused, especially when spending time with family and friends (links on the book's companion website). Apps like Forest and Moment had provided users with ways to monitor their smartphone usage. Moreover, browser extensions offering Pomodoro-style timers and the option to block certain websites for periods of time were also available across platforms.

As one example, in Google Chrome's web store, the StayFocused extension promises users the ability to "stay focused on work by restricting the amount of time you can spend on time-wasting websites. Once your allotted time has been used up, the sites you have blocked will be inaccessible for the rest of the day." Similar apps like WasteNoTime, Strict Workflow, Block & Focus, WebTime Tracker, Timewarp, BlockSite, and Pause all offer similar options for setting up blocks on certain websites for different periods of time. Clearly, there is a felt need among many, many web users that maintaining control of our—or our students'—browsing time is needed. All of these tools (whether a smartphone app, a web browser extension, or parental controls in the computer operating system) offer what might be called a "brute force" tool for maximizing attention. We wrestle control from ourselves by putting it back in the hands of the technology tools, all with the goal that we each figure out ways for self-regulation.

In this sense, the technologies described above offer respite from other technologies that were designed to distract us. To be fair, reviews of many of these apps suggest that some users find them to be meaningful ways of regaining some of their own attention. Moreover, there are points to be made about companies' motivations for keeping eyeballs on screens. As Albergotti (2019) summarizes succinctly, "Companies with wildly popular and profitable consumer products don't usually offer tools to help people use them less," a topic potentially worthy of student inquiry too.

However, the unintended consequences of these apps—especially when imposed by a parent, caregiver, or educator without a substantive dialogue related to their use—will likely lead students to additional feelings of frustration. An episode of the Netflix series *Black Mirror,* "Arkangel," takes this kind of monitoring to the extreme, where parents can have chips implanted in their children's brains to control the information they see (Framke, 2017), and could be worthy of conversation for some older students. Moreover, as noted above, clever workarounds abound. And, as has always been the case where students have wanted to get around school Internet filters, there are various ways to do so. Also, for any individual user with administrative rights to their own devices, they can turn these controls on and—even if the software makes it somewhat cumbersome to do so—off, thus creating a paradox in which they are blocking the blockers.

Still, as part of our effort to teach our students ways to be digitally diligent, the use of screen-time monitoring and website-blocking tools can be useful for them, if introduced as part of a broader strategy for when, how, and why they use the web, a strategy that they control. The teaching points below build on the premise that students will self-select what extensions or apps they might use in order to set up personalized routines and habits for web usage. While it is certainly the case that a school IT department could push some of these controls out to student devices—and that tools like NetNanny, Qustodio, Norton Family, and others can be installed at home—the goal here is to move our students toward more mindful use and self-monitoring.

Teaching Points

Part of the effort in this topic is to help students intentionally consider how they are using their devices at various times and for different purposes. Certainly, there are moments when we use technology in a purposeful way to pursue personal, academic, or other meaningful goals. These goals can ebb and flow, even within one period of time on the computer. And, certainly, there are moments when we use technology to distract ourselves, to procrastinate, or to engage in leisure activities. The challenge with our devices is that, in many ways, the lines between these tasks has been blurred so much that we struggle to figure out how to balance them. An email or text notification could be from a teacher, a family member, a friend, or a spambot. How we set up—and respond to—these notifications can have a significant effect on our productivity and, as some would argue, our happiness.

There are numerous articles offering guidelines for individuals on ways to best manage notifications, set up their home screens in an efficient manner, and otherwise assume more control of their digital lives. As part of the questioning strategies below, we can invite students to review the Center for Humane Technology's "Take Control" site and

Common Sense Media's "Customizable Device Contract" to review their tips and possibilities for setting up agreements. Also, as noted earlier, Manoush Zomorodi's podcast series through her WNYC show, *Note to Self,* in which she outlined the "Bored and Brilliant" (2015) challenges, could also provide some prompts for disengaging from tech. Her TED Talk (2017b), too, outlines the challenge and results that some listeners shared.

As students explore their use of various apps and web services—and try to really understand where and how they are spending their time—we can ask them to create a "map" of their own digital presence on the web. Some of this data can come from the types of screen-time monitoring apps listed in this topic, as well as a resource like Web Historian (described in Topic 3.1). In addition to looking at screen-time data, they might also use a tool like Namechk to create a visualization of the sites where they have accounts, getting even more insight on what the web knows about them (link available on the book's companion website).

For this activity, they could use any graphic design tool (like Canva or Google Drawing) or could simply organize their items on a slide in PowerPoint or Google Slides. To quickly find access to logos, Brands of the World is a website that can be useful, yet a basic image search can work too. Based on what students can find, they can then create a "map" of their online life, with logos placed in relative size and proportion to one another. My own screen-time map (Figure 4.3.1) is pretty boring, of course, when compared to what students might generate, but it does provide a starting place.

As I consider the ways in which I use the web, my dominant images are Gmail (through which much of my work is conducted) as well as Google Docs and Word (because I am writing for many hours a day). On the left of my map (Figure 4.3.1), I include YouTube and Twitter. Both of these sites can be distracting, and yet I can also learn many new ideas from the videos I watch and the people I interact with. Therefore, I need to use them, but do so sparingly. On the right of my map, I include the main page for my university, Central Michigan, and our learning management tool, Blackboard. I spend lots of time in those spaces too, creating lessons and materials for students, as well as reviewing their work and providing feedback. Overall, I think that I lead a well-balanced life on the web, though with Namechk I found about 25 accounts to services that I no longer use, and I was pleased to be able to delete those. I probably need to be

FIGURE 4.3.1. Self-monitoring: my screen-time map example.

even more intentional about how much time I spend on email, as I check it far too often and it can keep me away from more important work.

A teacher at Skyline High School in Ann Arbor, Michigan, and colleague from the Chippewa River Writing Project, Jill Runstrom, invited her students to create similar maps in February 2020, reflecting on the sites they use most after exploring their own browser histories with Web Historian and their screen-time stats on their mobile devices. Then she had them assemble their individual maps into an overall collage on her classroom whiteboard (see Figure 4.3.2). As students looked across the maps created by their classmates, they could compare and contrast their own experiences of what it means to "be online" and to "use technology." Moreover, another extension could be to ask them to look at what they are seeing in their collected maps and look at The Internet Map, a free and open site built by Ruslan Enikeev, in which we see the entire web like a constellation and zoom in to particular websites, domains, or even countries. In all of this, we want to continue to remind students that the web is a dynamic, ever-shifting space and that their—as well as their peers'—consumption and production of content is part of this universe.

As these ideas relate to the NCTE definition's overarching themes of literacies (plural) being "interconnected, dynamic, and malleable," this topic encourages students to see the many ways in which they individually—and, potentially, with their peers collectively—engage with the Internet. This leads to some additional opportunities for discussion about both what they consume, as well as what they create. In particular, after engaging in this topic and seeing what they are really spending their time on in these online spaces, it could be useful to push into the broad concept to "determine how and to what extent texts and tools amplify one's own and others' narratives as well as counter unproductive narratives" (NCTE, 2019b), as well as some of key subquestions in that section. This element of the definition encourages us to help our students see how narratives (broadly) are created and circulated online, and even these broad narratives

FIGURE 4.3.2. Student screen-time maps. Photo courtesy of Jill Runstrom.

about the sites that are used most often can shape that conversation. In composing their own maps, for instance, how might "learners share and critically analyze narratives they produce and consume in digital spaces" as well as "use multiple digital tools and print-based literacies to amplify the cultural wealth in their communities" (NCTE, 2019b)? By seeing the ways in which they do—and do not—use a certain number of tools in (potentially limiting and) similar ways, they can begin to imagine new opportunities for sharing stories in new spaces, with even more tools.

Guiding Questions

When working with students and exploring this topic, consider the following questions when designing lessons, assignments, and assessments:

On What Points Can We Reasonably Agree Related to Technology and Social Media Use?

- Recognizing that the human mind craves novelty, and that our devices offer us more new ways to stay entertained and informed than we can ever possibly keep up with, what would you consider to be a "reasonable" amount of time spent using technology each day? How would this "reasonable" amount of time differ when you consider the following:
  - During a school day as compared to the weekend?
  - During time in school when you are engaged in class activities or discussion as compared to individual work time?
  - When doing a school-related assignment, a personal hobby, or other task that requires you to do additional research, learning, and creating with digital tools?
  - When communicating with family or friends about time-sensitive plans for other activities?
  - When communicating just for fun by viewing entertainment or playing video games?
- Again, recognizing that our minds can only devote attention to a limited number of streams of information—in any given moment and over time—what would you consider to be the best ways to balance this use of time?
  - For instance, how much time could or should be allotted, in an average day, to the various activities outlined above?
- Finally, as we prepare to examine the amount of time that we spend on these activities— especially as they align to our overall goals and ways of being in the world—how do our actual activity-use patterns align with our intentions?
  - Where, for instance, do we see an alignment between the apps we use and the time we hope/expect to spend using them?
  - Alternatively, where is there a disconnect between what we hope to be doing with our time and attention and what shows up in our screen-time usage?

To Create the Learning Community We Want, without Setting Up Additional Controls on Our Devices, What Might We Agree to in Terms of Classroom Norms?

- In what ways can we agree to norms for whole-class instruction, activities, or discussion, as well as small-group work and individual work time?
  - When, how, and why might we use—or not use—our devices in any of these moments?
  - When might we set up times during class for us to check our devices for a few moments? How will we reengage once these moments have passed?
  - Depending on the topic for instruction (or an activity or a discussion), are there times we can agree that we will put devices out of sight and away from our person?
    - That is, could we agree to set the devices under our chairs with the screens down or in some other designated space in the classroom so we are not tempted to use them?
- When we see classmates engaged in behaviors that are outside our norms, how can we approach them assertively, not aggressively, and encourage them to limit their device usage?
- If an individual's device usage is distracting for others, how will we work as a community to discuss this with one another?

If We Are Not Able to Adhere to the Guidelines Above, What Might We Need to Do by Setting Up Additional Controls or by Enforcing Disciplinary Measures?

- Before an outright ban on devices for all students, in what ways might we agree to use universally available tools like Do Not Disturb, at least for portions of class time?
- How might we work together to help individual students customize their settings to block notifications or certain websites?
- As a last resort, at what point is it appropriate for us to take technology away from a student?

CHAPTER 5

Popping Filter Bubbles
and Breaking Algorithms

We see what we see online because someone, tacitly or explicitly, wants us to see it; learning how to discover a broader picture, comprised of various perspectives, is crucial.

Though the Internet has been part of our students' lives since before they were born, it has been my experience that they don't fully understand exactly what the World Wide Web (one part of the Internet) really is, how precisely it works, and what has changed about it over the years. And while they have probably heard about their "digital footprint," and even considered some of the many places where their digital feet may have stepped, sometimes we all take our anonymity and privacy for granted. In what spaces have our students walked across the web, from where and whom do they typically get their information, and how can we help them make more intentional choices in the future?

As language arts teachers, these issues are of particular importance to us as we consider the ways in which we invite our students to engage in inquiry, move toward deeper and more sustained reading, and, ultimately, express themselves through digital writing. What they do on the web is tracked and, in turn, leads to additional predictive algorithms that will anticipate what they might do next. Helping students to see themselves the way that the web itself sees them is a way to bring new lenses to their literate lives, lives that are increasingly lived online. The three topics in this chapter will help them as they come to understand what the web knows about them, as well as how they can make more informed choices about their current and future web-based activities, both consuming and creating.

In Topic 5.1, "Popping Our Own Filter Bubbles," we begin by looking at topics already explored through the lens of ideology and bias in the news media. Topic 5.2,

"Seeking and Seeing Alternative Views," invites students to move deeper into this process of finding different news sources and looking closely at the ways in which they express their ideas and perspectives. Topic 5.3, "Creating Civil Conversation," then helps students imagine ways for connecting with others through active listening, even through the text-based messages we might send in Twitter.

At the time I am finishing the major chunks of writing on this book, in late 2020, it seems that—for the topics explored in this chapter—there are too many examples of mis- and disinformation from which to draw. There are also many ideas about how best to combat them. With these continually shifting landscapes, there are a few resources that have guided my thinking and teaching about these topics, especially with my first-year college students and in a media literacy course for teachers. Renee Hobbs's recent *Mind Over Media* (2020) presents tools for critiquing and resisting propaganda, and this book's companion website—linked from my own: hickstro.org/digitaldiligence—is rich with examples and tools. Clare Wardle of *First Draft News* has been thinking about the effects of mis- and disinformation—as well as the purposes behind it (Wardle, 2017, 2019). From the journalistic side, Kevin Roose of *The New York Times* has examined the ways in which people are drawn into mis- and disinformation schemes through both his articles (e.g., 2019) and limited podcast series *Rabbit Hole* (Roose, 2020).

To help students even more directly, Mike Caulfield (2017b) has created his open ebook *Web Literacy for Student Fact-Checkers* and popularized his SIFT model for sourcing information, which includes (1) stopping, (2) investigating the source, (3) finding better coverage, and (4) tracing claims, quotes, and media to the original context (Caulfield, 2019). Similarly, work from Sam Wineburg and the Stanford History Education Group has pointed to the need for explicitly teaching these digital literacy and information-seeking skills (McGrew, Breakstone, Ortega, Smith, & Wineburg, 2019; Wineburg, 2018; Wineburg & McGrew, 2017), and this is exemplified in their free, openly available Civic Online Reasoning curriculum. In addition to short video clips available from SHEG, there are 10 Crash Course videos, produced and hosted by author and Internet celebrity John Green (Crash Course, 2018), collected in a series entitled "Navigating Digital Information."

One final resource is Ad Fontes's interactive Media Bias Chart, originally developed by an intellectual property attorney, Vanessa Otero. Its parabola-shaped graph of news sources that range from those focused on original reporting to those that may have more opinionated content (or outright propaganda) has become quite popular among educators who are trying to help students at least begin to get a sense of the flooded media ecosystem in which we now live. She and her team use a robust methodology to rate several dozen articles per month, employing scores for many elements, such as "Expression," "Veracity," and "Political Language" (Otero, 2020). It is a useful tool and, for the sake of transparency, one in which readers should know I have invested through membership and a stake in the company.

As noted earlier, links to all of these resources are available on the book's companion website: hickstro.org/digitaldiligence.

TOPIC 5.1. POPPING OUR OWN FILTER BUBBLES

> To help them become digitally diligent, we need students to become
> aware of their own perspectives, especially as those perspective can lead
> to implicit or explicit bias when finding and evaluating source material,
> as well as enacting bias in their own research and writing.

Overview

As noted earlier, Eli Pariser coined the phrase "the filter bubble," describing the ways in which the social networks and search engines we use inherently limit our worldview based on the algorithmic decisions they use to track users' interests and, ultimately, serve up ads and keep people tied to a particular site. For instance, Pariser suggests in his TED Talk that "there are 57 signals that Google looks at—everything from what kind of computer you're on to what kind of browser you're using to where you're located—that it uses to personally tailor your query results." While there is some discussion in the tech community about whether 57 is an accurate number (and this has likely changed in the decade since Pariser first made his argument), the point here is clear: Internet companies are using a variety of data points to track users, and the combination of those data points can yield an astonishing amount of detail about each of us, our preferences, and our daily habits.

On the one hand, industry insiders could argue that this kind of personalized information is employed to target advertisements and the most relevant content, thus keeping the content itself—as well as their own service—free to users. On the other hand, there is the oft-noted idea that if you are not paying for a product, then you are product, an idea with which Pariser and other technology critics noted throughout this book would likely concur. All of this comes at a time of continued political polarization and social unrest, where many of us still experience the web-based world through only a few main portals, including Google, Facebook, Twitter, and YouTube.

By understanding their own perspectives and actively seeking out the ideas of others, students can recognize—and attempt to pop—their own filter bubble. Moreover, they can begin to differentiate fact from opinion when they are able to see how ideologies are expressed in words and images. This topic invites students to first explore their own perspectives on political topics and then curate their own news sources outside of apps they are most likely to use, creating new feeds for both information and opinions. With opportunities for beginning with two quizzes that will better help them understand they own perspectives—as well as the exploration of many websites for comparing media outlets—the teaching points below allow for a great deal of flexibility and in-depth exploration.

Teaching Points

Students can begin with a visit to the NewsCompare website, a project of Isaac Saul, founder of the *Tangle* newsletter in which he aims to offer his readers "the best arguments both sides are making, then my take" (Saul, n.d.). The NewsCompare tool takes a snapshot of major news websites, hour upon hour, and allows users to compare screen-shots of sources that have been deemed more liberal to neutral to more conservative. These snapshots are then displayed on the NewsCompare home page, with a searchable archive dating back to 2 A.M. Eastern time on April 24, 2017, and continuing to the present. These hourly snapshots of the major news sites are compelling for a number of reasons, including the ability to have students quickly scan headlines and dominant images, seeing in "real" time the ways that these different media outlets frame their understanding of current events. Additionally, tracing stories back to their beginnings by continuing to look back in the history of these snapshots could be a compelling exer-cise too. If journalism is the first draft of history, then NewsCompare is one compelling way to see how the story is being written.

As an introductory lesson on media literacy and messaging, these snapshots are illustrative and can serve as a way to begin thinking about the language and messag-ing that various media outlets use to describe the same story. For instance, students could choose any day in the past few days or week (since the news, hopefully, will still be relevant). As they examine the screenshots on NewsCompare for that particular day and time, they can use the five key questions from the Media Education Lab's "Media Literacy Smartphone" to interrogate the three images from the liberal, neutral, and con-servative viewpoints. These questions, expanded from the original questions to better encompass this activity, are outlined in the "Guiding Questions" section below.

From there, students could then move into one, or both, of the following quizzes: the Pew Political Typology Quiz and/or the quiz available from the website I Side With. Each of these quizzes offers users insights on their own beliefs. Pew, for instance, offers nine typologies ranging from "core conservatives" on the right to "solid liberals" on the left, and "bystanders" in the middle. The Pew Political Typology Quiz was created from data collected over three decades, including recent 2017 data from a survey of more than 5,000 American adults. In describing their typologies, Pew (2017b) makes the point that

> The goal of the political typology is to go beyond people's partisan leanings to gain a better understanding of American politics. While partisanship remains a dominant factor in politics, the current report finds—as did prior typology studies—that there are internal values divides within both partisan coalitions. (p. 9)

To look at this in action, one question from the Pew quiz (2017a) related to income asks the following:

Which of the following statements comes closest to your view?

- The government should do more to help needy Americans, even if it means going deeper into debt.
- The government today can't afford to do much more to help the needy.

Of course, by asking students to choose from dichotomous, either/or options, we risk reinscribing the kinds of binary thinking that this activity would push against. Pew (2017b) acknowledges this in their segment on the economy and the social safety net, noting that "most Americans and typology groups see economic inequality as a problem" (p. 47), with various views on issues related to taxes and health care. In this sense, it is clear that Pew has taken great care in designing the quiz questions and helping students to see that viewing these stances on a wider continuum is important too.

To bring a bit more nuance to the conversation, another tool can be useful, at least from the standpoint of taking a quiz to determine one's stance on political issues. The website I Side With was created "in March 2012 by two friends with two very different views of politics," Taylor Peck and Nick Boutelier. At the time of this writing, the I Side With website had been updated with information about the 2020 presidential election in the United States, though it is worth noting that, looking at both Peck and Boutelier's Twitter accounts, no updates had been posted by either of them since 2017 and 2019, respectively (Peck & Boutelier, n.d.-a). Still, the I Side With website offers users the ability to choose from an either/or selection, as well as the option to elaborate on the binary with options on many questions to select from "Other stances," or to add one's own stance (Peck & Boutelier, n.d.-b).

In contrast to the Pew Political Typology Quiz, the I Side With quiz appears to be more direct in the ways that it uses political language to frame the question. For instance, some of the questions that relate to economics include the following:

- Should the U.S. raise taxes on the rich?
- Should the government raise the federal minimum wage?
- Do you support a universal basic income program?

Beyond that, there is an option to "Show more economic questions," where users can find even more questions about the corporate tax rate, welfare, and the gender pay gap. In that sense, the I Side With quiz does offer more nuance and opportunities for discussion than the dichotomous choices offered by the Pew Political Typology Quiz.

Finally, of note, AllSides offers a "Rate Your Bias" quiz, though the interface asks users to identify where they stand (left, lean left, center, lean right, or right) with drop-down menus inviting the reader to explore more on these perspectives. Rather than being framed in statements of values, like Pew and I Side With, the AllSides quiz really requires users to know where they stand as they complete the Likert-style continuum questions. Many students are likely not going to know, in any firm sense, where they stand on particular issues from a "left" or "right" perspective alone, and are probably unlikely to click into all the further explanations. Still, it could be a useful addition to the other quizzes and might help students further explore the issues from the political left and right perspectives.

Using quizzes like this—especially when presented with a site like NewsCompare—provides students with an opportunity to better understand political bias, as well as the perspectives they themselves bring to the conversations. As noted with the binary choices that Pew's quiz offers, no single measure of one's political beliefs is entirely representative of a lifetime's worth of experiences, not to mention the influence of family, friends, and community. As I often note in conversations with colleagues, none of us completely shed our identities when walking through the classroom door, nor should we expect students to do so either. Still, as students learn about these different perspectives—and attempt to differentiate their own views from their family, friends, and community—these quizzes can be helpful.

As one additional way to recognize our own filter bubbles, there are extensions that can be used in Chrome to analyze our Facebook feeds and the ways in which our friends (or at least our acquaintances that Facebook labels as "friends") identify themselves politically (He, Liu, Mo, & Zong, 2016). More accurately, these tools analyze one's social media feed and place an identifier upon a person. In this way, a tool like PolitEcho could be useful for students who are also Facebook users so they can see how others perceive them. Created in 2016 as an open-source project, PolitEcho "shows you the political biases of your Facebook friends and news feed" based on an analysis of political learnings scored from content on their news feeds, as well as your own. A Google Chrome Extension, it was most recently updated in 2017 (so it may not be maintained as of the time of this publication). There are other similar apps in the Chrome Web Store, including Ven, Centr, and Escape Your Bubble (similarly, none of these seem to be maintained as of fall 2020, yet could still be useful).

As one part of an overall look at their filter bubbles, I recommend these extensions as ones to share with students and for them to explore. Most likely, they will need to do so on their own at home because it is likely Facebook is not accessible on a school network. Even if it is, depending on the age of the students, using these extensions assumes that students have a Facebook account (which, technically, they should not have if under the age of 13). Even without these views of their own social media feeds, it can be helpful for students to look at the extensions in the web store, with some screenshots of how they visualize a Facebook user's political leanings. So, even if they are not able to run the extension and just explored the available screenshots, students can return to review the general views that are outlined in the Pew typologies, I Side With, and AllSides.

Then, as a way to round out the topic of identifying our own filter bubbles, there are a few additional tools that can be introduced (and are explored in more detail in Topic 5.2). To begin, the nonprofit and cross-partisan team at AllSides offers a number of tools, including their balanced dictionary, a topic guide, and a transparent media bias rating system. Inviting students to find a particular topic of interest and begin exploring could be one way to extend the conversation on filter bubbles. There are also many articles that can be found about media bias—and the language surrounding different political parties and movements, a topic covered in Topic 5.2.

A scholarly article that provides some key concepts related to major political ideologies can be found in "Mapping Press Ideology" (Schena, Almiron, & Pineda, 2018). Offering both "core frames" and "ideological markers" that define particular political stances, such as conservatism, liberalism, and feminism, Schena and her colleagues also provide specific language that can be helpful in identifying and naming these perspectives. For instance, with "conservatism," we see words and phrases like "common morality" and "family values," along with about two dozen other terms to watch for in the media. This list is one helpful place to help see the kinds of underlying approaches that appear, implicitly or explicitly, in media artifacts.

In a similar manner, Vanessa Otero and colleagues at her company Ad Fontes Media have created an interactive Media Bias Chart (link available on the book's companion website: hickstro.org/digitaldiligence). Seeing the way in which an additional organization also ranks the potential bias of these media sources, the Ad Fontes chart complements what students might already be seeing in the AllSides rankings. With this chart, users can examine a variety of media sources as they are categorized by their general political leaning, either left or right, from "most extreme" to "hyper partisan," "skews," and "neutral." Additionally, the news sources on the site are categorized, at the highest level, as "original fact reporting" with additional levels showing "complex analysis, or mix of fact reporting and analysis," and all the way to the bottom of their scale with "contains inaccurate/fabricated info." As a place to begin the conversation about media ideologies, this chart, too, can be helpful.

As we consider these teaching points, a return to the NCTE definition provides another insight. In the introduction of the definition, NCTE (2019b) notes that our literacies are "inextricably linked with histories, narratives, life possibilities, and social trajectories of all individuals and groups." At the same time we teach about individual perspectives and the beliefs we hold, we also teach about potential biases, both implicit and explicit. As it has ever been, it remains a challenge for us to "build and sustain intentional global and cross-cultural connections and relationships with others so as to pose and solve problems collaboratively and strengthen independent thought." Beginning to understand our own perspectives is a good start, and we then need to think even more intentionally about practices where students can "collaborate with others whose perspectives and areas of expertise are different from their own" and "develop new ways of thinking and/or new responses from disagreements and grapple with diverse perspectives in ways that positively impact work."

Further, as a way to situate the work for this entire chapter, helping students understand connections within the "Promote culturally sustaining communication and recognize the bias and privilege present in the interactions" segment of the definition, too, can be insightful. For instance, we can teach students to begin "recognizing patterns in discourse which are rooted in the oppression of nondominant groups (e.g., race, gender, sexuality, ability) and a variety of strategies they can use to interrupt this discourse." The next two topics, 5.2 and 5.3, move us deeper into this kind of work.

Guiding Questions

When working with students and exploring this topic, consider the following questions when designing lessons, assignments, and assessments:

Opening Questions

- What do you know about the political terms *conservative* and *liberal*? What about *left* or *right*? Where have you heard these terms used?

- What, specifically, makes an idea *conservative* or *liberal*? What about *left* or *right*?
- As you think about familiar news sources, how might you categorize those sources using these terms?
- What are some terms you hear in the news that seem to be particularly common?
  - Who do you hear speaking? Or where do you read these words and phrases?
  - Why do you think they might be using these particular words, in this context?

As Students Explore NewsCompare

These questions are adapted from the five presented on the Media Literacy Smartphone (Media Education Lab, n.d.). As you examine the screenshots on NewsCompare for your particular time and day, answer the following questions:

- Which news organization is the author, and what purposes can you infer it may have by presenting the images and headlines that it shares on its home page?
- What techniques does this news organization use with these particular headlines (e.g., sensational words, active vs. passive constructions) and images (e.g., framing of the image, who or what is included in the image) to attract and hold your attention?
- Given that NewsCompare has already labeled the source as more liberal, more conservative, or neutral, in what ways do you see these specific points of view represented through images, headlines, and the overall design of the news website?
- When examining these headlines and dominant images from a different political perspective, how might different people interpret these messages?
- Finally, what information or perspectives are omitted from this version of the message when compared to other versions?

As Students Work through the Quizzes from the Pew Typology or I Side With

- Which categories of questions/issues are most compelling to you? How would you describe the reasons these particular categories of questions/issues are important?
- As you explore these various issues, which ones have you given a great deal of thought to in the past? Which have you not considered that much? Which have you not considered at all before seeing them on the quiz?
- In the questions—and answer responses—that have been provided, what do you notice about the ways that different issues are framed? What words and phrases stand out to you the most?
- Now that you see the ways these issues are presented, what have you come to understand about the bias (or ideology) in the news media as they are covered through different outlets?

TOPIC 5.2. SEEKING AND SEEING ALTERNATIVE VIEWS

To help them become digitally diligent, we need students to evaluate the
nuances of different perspectives of people who share various forms of
evidence, designing their own defensible claims in response.

Overview

Building on Topic 5.1, students can begin to delve even deeper into topics of interest and examine the ways in which ideologies are enacted, both through words and images. This is difficult work, requiring us to recognize our own perspectives while also acknowledging our blind spots. Even when students are encouraged to "read closely," this alone is probably not enough. As summarized in his analysis from *The Guardian,* Steve Rathje (2017) makes the point that "people tend to frame political arguments in terms of their own values, but when arguing across party lines, it is much more effective to frame your argument in terms of your opponent's values." He cites work from social scientists, including George Lakoff (Lakoff & Johnson, 2003) and Daniel Kahneman (Kahneman, 2011), noting that the ways in which we talk about topics matters a great deal, both with like-minded and oppositional individuals.

Using the news aggregation site AllSides, as well as other sources such as Kialo and ProCon that put various viewpoints on issues in conversation with one another, students can explore a topic and look at the way it is represented by the political left and right, as well as from more neutral points of view. In doing so, they can analyze the dominant headline and image, as well as use a word cloud generator and employ key media literacy skills in an effort to uncover the perspectives that each side brings to bear on a given issue.

As a foundation of this activity, I draw from the work of Sam Wineburg and the Stanford History Education Group and, in particular, their concept of "lateral reading." In their 2017 working paper, Wineburg and Sarah McGrew describe the ways in which many readers will typically "read vertically," relying on traditional models of website evaluation and "staying within a website to evaluate its reliability." Fact checkers, on the other hand, "read laterally, leaving a site after a quick scan and opening up new browser tabs in order to judge the credibility of the original site." I build on this definition of lateral reading in the sense that the activities described in this topic invite students to examine a topic by opening up two articles, from two perspectives, on a single topic.

At this point, I do want to note that the kinds of lateral reading I am describing here are not so much about fact-checking in the sense that Wineburg and McGrew define it. Instead, my approach uses similar technical skills (opening sources in new tabs) to help them examine two articles, in depth, and to see the ways that ideologies are at work on the same topic. By doing so, students are able to begin seeing how different topics are framed through language and images.

For the main portion of this activity, we begin with AllSides, which strategically puts current news items from left-, center-, and right-leaning organizations into a side-by-side comparison with one another, both for current, major headlines and for deeper dives into topical guides. This organizational structure is especially useful for delving deeper into the readings, as the links to these articles will open to the full version of the article, in context, on the news source's website. Unlike NewsCompare, which will only take users to the news organization's main site, in real time—not linking to the specific article from the past—AllSides provides users with opportunities to dig in deeply to similar topics across political perspectives by linking directly to the article. The Ad Fontes Media Bias Chart, noted above, can be another source to help students gain insight on where various media organizations stand, politically, with their reporting and can be used as a companion tool for lateral reading. Two other freely available sources that could be used as part of this activity—yet do not demonstrate the differences between different political learnings in nearly as clear a way as AllSides does—are Kialo and ProCon.

Kialo provides an overview of an argument with a graphic that looks like an organizational chart, allowing users to click into topics and subtopics in order to view arguments and counterarguments. Kialo can be a good place to get a sense of what arguments are in play around a topic, though it is made for a general audience and invites contributions from users (so be sure to review topics before sharing any of the debates with students). Kialo EDU, in conjunction with topics from the Kialo website itself, allows teachers to create debates and invites students to join conversations and rate arguments, though educators need to set up those debates for their students in advance.

ProCon provides topical guides to dozens of issues. Once having clicked on any particular issue, a brief overview of the topic appears under the headline and banner, and then there are lists for "Pro & Con Arguments," with links to still more primary sources and other information on the ProCon website. Users can even click on the names of individual sources to find more information about the people who have been quoted. For instance, on just one ProCon article—"Is a College Education Worth It?"—there are 26 individual sources that users could explore in more detail. In order to think even more deeply about the topics being presented, we might also share with students *The New York Times* Learning Network's "401 Prompts for Argumentative Writing" (Gonchar, 2017), where students can see a variety of thoughtfully posed questions about everything from social media to gender, from sports to school.

In addition to these openly available sources, there are subscription database services that provide context on these issues too. For instance, in Michigan, our state's electronic library, MeL, offers all state residents access to subscription databases, including Gale's Opposing Viewpoints and EBSCO's Points of View. Depending on the school, local, or state library access that you and your students have to such resources, they could be useful too if the subscriptions are available. Both Gale and EBSCO's entries on any given topic provide context on both sides of the debate, with links to additional articles. Again, as students dig further into these sources, they can find out more and more about the original sources by looking back at the media bias ratings on AllSides and Ad Fontes Media's Media Bias Chart.

Once having explored these spaces for finding alternative perspectives and preparing for students to head back to AllSides to find two specific examples that can be used for the activity outlined in the Teaching Points section below, it is also worth noting that there are many useful conversation guides available to help them think about how to put various ideas in dialogue with one another (in their own minds, let alone when talking with others).

Using resources from initiatives like Hi From The Other Side—such as their "Conversation Guide" (2017) and their conversation agreements (Living Room Conversations, n.d.)—or questions from StoryCorps's "One Small Step" series (One Small Step, 2020), there are many ways to encourage this kind of reflection. Using discussion agreements (or, put another way, ground rules) as well as open-ended questions and prompts, the opportunity for critical thinking and dialogue are enhanced. For beginning dialogue across differences, for instance, "One Small Step" has outlined the following three questions:

1. "Was there an event or person in your life that shaped your political views?"
2. "Have your political views changed over time? Was there something specific that made you change?"
3. "Has there been a particular moment when you felt misunderstood by someone with different beliefs than you?"

These tools can all be useful in beginning the kinds of exploration related to sensitive topics and to encourage students to think more expansively about both why and how they might frame their own argument (which will be explored even more in Topic 5.3).

Finally, I suggest reviewing the National Writing Project's (n.d.-a) College, Career, and Community Writers Program, which has the stated goal of "Creating Respectful Discourse for Change in the 21st Century." Abbreviated as the "C3WP," the program contains components of intensive professional development and tools for formative assessment, as well as numerous mini-units that "were designed as 4- to 6-day instructional sequences through which students could form their own arguments and write multiparagraph pieces" (H. A. Gallagher, Woodworth, & Arshan, 2015). Having participated in this program and worked with K–12 colleagues to implement it in their classrooms, I have come to understand that we must teach students that argumentative claims should be "debatable," "defensible," and "nuanced" (National Writing Project, n.d.-b). Exploring ideology provides students with yet one more way to engage in this kind of academic argument.

In addition, it could be useful to have students employ some of the "sentence templates" offered by Graff and Birkenstein in their popular textbook *They Say/I Say: The Moves that Matter in Academic Writing,* released in its fifth edition (2021). They offer, for instance, templates for introducing what other authors have said, conceding a point, and describing why one's own argument matters with phrases like "X argues that . . ."; "Proponents of X are right to argue that . . ."; and "Ultimately, what is at stake here is . . ." In a "view only" version of a GDoc, teacher and author Dave Stuart Jr. has—within the broad rights of fair use for educational purposes—gathered all of the sentence templates in one convenient space. A link is available on the book's companion website, and I strongly encourage educators to save a copy to their own Google Drive for further sharing with their own students.

In the past, it seems as though we have tried to teach the idea of writing a thesis as an "all or nothing," "this or that," "my way or the highway" kind of opportunity. Yes, a counterpoint may have been offered, but it was perfunctory. The resources noted above can invite a broader conversation about how to make argument writing more compelling and convincing when framed as a dialogue, not a dichotomy. The teaching points below outline opportunities for pursuing this more contextual and engaging approach, especially as we help them understand the tenuous world of political ideology.

Teaching Points

For this activity, students will explore AllSides in an effort to find two articles about the same topic and then examine those articles in two ways. First, they will analyze the visual rhetoric presented in the headline and dominant image, and second, they will take the text of the articles themselves and create word clouds. In reviewing the texts, students are then encouraged to look at what each one cites as evidence for its main argument. I've built out the ideas from this lesson using ideas from my colleague Tom Liam Lynch (2017a, 2017b), and especially his lesson "Plotting Plots" (Lynch, n.d.) and website (linked from the book's companion page) in which students use word frequency data to do a "distant reading" of a text. Additionally, we engage with a protocol/list of questions adapted from the Media Literacy Smartphone (Media Education Lab, n.d.) and the Center for Media Literacy's "Five Key Questions" (Center for Media Literacy, n.d.). The questions that form the core of this activity are, quoting from the Media Literacy Smartphone, as follows:

- Who is the author and what is the purpose?
- What techniques are used to attract and hold your attention?
- What lifestyles, values, and points of view are represented?
- How might different people interpret the message?
- What is omitted from the message?

By slightly adapting these questions for each part of the activity, we can help students discern the nuances between the different media outlets and the ways they intentionally construct their messages. It is also important for students to look at the ways AllSides works to provide additional context for different articles by adding the labels of "Opinion" and "Analysis" on some of them. With these additions, the site tries to identify pieces that move beyond the basics of the "who, what, when, and where" elements that would be reported consistently across any news story, making it clear there will be additional insight and nuance related to the *why* and *how*, again from a particular perspective.

To begin this topic, ask students to find two articles on a similar topic in AllSides. This can be a bit of a challenge because—even within the pages for a broad topic—the many articles presented on AllSides do not always line up in an "apples to apples" manner. Depending on the time allotted for this activity, then, it could be advantageous to identify two or (as we explore below) three articles for them to examine. For instance, at the time of this writing, the death of Ruth Bader Ginsburg is dominating the news. I was able to find three headlines from sources on different areas of the political spectrum state the headline in different ways, demonstrating their ideological underpinnings.

Thus, drawing from the crowdsourced ratings on AllSides, we see articles about Ginsburg from three different angles. From the right-leaning perspective, the headline from the *National Review* states the *who* and the *what,* without any additional commentary: "Supreme Court Justice Ruth Bader Ginsburg Dead at 87" (Crowe, 2020). From the center, *The Wall Street Journal* adds a general description of her achievements, noting in an appositive phrase, "Ruth Bader Ginsburg, a Pioneering Justice on Supreme Court, Dies at 87" (Bravin, 2020). Finally, with just a bit more detail and from a left-leaning perspective, *Rolling Stone*'s headline reads "Ruth Bader Ginsburg, Supreme Court Justice and Pioneer of Gender Equality, Dead at 87" (Dickinson & Stuart, 2020). By adding just a bit more to the description of what she was a pioneer at doing with the law, this final headline provides some additional perspective on her role. Each of these articles is linked from the book's companion website—hickstro.org/digitaldiligence—and warrant a bit more attention in light of the activity described below.

For the *National Review,* the straightforward headline is accompanied by an image of Ginsburg, taken from mid-range, sitting in a chair and looking to her right with her mouth slightly agape. One could contend that she is meant to look slightly out of sorts, with the first line of the article noting her age (87) and the third paragraph reminding readers that she "staked out a position on the court's progressive wing and in recent years emerged as an icon on the activist left for her strident positions on abortion rights, gay marriage, and other major progressive causes" (Crowe, 2020). Returning to the Schena et al. (2018) article on media ideologies mentioned in Topic 5.1, we can see some of the markers for conservatism at work here, calling out her strong positions with the verb *staked* and the descriptors *strident* and *activist.* Also, because the values of conservatism lean toward faith, family, and traditional practices, these are noted as ideas that Ginsburg pushed against (as seen in this headline, dominant image, and leading sentences).

The Wall Street Journal, as a more centrist source, does make the move in their headline to call Ginsburg "pioneering." Their image of her, a 2013 image celebrating her 20th year on the court, shows her standing in front of a wooden-paneled fireplace, angled from the ground up looking toward her. With a framed picture in the background, and obscured by her own visage, she is cast in a portrait-like manner herself. The secondary headline states "Second woman to sit on the top U.S. court spent her last years on the bench pushing back against an emboldened conservative majority," hinting at her place following Ronald Reagan's pick, Sandra Day O'Connor. Later in the article, it is noted that "in 1993, President Clinton helped blunt a conservative ascendancy at the Supreme Court by selecting Justice Ginsburg to succeed Justice Byron White, a Kennedy appointee who had moved to the right during his tenure" (Bravin, 2020). Throughout the article, the values of both conservatism and more liberal/social ideologies are presented as Ginsburg is described in relation to others on the court.

Finally, for *Rolling Stone,* as a more left-leaning source, the values of a politically liberal or socialistic ideology are represented in many ways, beginning with the dominant image. Again, Ginsburg is shown in a 2013 image, yet this time she is framed in a different manner, from mid-range, looking slightly to her left with the illumination of a window lighting up most of her face. The photograph was taken from an angle just above eye level, looking at her from a slight tilt above. She is then described as a "trailblazing feminist icon who had fought off colon, lung and liver cancer" (Dickinson & Stuart, 2020). The article goes on to describe her as a "liberal stalwart through successive conservative-leaning majorities" who "will be remembered for her fiery dissents and work defending reproductive and civil rights, including those of the LGBTQ community." Again returning to Schena et al.'s (2018) descriptions of ideological markers from feminism, multiculturalism, and socialism, we see themes of resisting patriarchy and embracing cultural identity through the connotation of strength with "stalwart," as well as cooperation and egalitarianism. The light on her face, in this sense, could symbolize these liberal values and metaphorically shows Ginsburg as a beacon of hope.

An analysis of each of these articles—with the headline and the main image of Ginsburg—can be an opening for a conversation. When reviewing the three sources through the additional lenses of exploring visual rhetoric—when the headline is paired with the dominant image—and looking at language used in the article, even more can be discerned about the political perspectives from each one. At this point, I would invite students to describe what they see and have read, in three to five sentences, for each source:

* Based on what you can tell from the image and tone of the words, what perspective does the author of this article/publisher of this website have on the topic?
* What creative techniques (color, fonts, catchy words, framing of the photograph) are used to capture your attention?
* How might someone with a different perspective than you understand this message in a different way?
* What perspectives or values are omitted from this message?
* Beyond simply "informing" or "persuading," why do you think this message is being sent, in this way, to the intended audience?

We would then prepare to analyze the text of the article in a different way. As students prepare to copy–paste the text from the original articles, and before heading into a word cloud generator, they should work to eliminate as much extraneous information as possible. This can be done with a "reader view" extension and then simply copying/pasting information into a separate Word or GDoc. There are many word cloud generators that could be used, and two that I prefer are WordArt.com (formerly Tagul) and Voyant

Tools. WordArt.com's main advantage is that you can delete words from the cloud easily (e.g., if you want to remove all the instances of *and* or *the*). It also allows for users to play with the shape of the word cloud, as well as change fonts and colors. For a simpler interface—and output—Voyant Tools offers those who study language a number of ways to analyze a chunk of text (or, in the linguists' terms, a *corpus*). On the Voyant Tools home page, a user simply copies and pastes in the text and then clicks "Reveal" to see a word cloud and other data related to the text. Using the resulting images, I ask students to engage in a critical questioning of the word clouds with the same five questions noted above.

Finally, as students go back to their original sources with a new perspective from the visual analysis of the headline and image as well as the word cloud, they are then asked to compare and contrast the kinds of evidence used in each one. Without going into a deeper lesson on epistemology—the branch of philosophy dealing with the nature of knowledge—the goal here is to help them think about the overarching questions related to the nature of evidence itself: What counts as evidence? For instance, we know that quotes, statistics, images, videos, polls, and other elements can all be introduced as evidence. Moreover, we must then ask about the evidence and how it counts. For whom would this evidence be most compelling? In what context would it be most likely to be considered appropriate for an argument?

As they move into the final stages of analysis, students can then look at the sources with the critical lens that can be brought from a historical perspective (even if it is a contemporary source). Drawn from Dan Wewers's (2007) "Brief Guide to Writing the History Paper" that was created for the Writing Center at Harvard, a few additional questions can help interrogate the sources more fully:

  • **"Who** produced this source? Is the author's biography (i.e., viewpoints and personal background) relevant to understanding this source? Was the author biased or dishonest? Did he or she have an agenda?"

  • **"When** was this source created? **Where**? Is it representative of other sources created at the same time? In what ways is it a product of its particular time, place, or context?"

  • **"Why** did the author produce this source? For **what** audience and purpose? Did the author make this purpose (or argument) explicit or implicit? Was it intended for public or private use? Is it a work of scholarship, fiction, art, or propaganda?" (Wewers, 2007)

At this stage, students have moved through a fairly extensive analysis of two (or three) sources and now have a great deal of evidence on which to base an argument of their own. If they have not yet been introduced to the They Say/I Say sentence templates, it could behoove them at this point to explore that document, especially the "Introducing an Ongoing Debate" samples. This will then help them frame their own claim—as the

National Writing Project says, a "debatable," "defensible," and "nuanced" claim based on their new understanding of the topic.

Because this is such an involved activity, typically stretching out over at least two to three class sessions for my first-year undergraduates, I will often lead them through this by having a document with many of the instructions laid out. Though I continue to change it, for a recent version of a Google Doc template of this particular lesson that can be adapted and used with students, please visit the book's companion website.

Connections here to the NCTE (2019b) definition are many, as this series of activities invites students to be critical consumers of information, evaluating it in a variety of ways and developing their own conclusions about a particular topic after careful examination of the evidence. In particular, I believe this topic builds on a number of questions within the "Explore and engage critically, thoughtfully, and across a wide variety of inclusive texts and tools/modalities" as a foundation. They have opportunity to "strive to see limitations and overlaps between multiple streams of information"; to "use tools to deepen understandings, to share ideas, and to build on others' thinking"; and to "develop new skills strategies to meet the challenge of new texts and tools," among others.

From the element in the NCTE definition that argues we "advocate for equitable access to and accessibility of texts, tools, and information," we can also think about ways to help students gain "ready access to information and information professionals that provide expertise in print-based and digital-based texts." This part of the definition is speaking to issues of diversity, equity, and inclusion—and providing access for all learners. By remaining focused on the ways that learners are able to take advantage of openly available resources, as well as those provided by their school, local, and state library, we can help them to "make decisions in information-rich environments" and "attain a greater understanding of text through accessible text structures" (NCTE, 2019b), structures they create by moving the written language of a text into a word cloud.

Guiding Questions

There are already a number of guiding questions embedded in this lesson, so when working with students and exploring this topic, I offer just a few more to consider when designing lessons, assignments, and assessments:

- What are you beginning to notice about the nature of language, especially as it is used across different sources?
- Similarly, what are you beginning to notice about the nature of visual design/rhetoric, as it is used across different sources?
- As you compare sources from different political perspectives, what are the starkest contrasts you are noticing, and how might we be able to examine those contrasts in order to understand ways we can talk with one another in more productive ways?

TOPIC 5.3. CREATING CIVIL CONVERSATION

To help them become digitally diligent, we need students to recognize
and disrupt patterns of uncivil dialogue, modeling similar kinds of
active listening and empathy with digital communications as what they
would do if together in person.

Overview

Sherry Turkle, in her books *Alone Together: Why We Expect More from Technology and Less from Each Other* (2011) and *Reclaiming Conversation: The Power of Talk in a Digital Age* (2015), creates a compelling case for why we should *not* use technology to mediate all our conversations. The tools, she contends, provide us with too many ways to avoid difficult topics and employ empathy. As she articulates in her TED Talk (Turkle, 2012) on the same topic,

> We use conversations with each other to learn how to have conversations with our-selves. So a flight from conversation can really matter because it can compromise our capacity for self-reflection. For kids growing up, that skill is the bedrock of develop-ment.

As should be clear by this point, I agree she makes a compelling point, and there are certainly times that talking face-to-face is both appropriate and useful. Rather than a flight from conversation, there are many times we should flock toward it, engaging with friends, colleagues, and sometimes even strangers in an effort to make these connections.

To that end, a number of nonprofit and nonpartisan projects related to civil dis-course have emerged in recent years, especially since the 2016 election. Three are of note here. First, the National Institute for Civil Discourse (NICD), based at the University of Arizona and self-described as a "non-partisan center for advocacy, research, and policy," has developed a number of resources and programs, including their Engaging Differ-ences website with associated resources and activities. The NICD website also includes links to various research reports about the role of civil discourse in politics and the media, many of which could be used, in part or in whole, as texts for exploration in this particular topic.

From a slightly different approach, StoryCorps (n.d.-a) began in 2003 as an initia-tive "that includes an intense focus on the collecting, sharing, and preserving of people's stories." As noted above in Topic 5.2, the main component of any StoryCorps story is an interview, fueled by thoughtful, dialogic questions. Over the intervening years, as Sto-ryCorps has expanded its work to include stories from diverse participants through their initiatives, such as their September 11th Initiative, StoryCorps Griot (African America), StoryCorps Justice, StoryCorps Historia (Latino/a), and others, they now have hundreds of conversations archived. In particular, as it relates to civil dialogue, their "Take One Small Step" campaign was launched in 2018 as a way to help people with differing political perspectives to meet and discuss issues of shared importance. A collection of StoryCorps' (n.d.-b) best question prompts can be found on their website, and I have a link for it on the book's companion website.

The third resource, a conversation guide, also noted above in Topic 5.2, comes from the organization Hi From The Other Side (n.d.). Their goal is to "pair nice people across the political divide to talk like neighbors. Not to convince, but to understand." Their conversation guide, simple and concise, shares a brief list of tips for "What We've Found Helpful in Discussions" as well as "Some Questions to Get Going," which include some open-ended examples such as "Tell me about where you grew up and your family" and "If you could do one thing to help the other side, what might it be?" While the questions are geared more for bridging political divides, they could be easily adapted for specific issues.

While it is important—some would go so far as to say essential—that we regain what has been lost in our civil discourse by engaging in face-to-face conversation, due to constraints in either time or space, these conversations cannot always happen in person. The history of telecommunications is one that demonstrates how humans can continually and consistently improve the ways in which they might connect with one another. Despite Turkle's overarching concern that we are losing the ability to talk with one another, it is clear that we need to learn how to have both face-to-face and, increasingly, online conversations through a variety of media.

One such medium, Twitter, offers us a unique perspective on moments as they happen, showing us the pulse of the planet in real time. Despite the criticisms of Twitter as narcissistic, many educators have praised the benefits of Twitter for their own professional learning. There is no doubt that, throughout the second decade of the 21st century, it has also been used for political discourse, and—for some—to deliver political directives. No doubt, as investigations into "Big Tech" continue through congressional hearings and in the court of public opinion, we will see these platforms continue to evolve (though it is unlikely that the major players will disappear). As just one example, Twitter, by design, moves fast. It can be difficult to keep up with conversations, let alone engage with others in productive and positive ways.

This topic, then, considers ways in which we can use active listening and thoughtful questioning, even in social media, as a way to create space for conversation, encourage empathy, and develop deeper relationships. In that sense, it is meant to move students into a slow-motion, role-playing Twitter conversation. And while it may not be conversation that forms the "bedrock of development" that Turkle advocates for, the goal here is to help students adopt a stance of active listening, even in the swiftly moving space of a Twitter conversation. They must work together to create a simulated Twitter conversation between people of two different perspectives while, at the same time, translating the habits of active listening from a face-to-face dialogue (with one's body language and vocal responses) into social media space. Their goal will be to create one series of Twitter interactions that show a lack of listening, with a second series that demonstrates interest and empathy.

Teaching Points

With this activity, I would invite students to imagine two versions of a conversation that would unfold between people, one version being relatively negative and contributing to an uncivil conversation, and the other being more open, responsive, and dialogic. For creating the negative series of tweets, we could consider different kinds of words and phrases that express a negative mood, such as outright name calling or shaming, or more subtle forms of negativity—such as unhelpful or antagonistic comments, or just sarcastic inferences. For making positive connections in the second version of the conversation, we can help students think about ways to demonstrate elements of active listening and genuine response—such as staying focused on topic, reflecting back key ideas from the other's perspective, and acting with empathy.

Of all the tools that could be used to generate fake social media messages, I have found TweetGen to be the best option, for both ease of use and the fewest ads (linked on the book's companion website). The goals of this topic could also be accomplished using other tools. For instance, a search for "Google Slides Twitter Template" will yield quite a few results that can be adapted if TweetGen is blocked via school Internet filters, or otherwise seems as if it is not the right fit. With Google Slides as the template, multiple copies can easily be made. Moreover, Google Slides does allow for export of the individual slides as a single image, so that could be more convenient depending on the goals in place for the project.

No matter which tool is chosen for this activity, the social and collaborative aspects of partnership will be important as students develop their own simulated conversations. Thus, it is ideal that they are in pairs or trios, though groups larger than that are probably not advantageous.

To begin, students would need to agree on a topic that their fictionalized social media commentators will discuss. Returning to many of the resources outlined earlier, they could look for topics—and opposing positions on those topics—from AllSides, Kialo, ProCon, or some of the subscription database services like Gale or EBSCO. Also, they might simply note some examples of ongoing debates through a quick brainstorming session. One fictionalized person would, of course, be on one side of the issue, and the other would take the opposite position.

After identifying the topic and the positions, the partners would use the TweetGen interface to create tweets from the two users, simulating a negative conversation, and then export them as image files and put them in a timeline. As they consider ways in which negativity might be expressed, the students could discuss ideas related to the timing of a reply and the use of emojis, GIFs, or single-word responses. In a blog post for a career-building site, Lea McLeod (n.d.) documents "5 Ways You Don't Realize You're Being Negative," including the common practice of making negative inferences and responding with a "yeah, but . . . " as a reaction. There are likely many other examples of Internet trolling that students can discuss and share in the process of creating this first round of an "uncivil" conversation.

In the second version of the conversation, we want students to understand the ways in which the digital tools available in social media, especially Twitter, can be used to demonstrate that one is really "listening" and engaging (or not) in the dialogue. For instance, a key feature of all Twitter conversations include the use of *@replies* and #—or *hashtags*—as ways to connect with other individuals and contribute to an ongoing conversation. Both *likes* and *retweets* can be seen as ways to participate in a conversation; still, there is some question as to whether either of these constitutes an "endorsement" of the original idea. That said, there seems to be a growing consensus that likes and retweets do, in fact, constitute an endorsement—at least an endorsement that you want someone to engage with that content in some way (Johnson, 2014; van Alstyne, 2020). Even so, these types of conversational conventions (as part of Twitter) and as components of active listening shifted into an online space are all worth exploring more, as shown in Table 5.3.1.

Third, as students work to build the conversations, both negative and positive—and hearkening back to the ideas in Topics 5.1 and 5.2—we must ask them to consider the broader argument that these imagined speakers are making, even in these microblog posts. That is, even though they are creating individual messages of 240 characters that, in turn, accumulate into a series of messages, it is important to help them see the broader claim that the speaker is aiming to create through these messages. Taken as a whole—and by examining the conventions noted above—what might students say is the tone that is being presented in the Twitter chat?

According to the NCTE's "Definition of Literacy in a Digital Age," the goals of promoting "culturally sustaining communication" are a key part of what we should do in our ELA classrooms, and I quote their entire introduction to that segment of the broader definition statement.

> Culturally sustaining communication provides an opportunity for (and is possible when) learners draw on racially, culturally, and linguistically diverse sign systems/modalities to consume, curate, and create in face-to-face and digital spaces. Teaching practices grounded in this framework create opportunities for learners to inquire

TABLE 5.3.1. Conventions of a Twitter Chat and Elements of Active Listening

Conventions of Twitter chat	Elements of active listening
• @ replies and hashtags • Likes and retweets • Message length • Specific word choice • Overall tone • Use of hyperlinks • Wait time, ranging from seconds to minutes, to perhaps even hours or days, depending on the pacing of the conversation	• Stay focused • Really listen • Allow for periods of silence • Repeat/paraphrase • Understand the emotions

about how language and power converge in print or digital texts to create and perpetu-
ate biases against marginalized communities. Learners need opportunities to practice
recognizing patterns in discourse which are rooted in the oppression of nondominant
groups (e.g., race, gender, sexuality, ability) and a variety of strategies they can use to
interrupt this discourse. (NCTE, 2019b)

In our efforts to help students draw on their "diverse sign systems/modalities" and to
"inquire about how language and power converge," an activity like this could help students begin to understand some of these nuances. Through conversation with their partners and the process of designing both an "uncivil" and a "civil" dialogue, students do
engage in some elements of empathetic thinking, and they work to see how communicative acts (in this case, tweets) can be directed at others in both appropriate and hurtful
ways.

   As noted above, and to extend the ideas for this lesson, we could certainly move
beyond Twitter as the primary form of expression and invite students to compose sample
messages with templates for other platforms. Typically, a search for "Google Slides Template [name of app]" will yield many examples of great designs that teachers have created.
To see what these might look like and get started, the book's companion website has
links to a few such templates for Facebook, Instagram, Snapchat, and Twitter.

   As their designs become more nuanced—and they draw in more media, such as
photos and video clips, to supplement their fictionalized social media posts—it is also
important to talk with students about what the NCTE (2019b) definition refers to
as the "rights, responsibilities, and ethical implications," of using such material. For
instance, they can begin conversations about how to "respect the intellectual property
of others and only utilize materials they are licensed to access, remix, and/or share" and
consider their "discursive practices in online social systems with others without deliberately or inadvertently demeaning individuals and/or groups." These conversations—
when engaged with around fictionalized characters that students are creating in fake
chats—might be easier to enter than ones in which they are discussing their own online
behaviors.

Guiding Questions

When working with students and exploring this topic, consider the following questions
when designing lessons, assignments, and assessments:

Before the Activity

- What are some of the positive experiences you have had—or have heard about from
  others—as it relates to conversations on social media?
  - What happened in those conversations that made them positive, and what were the
    outcomes of those conversations?

- On the flip side, what are some negative conversations you have had—or heard about—on social media?
  - Again, what were the characteristics of those conversations that made them negative, and what happened as a result of those conversations?
- Then, overall, how you feel about the use of social media in your life?
  - Do you feel the positives outweigh the negatives, or vice versa?
  - Are you comfortable with this balance?

During the Activity

- In composing both of the conversations, what specifically did you do with your digital writing in order to represent perspective and tone?
  - How did you choose specific words as well as consider who would speak (or tweet) first?
- Which conventions of Twitter conversation did you employ? How often?
  - In the negative chat, how specifically did you represent negativity or dismissiveness?
  - In the positive chat, how specifically did you represent active listening and engage in dialogue?

After the Activity

- While this is obviously a simulation (because it was a collaboration between partners creating fictional exchanges) and very much *unlike* a real Twitter exchange (because you were discussing and negotiating what the characters would do), what can we take from this as we consider the ways in which we use Twitter (or other social media) in the future?
- How can you practice "active listening" when engaged in Twitter and other social media conversations? How might you promote more active listening with and for others?

CHAPTER 6

Understanding How Knowledge Gets Created and Circulated

> Facts matter. Moreover, the sources from which we draw our facts
> matter too, as they are often infused with analysis and opinion.
> Understanding how knowledge is created and circulated in the world, as
> well as how to accurately source and properly cite it, is crucial if we want
> to become digitally diligent.

As the topics in Chapter 5 demonstrate, we all bring perspectives (or, as some might say, biases) to our experience of using the Internet. As students come to understand more and more about what the Internet is, how it works, and the ways that various actors use it for different purposes, they also need to understand how some of the "old rules" about source credibility don't work the way they used to. It is no longer enough to say that we can inherently trust a website based on an *.org* or *.edu* domain name, nor that Wikipedia is inherently unreliable. Moreover, we need to help them understand that everything—every article, every photo, every video, and more—has a home online, defined by a "uniform resource locator," or URL, that can be the central component of a citation for that source.

In our ELA classrooms, we have worked to teach digital and media literacies for decades, as well as critical literacies that help our students read between the lines when evaluating the motivations behind texts. As we prepare to help them create and share their own work, we need to help them understand how the information they are sorting through, as a foundation for their own ideas, are brought to life online. The activities in this chapter center on the dispositions that students will need to bring to the task of seeking new information, discerning high-quality information from that which is less useful, and keeping track of it all in a more formal manner.

With Topic 6.1, "Wikipedia: Full of Falsehoods, or a Credible Source?" we begin the conversation by unpacking our assumptions about this much-maligned website. In Topic 6.2, "The Whole Story: Fact-Checking 101," we build on ideas from Chapter 5 and continue to look at our sources even more critically and carefully. Last, with Topic 6.3, "Keeping Tracks: Documenting Our Sources," we move from the idea of bookmarking and curating many resources and begin to use bibliographic management tools to fully cite those that become a formal part of our academic research. Throughout, the goal is to have us continually question the ways in which we encourage our students to use the web, treating the items we might find online as primary sources, artifacts that demand our students' attention and proper documentation.

Additional resources that have informed my thinking in this chapter include many of those from Chapter 5, as well as a number of resources about Wikipedia, in particular, and broader critiques of the media. One source that crosses both of these lines is WNYC's weekly show and podcast *On the Media*. I have been a regular listener for nearly 20 years, and each week I am continually surprised and enlightened by their conversations with both media makers and critics. One such interview, in 2005 (Garfield, 2005), changed my nascent views on Wikipedia and introduced me to the work of Clay Shirky, leading me to read his books (Shirky, 2008, 2011) and view his TED Talks (links to these resources are on the book's companion website: hickstro.org/digitaldiligence).

The other primary guide I have used as a basis for my presentations and workshops in the past few years is a document produced by an American Library Association division, the Association of College and Research Libraries (ACRL; 2015): "Framework for Information Literacy for Higher Education." This resource speaks to both the media that we consume and more traditional academic sources, as well as how we can approach all of them from a critical perspective. Rather than prescriptive checklists, the authors of this framework offer a vision of "information literacy as extending the arc of learning throughout students' academic careers and as converging with other academic and social learning goals."

Thus, the framework is designed "to emphasize dynamism, flexibility, individual growth, and community learning," and the six frames have been useful for me as I introduce in workshops, webinars, and courses the principles of digital diligence. They are as follows:

- Authority Is Constructed and Contextual
- Information Creation as a Process
- Information Has Value
- Research as Inquiry
- Scholarship as Conversation
- Searching as Strategic Exploration

While the explanations of these frames can feel a bit esoteric, especially if we were to share them with middle and high school students, I do think that examining the concepts and making them applicable for our learners is useful for us as educators.

For instance, under the "Authority Is Constructed and Contextual" frame, there is the learning goal to "define different types of authority, such as subject expertise (e.g., scholarship), societal position (e.g., public office or title), or special experience (e.g., participating in a historic event)." Breaking this down and sharing it with an audience of middle school students, for instance, we might talk about how someone who is documenting an experience during a Black Lives Matter protest using social media as a "person on the street" does have a certain kind of authority, in a certain situation, but does not have the same kind of knowledge as a sociologist who has studied the issue of civil rights for two decades, or a public figure who is working on legislation to address systemic inequality. Again, some of the explanations are aimed at an audience of higher education librarians and scholars yet can be adapted and explained for our younger students, and I've included a link to a brief video from a YouTube user, Modern Librarian Memoirs, who describes the ACRL framework in easy-to-understand terms. Working through each of the frames with these kinds of examples, we might lead our students through a more robust understanding of each of the six elements of the framework.

TOPIC 6.1. WIKIPEDIA: FULL OF FALSEHOODS, OR A CREDIBLE SOURCE?

To help them become digitally diligent, we need students to embrace a more nuanced understanding of what Wikipedia is, how it is developed in an ongoing manner, and the ways in which they could use it in purposeful ways to bring evidence into their own arguments.

Overview

For many students, they have been told (most likely by other educators), over and over, that Wikipedia is an unreliable source. These concerns have roots in the technical functions of how any wiki, including a site like Wikipedia, functions; who has access to it; and what that access might allow a user to do with any given article through malicious editing. From its inception in January of 2001, Wikipedia has—according to the entry about itself—faced a number of critiques from academics, librarians, and journalists. These include blaring headlines about why students should never trust Wikipedia (that also seem to shout "clickbait!") and subtle reminders that teachers do not like sources from Wikipedia cited in papers, yet are still infused with a simple point; because anyone can edit Wikipedia, we can't possibly trust it.

Yet how much do we really know about the ways in which Wikipedia works, from both technical and social standpoints? With this topic, we explore the anatomy of a

Wikipedia page, including the guiding principle that each page is written from a "neutral point of view" (Wikipedia, 2020d). Moreover, we can explore additional features that are embedded in the very structure of Wikipedia itself for tracking page edits and discussing disagreements about any topic. These structural features of Wikipedia are important to understand as we invite students to consider using this source for their own arguments.

To begin, I encourage you to listen to a brief podcast mentioned in the Chapter 6 introduction, the one from WNYC's *On the Media*. Though recorded in 2005, Bob Garfield's interview with Clay Shirky still offers us a number of insights as we consider the ways in which we talk with our students about Wikipedia, and the ways in which we invite them to consider using it. He describes many of the technical aspects of Wikipedia, including the fact that many contentious topics are "locked," and how every Wikipedia entry has a corresponding "Talk" and "History" page.

For instance, the screenshots outlined in the Teaching Points below offer a quick glance at a semiprotected, or "locked," page that requires users to be registered contributors on Wikipedia. Additionally, some articles are indicated as "Good Articles" or "Featured Articles," indicating that Wikipedia editors have found them to be exceptionally well written and maintained. A few of these features can be examined on the "Black Lives Matter" page (Wikipedia, 2020a), shown in Figures 6.1.1–6.1.4. While some of this information can be accessed through the various pages on any article, a user can also look up information by pasting an article's URL into the xTools "Article Info" search tool (link available on the book's companion website).

Shirky describes Wikipedia's editorial policy toward a "neutral point of view." With this policy, Wikipedia contributors on any given topic are expected to adhere to the idea that they are "representing fairly, proportionately, and, as far as possible, without editorial bias, all the significant views that have been published by reliable sources on a topic" (Wikipedia, 2020d). In this sense, the fundamental policy of Wikipedia is to summarize and share existing information, pointing their readers to additional, outside sources of reliable information. In the case of the "Black Lives Matter" page, for instance, there were 434 external sources as of the time of this writing.

Further, in his 2005 interview, Shirky goes on to make the point that "what makes a wiki good is not the technology but the community." In this sense, he suggests that the community of writers and editors that work on a particular set of Wikipedia pages both are bound by the common expectations of Wikipedia's policies and yet also adhere to a broader set of social norms. In short, they want the articles under their care to be both useful and of high quality, just as almost any writer would. Ensuring they watch for recent edits and make corrections as needed, Shirky suggests that the community built through attentive monitoring of the page activity prevents any vandalism to the page from lasting long. This, in turn, provides an overall integrity for both individual pages as well as the entire site. With this in mind, teaching students when, why, and how to use Wikipedia as a credible source can become a lesson in both digital diligence and source reliability.

Teaching Points

When explored as a part of a comprehensive research experience—where students are invited to look at a variety of sources, including social media, blog posts, videos, and more traditional sources from encyclopedias, books, magazines, and news outlets on the web—asking students to engage with and use Wikipedia as a reference can spark many additional conversations. In this sense, these questions about what counts as evidence, for whom, and in what context connect to broader goals for teaching digital diligence. Questions about who gets to produce knowledge—and how that knowledge can be employed in different settings, for various purposes, and with certain audiences—are crucial for our students to understand. Connecting back to the ACRL (2015) "Framework for Information Literacy," a conversation about Wikipedia can touch on many of the frames, including the ideas that "authority is constructed and contextual" and that "information creation as a process"; each are enacted every day with Wikipedia, where with many contributors and editors collaborate on a constant basis.

An additional tool that can be helpful in visualizing the information about any given Wikipedia entry is xTools' page history statistical analysis tool. While I had known about the page statistics, I was introduced to the many aspects of xTools by Marcio Gonçalves, a Brazilian educator I met through our participation in the 2019 Summer Institute in Digital Literacy at the University of Rhode Island. In a paper he wrote for a 2017 conference, "Fact-checking on Wikipedia: An Exercise with Journalism Undergraduate Students," he pushed his students to examine the xTools statistics for articles, as well as the references that are listed to ensure that they are, indeed, from credible sources (Gonçalves, 2017). He noted that, for the particular articles they were examining from Wikipedia, his students were, in turn, going "upstream" (Caulfield, 2017a) to check sources from Portuguese-language sources that were, in some cases, inaccurate.

Though this could call into question the reliability of some Wikipedia articles based on the sources that are referenced, I would instead argue that it reiterates the need for students to follow through on their fact-checking and to think critically about how they can cite Wikipedia sources. In general, I suggest students use them as a way to enter the academic conversation with general definitions and descriptions of their topics that can then be triangulated with other sources. This is one main part of the conversation about Wikipedia that we need to continue having with students on a regular basis.

Finally, helping students situate their use of Wikipedia as a source in an overall argument will be important for them to fully think through the implications of doing so (and, perhaps, to convince some of our colleagues their citations are appropriate and useful). Building off the success of models like Gerald Graff and Cathy Birkenstein's "sentence templates" in their composition textbook *They Say/I Say: The Moves That Matter in Academic Writing,* these prompts can help our students justify their choices.

These sentence templates can be adapted to form the basis of a thoughtful, integrated citation, as I will demonstrate in more detail below. Some templates that I've developed and taught with include the following:

- According to the Wikipedia entry on [Topic], which was created on [Date of First Edit] and has a total of [Total Edits] with its most recent addition on [Date of Latest Edit], "[Key Quote]."

- Given that [Number of Editors] contributors have added value to its Wikipedia entry, and that it is monitored by [Number of Page Watchers], a reasonable reader can agree with these Wikipedia contributors who state that "[Key Quote]."

- Also of note, for the Wikipedia entry on [Topic], there are a total of [Current Conversations] about it, suggesting that the inclusion of "[Key Quote]" is still under active consideration.

- With a total of [Number of References] outside references to substantiate its claims, the Wikipedia entry on [Topic] offers an explanation that states "[Key Quote]."

It is possible, too, that students could work on this process in a collaborative manner, sharing what they have discovered about their own individual sources, and then begin thinking about the longevity of given articles, the number of edits, the number of outside sources, and other factors that could weigh on the credibility of the articles they are sharing.

Examining Wikipedia's "Black Lives Matter" Page and Citing It as a Source

As an example of how I would walk students through the examination of a source, I have captured four screenshots of various elements of Wikipedia's page for "Black Lives Matter" in late November 2020 (see Figures 6.1.1–6.1.4). After examining these snapshots—and then using the sentence templates above—I share a paragraph that more fully considers this Wikipedia page as an entry point for an academic argument. Most likely, a writer would sprinkle one of each of these sentence types throughout a longer essay, intertwined with other sources and as a way to create a more robust argument. That said, as a complete example, Figure 6.1.5 draws ideas from each of the four preceding figures: the main page, the talk page, the history page, and the xTools data for Wikipedia's page for "Black Lives Matter." Using the sentence templates above, I try to build this resource into a more compelling argument that moves deeper into the academic conversation. Whether or not this kind of citation for Wikipedia is, ultimately, effective in the context of an overall academic argument could then become a conversation among students, especially as they find more and more resources to support their case.

With this example and the general ideas about Wikipedia's usefulness, we turn again to the NCTE's "Definition of Literacy in a Digital Age" to think through additional connections. I am immediately drawn to one segment, "Explore and engage critically, thoughtfully, and across a wide variety of inclusive texts and tools/modalities" (NCTE, 2019b), which has been explored in many of the earlier topics. Three additional questions drawn from that section that I find compelling in the context of examining Wikipedia are "Do learners choose texts and tools to consume, create, and share ideas that match their need and audience?"; "Do learners create new ideas using knowledge

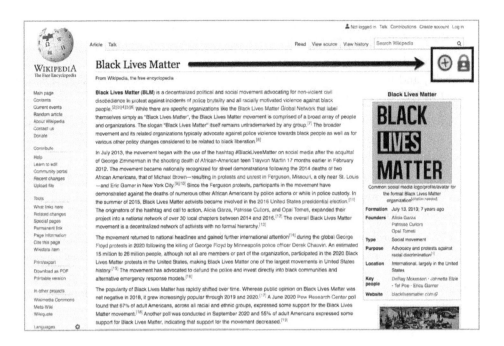

FIGURE 6.1.1. Screenshot of Wikipedia's page for "Black Lives Matter" in late November 2020, with a magnified callout on the "good article" and "semiprotected" lock icons.

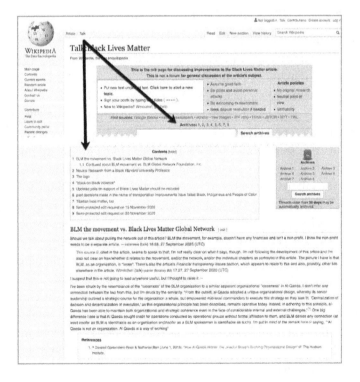

FIGURE 6.1.2. Selected elements of a screenshot of Wikipedia's "Talk" page for "Black Lives Matter" in late November 2020, with a callout indicating the nine discussions, including those seeking "semiprotected" editing status, as well as the nine archived pages of discussion.

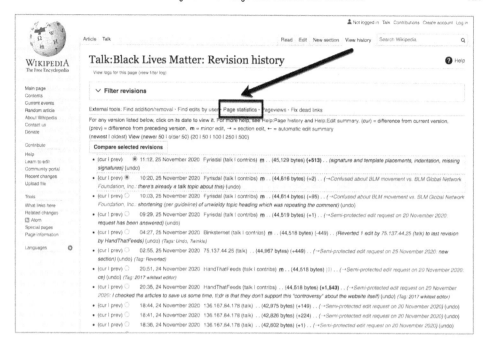

FIGURE 6.1.3. Screenshot of Wikipedia's "History" page for "Black Lives Matter" in late November 2020, with a callout indicating the link for "page statistics."

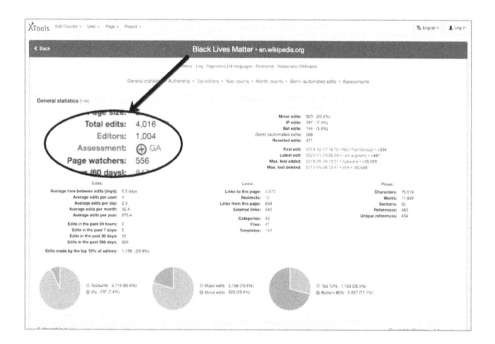

FIGURE 6.1.4. Screenshot of Wikipedia's xTools statistics for "Black Lives Matter" in late November 2020, with a magnified callout indicating the number of page edits, the number of page editors, and the number of page watchers.

In the past decade, civil rights issues have become more and more prominent as part of conversations regarding police brutality and mass incarceration in America. One key part of this movement is encapsulated in the Black Lives Matter movement, or BLM. According to the Wikipedia entry on "Black Lives Matter"—which was created on December 17, 2014, and has a total of 4016 edits, with its most recent addition on the day of this writing, November 25, 2020—the BLM movement "is a decentralized political and social movement advocating for non-violent civil disobedience in protest against incidents of police brutality and all racially motivated violence against black people." Given that 1,004 contributors have added value to its Wikipedia entry, and that it is monitored by 556 page watchers, a reasonable reader can agree with these Wikipedia contributors who state that "the broader movement and its related organizations typically advocate against police violence towards black people as well as for various other policy changes considered to be related to black liberation." Also of note, for the Wikipedia entry on BLM, there are a total of nine current conversations about it, as well as dozens of archived ones. In particular, the section of the page related to the "loose confederation of groups advocating for racial justice" is still under active consideration amongst page contributor, as indicated by a thread begun in September of 2020. "With the resurgence of Black Lives Matter in national headlines amid global protests," and with a total of 434 outside references to substantiate its claims, the Wikipedia entry on BLM concludes that "the movement has seen an increase in support in 2020."

FIGURE 6.1.5. Sample paragraph using the Wikipedia sentence templates.

and insights gained?"; and "Do learners analyze the credibility of information, authorial intent, and its appropriateness in meeting their needs?" By engaging in an analysis of Wikipedia pages in the ways described above, we move students toward answering these questions and, additionally, push them to speak back to other educators who may be misinformed about Wikipedia's community, policies, and, in the end, accuracy.

Additionally, in the "Examine the rights, responsibilities, and ethical implications of the use and creation of information" segment of NCTE's definition, there is opportunity to consider how a deeper study of Wikipedia could meet the goals embedded in many of the questions listed therein. Quoting at length from the introduction to that subsection of the NCTE statement, there are many overlaps worthy of exploration:

> Networked, digital spaces offer the opportunity to instantaneously share, aggregate, and access torrents of information from others. These spaces also raise questions about aspects of intellectual property and ownership of ideas, content, and resources online. The rapidly changing digital texts and tools create new categories of ethical dilemmas around these issues. It is important for learners to understand the ethics, or "principles governing an individual or group," as they interact with information in current and future contexts. (NCTE, 2019b)

The subquestions within this section of the statement are useful too, especially "Do learners consider the contributors and authenticity of all sources?" There are numerous ethical implications that the use of Wikipedia raises and, with these connections to the NCTE definition, we now turn to questions that can guide students through a deeper exploration of Wikipedia as a credible source.

Guiding Questions

When working with students and exploring this topic, consider the following questions when designing lessons, assignments, and assessments:

Opening Questions

- What have you been warned about when using Wikipedia?
- From these warnings, what additional information have you been given about the way Wikipedia functions, in a technical sense?
- How often do you see Wikipedia entries showing up in the top results for your web searches?
- Given all this background, how often—and for what purposes—do you use Wikipedia?

As Students Explore Wikipedia

- Find one specific page. As you explore that page, use the "Talk" page, the "History" page, and the xTools, try to discover the following:
  - When the page was created
  - When the most recent edit occurred
  - How many total edits have occurred on the page
  - How many total editors (contributors) and page watchers the page has
  - How many active discussions about the page have been or are currently going on
  - How many references are available to outside sources
- After engaging with some of the additional material found on book's companion website, and further discussing Wikipedia, answer these questions:
  - How are Wikipedia articles written, edited, and monitored?
  - How do the Wikipedia policies of a "neutral point of view" and "no original research" affect what is written there?
  - What have you discovered about the "History" and "Talk" pages for any particular Wikipedia article?
  - What have you discovered about the ways that Wikipedia references outside sources?

Further Questions

- Based on the information you have discovered, do you think a Wikipedia page could be considered "credible"?
- How would you defend the credibility of this page to a teacher who says you can't use Wikipedia as a source?
- More important, how would you introduce various statistics surrounding the Wikipedia page within your overall argument?

TOPIC 6.2. THE WHOLE STORY: FACT-CHECKING 101

To help them become digitally diligent, we need students to be persistent
in their efforts to explore sources and verify information while also
identifying and empathizing with various perspectives that are offered
through analysis and opinion.

Overview

In the fall of 2019, *The New York Times* (Levin, 2019) expanded on an article from
the *Lansing State Journal* that exposed a network of "local [news] sites" in Michigan
(Thompson, 2019). Sites such as the "The Lansing Sun" and "The Ann Arbor Times"—
purportedly news sources that offered hyperlocal coverage—were shown to be owned by
a single company, led by a conservative activist. The sites would rely on similar content,
ghostwritten by a network of freelance journalists, and the single source would distribute
the same content under dozens of "local" sites. In their further analysis of the network,
journalists from *The New York Times* concluded that "behind the scenes, many of the
stories are directed by political groups and corporate P.R. firms to promote a Republican
candidate or a company, or to smear their rivals" (Alba & Nicas, 2020). Similar types
of such "local" news have been found more and more in other online networks and,
additionally, television stations (Graves, 2017). The line between accurate, local reporting and a nationally syndicated (and clearly biased) network of sources has been blurred.

The work of discerning fact from opinion is difficult enough, and especially so
when the facts themselves are in dispute. Even when agreeing on the *who, what, when*,
and *where*, the facts of a story are often interspersed with the *how* and *why* of analysis
and opinion. By checking the facts (and, if needed, then comparing the results of other
fact-checkers), students can begin to differentiate what has *actually* happened from the
ways that people *feel* about what has happened. This topic encourages students to use
explore fact-checking websites, comparing what they have found and understanding
how these facts are then represented from different ideological perspectives.

These perspectives, too, are difficult to discern just by looking at any single article
from only one particular source. Instead, it takes readers, listeners, and viewers a significant amount of time to become familiar with "ideological markers," or the core
elements that are indicators of how "each political ideology structures its mental map to
explain the social world" (Schena et al., 2018, p. 13 in PDF). For instance, Schena et al.
describe some ideological markers of conservatism as "authority" and "hierarchy," as well
as "faith in God" and "family traditions." Similarly, they describe the kinds of markers
that would typically be associated with American Democratic liberalism as in line with
their "socialism" markers (as compared to Libertarian values such as "autonomy" and
"civil liberties" in the "liberalism" markers). For the political left, at least as it is defined
in American terms, Schena et al. describe some ideological markers as "class politics" and
"wealth distribution" as well as "social justice" and "equality." By beginning to recognize
these linguistic markers in the headlines, images, and specific words and phrases used in
media, we can begin to show students how various ideologies are enacted.

In other words, we need to begin with the premise that all information is presented from a particular standpoint. This has been explored in previous topics, though it warrants a bit more attention here from the perspective of journalism, as a field, and journalists, as professionals working in that field. A look from the field itself and from two practitioners, in particular, can be helpful.

First, the Society of Professional Journalists (SPJ; 2014) has a code of ethics that begins with the premise that "ethical journalism strives to ensure the free exchange of information that is accurate, fair and thorough. An ethical journalist acts with integrity." Built on four key principles—"seek truth and report it," "minimize harm," "act independently," and "be accountable and transparent"—the SPJ statement asserts that journalists should engage in a variety of principled practices, including the ideas that they should "verify information before releasing it," "use original sources whenever possible," and "avoid pandering to lurid curiosity, even if others do." From their website, SPJ offers links to find more information about each of these principles, each providing links then to even more information and guidelines. As a document for discussing what journalists should—and should not—do, a conversation on this code of ethics could be paired with additional dialogue about the kinds of biases that might present themselves across various news outlets.

Second, from an instructional standpoint, Mike Caulfield encourages us to consider a model for seeking out more information on a source by following the acronym "SIFT." Caulfield (2017b) is an educational technologist and has released his entire book, *Web Literacy for Student Fact-Checkers,* as an open ebook. Also, he blogs regularly at Hapgood.com and is director of the American Democracy Project. Moving beyond the ways in which we used to teach students to check the domain extension on a URL, the "about" page for more information on an author or organization, and to look for the most recent update to the website, it becomes more obvious that our old models of website evaluation are not enough (Murchie & Neyer, 2018). Caulfield's SIFT model—in contrast to outdated advice that encourages students to look at the "about" page or check for the most recent updates—encourages students to "go upstream." Though he is directing this message at students learning how to do fact checking, it is quite useful for any news reader too.

Using SIFT as a way to explore a given article, in order to better understand where information originated, Caulfield (2019) outlines four steps:

- "Stop," to quickly discern what it is you already might know about this source of information.
- "Investigate the source," in order to understand their area of expertise and particular perspectives.
- "Find trusted coverage," by looking for a source other than the original source from which you heard the information.
- And, finally, "trace claims, quotes, and media back to the original context" in order to find out if the information you are seeing, as presented, accurately represents what was originally shared.

In his blog post outlining the SIFT method, Caulfield concludes by emphasizing the need that evidence must be examined with the idea that everyone comes to the topic with a particular perspective. He contends that context is crucial, as a news source may take another's original report and reconstruct, reestablish, or recontextualize that material to bring a different perspective to it. In addition to understanding the sources of information, we need to help students understand the ways in which some ideas are presented as facts and how this plays on our natural tendencies toward confirmation bias (Vedantam, 2019) and looking at why we fall prey to mis- and disinformation.

Continuing with the practitioner perspective, Clare Wardle, an author and strategist affiliated with *First Draft News*, released a compelling article—with accompanying infographics—in 2017. Provocatively titled to play on Facebook's infamous relationship status message in her article "Fake News. It's Complicated," she argues that news creators and critics need to approach the problem of fake news from a different perspective. She suggests that "we also need to think about who is creating these different types of content and why it is being created" (Wardle, 2017). She outlines a variety of forms of misinformation (ranging from satire to completely fabricated content), as well as a list of motivations that could be behind the item being created: "Poor Journalism, Parody, to Provoke or 'Punk,' Passion, Partisanship, Profit, Political Influence or Power, and Propaganda." Using the categories in this matrix as a basis for conversation, and given this context for understanding how journalists aim to do their work—and the ways in which students can "go upstream" to find the original information—there are a variety of fact-checking tools that students can explore.

In the teaching points below, students could explore any of the following, including Politifact, FactStream, FactCheck, Poynter, and the increasingly robust Snopes, a site originally designed to debunk relatively innocuous Internet memes and which has now turned into a leading fact-checking organization. To that end, we will focus on Snopes, looking at the ways in which their articles are constructed as a way to think about examining—and reframing—mis- and disinformation.

Teaching Points

Given that there are numerous sites available for fact-checking—let alone hundreds of thousands of items on the Internet that deserve to be fact-checked—we could invite students to find a story that seems sensational, or even a topic that is likely to be contemporary and controversial, that they can begin to investigate. Students could even take an item from their own social media feed that seems to be worthy of a fact-check. This, however, could take some time and—depending on school filters and the topics that students are investigating—may not be as fruitful for one student as it might be for another. Looking at a different subject, the first student may find articles quickly while the other continues to struggle, as if on a wild goose chase. So, it could be more valuable for all students to explore a topic assigned by the teacher, at least in this case.

No matter how they find their topic, this lesson invites them to work as a fact-checker would, but to do so in reverse. In the spirit of analyzing mentor texts, which can provide writers with what Allison Marchetti and Rebekah O'Dell (2015) describe as "model pieces of writing—or excerpts of writing—by established authors" and to use these texts because they "enable student writers to become connected to the dynamic world of professional writers" (p. 3), we would first ask students to find a recent article from the "Fact Checks" section of Snopes. By doing this, we can be sure they are investigating something that has already been disproven and help them understand how the fact-checker drew that conclusion.

As they dig in and find a particular fact-checked article to explore, a few recurring features are worth noting—and analyzing—to better understand how a fact-checker would arrive at the conclusion. Using section headings as a guide for understanding the fact-checking process, we can have students look at Snopes as a mentor text. They can figure out original items being fact-checked can be rated from "True" or "Mostly True" to a "Mixture" or "False," "Mostly False," "Unproven," or "Scam," among a number of other rankings (a list to Snopes fact-check rankings, as with other resources listed in this chapter, are available on the book's companion website). The basic layout of a Snopes' fact-check article remains consistent from one article to the next and includes the following features:

- A headline, typically in the form of a question, that highlights the essence of the fact-check. For instance, at the time of this writing, the first article on Snopes' fact-check section led with the headline "Is the CDC Setting Up 'Green Zones' or COVID-19 Containment Camps?" (Evon, 2020). In examining the headline, remind students of what comprises a good headline and the way that a question might be more likely than a statement to draw a reader in. This question represents the core idea in the fact-checking process.

- This primary headline is followed by a secondary one, providing a brief synopsis of the rumor and some insight on the resulting fact-check. Again, in the case of Evon's article, the secondary headline provides an overview by stating, "A months-old document exploring one possible response to the COVID-19 pandemic was misrepresented on social media." Talk with them about effective summaries and what key elements need to be included, including the *who*, *what*, *when*, and *where*.

- Next, note that the fact-checker is named clearly in the byline of the article, as well as a publication date. Discuss why these clear notations about the author and timeliness are especially important for fact-checkers.

- An image follows next, representing the story in a non-sensationalized manner. With social media icons below, it is assumed this is the image that would appear if a user were to choose to post to social media. Examine the image and think about the composition of the photo. Also, note whether the photo is gleaned from the original source, if it is an image from the public domain or published with a Creative Commons license, and what other elements of attribution are included. Both Google Image search and TinEye Reverse Image Search are tools in the fact-checker's toolbox and can be used to look for the origins of a photo.

- Then, notice how the main part of the article has three additional sections: the claim, the rating, and the backstory, labeled as "Origin."

    o Claim: The original idea under consideration in the fact-check—and framed as a question in the headline—is framed as a defensible claim. Returning to the example cited above, the claim is noted as "The CDC is setting up COVID-19 containment camps called 'green zones.'" Invite students to consider different ways in which the claim might have been stated, perhaps showing how some versions might be clearer than others.

    o Rating: The rating, with an accompanying icon, is displayed prominently. With the ranking, there is a link to the description of what the ranking means, and if it is not demonstrably "True" or "False," additional context will be provided for the rating. As students read the "Origin" section below, ask them to consider their own interpretation of the evidence being presented, and whether they feel the rating is warranted.

    o Origin: With an explanation that can range from a few sentences to a few paragraphs, the description in the "Origin" section provides more background on the item under consideration, with additional links to other reputable sources. As with any piece of informational or argumentative text, invite students to read it and look for logical fallacies, as well as places that might not go into enough detail. Examine the evidence too, considering what is included in terms of quotations, statistics, and other direct links to articles, reports, or other resources.

- Finally, though not part of every fact-check, if the mentor text from Snopes includes a screenshot, a meme, or a photograph (especially one that appears to be manipulated), use that as a topic for conversation too. Snopes will include a version of that image with the label for the kind of fact-check superimposed on it. For instance, on the CDC example, a screenshot of the CDC.gov website that was embedded in the social media post is included, with the Snopes logo and "Mostly False" layered over top of a slightly greyed-out version of the original image. Ask students to consider what purpose this might serve as the Snopes article is shared more widely on social media.

After engaging in a discussion about the structure and scope of the Snopes mentor text—as well as the kinds of sources they rely on for evidence—students could then begin to craft their own "Snopes-like" fact-check article. As they look through their own social media feeds or explore other topics of interest, remind them of the points above about what a good fact-checker must do, as well as how an article about a particular topic would ultimately be represented on a website like Snopes, with the primary and secondary headlines, the restated claim, the clear rating label, and an in-depth explanation of the origin. Scaffolding students through a writing process where they create their own Snopes-like, fact-check–style article could be a good way to have them fully investigate an inquiry topic and consider the ways that such a topic might otherwise be misrepresented in social media.

In considering these teaching points, we return to NCTE's "Definition of Literacy in a Digital Age." Drawn again to the ideas that students should "explore and engage critically, thoughtfully, and across a wide variety of inclusive texts and tools/modalities" and "determine how and to what extent texts and tools amplify one's own and others' narratives as well as counter unproductive narratives" (NCTE, 2019b), I suggest a few of the additional subquestions worth pursuing in light of this topic, having used an article from Snopes as a mentor text and in preparing their own fact-check.

Under the subheading of "Create" in the "Explore" section, we are now asking students to "use tools to communicate original perspectives and to make new thinking visible," to "communicate information and ideas in a variety of forms and for various purposes," and to "articulate thoughts and ideas so that others can understand and act on them." From the "Determine" section, this topic of fact-checking becomes an opportunity to help students develop "a heightened awareness about how texts and tools can be used to produce and circulate biased narratives aimed at justifying exclusionary practices and policies that disproportionately impact nondominant communities." They also have opportunity, by analyzing and existing fact-check and then developing their own, to participate in "sustained opportunities to produce counter-narratives that expose and interrupt misguided texts" (NCTE, 2019b). While I can agree with the writers of this definition that this kind of work is normally done through personal narrative, I would extend the ideas in this section of the definition to suggest that students can engage in this kind of informational and argumentative writing to rewrite the kinds of underlying, implicit narratives about race, class, gender, and other points of division that we find embedded in our culture and represented on social media (and are likely to be at the root of many articles requiring a fact-check in the first place).

Guiding Questions

When working with students and exploring this topic, consider the following questions when designing lessons, assignments, and assessments:

Opening Questions

- What do you think of when you hear the term *fake news*? The term *fact-check?*
- What are the elements of an article, a photo, a video, or another source that you consider when you are determining whether it is trustworthy?
- Along those same lines, what kinds of evidence do you look for when you are examining a source, in order to see where they have found their own information?

As Students Explore Snopes

- What do you notice about the structure of the Snopes article?
  - What sections does it have?

- Who do you think the intended audience for a Snopes article is?
  - How do you know who this intended audience is?
  - What language suggests a particular audience that they might be writing for?
- In what ways does the article work to either prove or disprove the claim that is presented?
  - What kind of evidence is presented?
  - From where is this evidence gathered?
- What additional sources does the article link to in order to provide even more evidence?
  - What do you notice about the quality and trustworthiness of those sources?

Further Questions

- Based on the experience of creating your own fact-check-style article in the style of Snopes, what have you come to understand about the genre of fact-checking?
- In order to do fact-checking thoroughly, about how many additional sources do you estimate that a writer must have to substantiate their claims?
  - What factors help you make this estimate?
  - How does this number of sources needed for a fact check compare to the kind of research we might do in a typical academic essay?

TOPIC 6.3. KEEPING TRACKS: DOCUMENTING OUR SOURCES

To help them become digitally diligent, we need students to recognize
that information artifacts have unique identifiers that distinguish them,
and as we participate in scholarly dialogue, we need to help others
understand the resources from which we have built our own arguments.

Overview

There will never be less information available in the world than there is right now, so we all need to keep track of what we have read, seen, and listened to (or at least some of what we have experienced in our wanderings across the web). While it is likely that we neither would want to—nor even could—document everything we see online, let alone in our lives (though there are some filmmakers and computer scientists who have made such attempts), it is certainly valuable to document the key artifacts that will inform our thinking and expression later on. In addition to the social bookmarking and curation tools introduced early in the book, this topic will turn toward bibliographic (or reference) management tools as a way to help students more formally keep track of their sources.

First, we need to back the lens out a bit. Sometimes web users forget that all information artifacts have a "home" online. Videos, tweets, blog posts, PDF versions of reports. All these kinds of items may have been found through a certain search engine, yet they are not just something that a person "found online." Whether a social media post, a photograph, a journal article, a Wikipedia entry, or a shared collaborative document, all items have a "uniform resource locator" (a URL) that designates exactly where a web browser can find it. Moreover, everything online was created by someone, whether an individual, an organization, or even through a bot producing text with artificial intelligence. Each of these items are unique and—when being used as a component of an academic argument—deserve to be recognized through a more formal citation, not just as a tab in a curated list of items.

Going into an even deeper dive on the ways in which the web works, we can see that these items are located in a certain part of the Internet, the World Wide Web. Though the backbone of the Internet had been under development for decades, it was in the 1990s that new languages for creating and transferring data allowed users to see and interact with that data in new ways. The inventor of "hypertext transfer protocol" (the "http" we see in front of web addresses), Tim Berners-Lee, aimed to create a way for computers to easily talk with one another across a network and to be able to find appropriate files. For more on hypertext and the history behind it, I have written an entry in the 2019 *International Encyclopedia of Media Literacy* and encourage readers to take a deeper dive into the topic there (T. Hicks, 2019a).

Fast-forward two plus decades, and sometimes we don't even think about where an item lives on the web. For instance, in a social media app, we may never even see the URL of a particular post or image. Even in our web browsers, we may only see a portion of a URL unless we adjust our settings. Of course, we know that social media sites, especially Facebook, have in the past hidden URLs and not made them explicitly clear, so the different between clicking on "ABC News" from the American Broadcasting Company via (ABCnews.go.com) and the purveyor of fake news from ABCnews.com.co—which has emulated the logo and general style of the official ABC News company—can be a challenge for those quickly scrolling through their social media feeds. Of course, the fact that domain names such as *.com* and *.org* can be purchased by anyone (and do not have the same respectable cachet as they used to) means that source checking through deeper levels of analysis and triangulation is more important than ever (as noted in the previous topics in this chapter, 6.1 and 6.2).

Still, the main point here is clear: All sources (whether we consider them to be good, bad, or otherwise) have a home online, and students need to discover as much out about a source as possible if they plan to integrate it—or critique it—as a part of an informational piece or an academic argument. Using bibliographic management software as a tool to scaffold this process, the work of documenting sources can become an exercise in both sourcing materials and moving beyond the adage that we need to cite our sources simply to avoid plagiarism, instead pushing students toward a more robust understanding of what it means to be a reader, a writer, and a researcher in a digital age.

Teaching Points

Understanding why academic writing encourages the use of citation requires that we teach students about two simultaneous sets of demands: engaging broadly in "scholarship as conversation," as noted in the ACRL framework and, at the same time, teaching them about the minutiae of APA, MLA, or other formatting styles. For the first point, we need to remind students that their work will be informed by that of other scholars, journalists, filmmakers, producers, and even social media content creators. In order to put these ideas in conversation with our own, we then need to provide proper attribution for them.

For the second point, though it can seem mundane, there are actually very good reasons that different citation styles have evolved in different ways; understanding some of the nuances of each can be insightful as students are struggling to figure out rules about capitalization, punctuation, and whether to use an author's full name or just the last name with first initial. Though it feels a bit dated in the style of production, a brief 4-minute overview of these ideas has been produced as a YouTube video from the Raritan Valley Community College Library (link available on this book's companion website). For instance, they note that scientists care about the currency of the citation, as more recent research is likely more useful in developing their own projects and comparing results, whereas someone studying literature is more concerned about the author's name and the work, no matter when the citation was published. In short, different disciplines have different priorities when sharing citations. Understanding, then, that different disciplines have different expectations for citation styles, we can talk with students about the nuances across various fields of study.

In addition to the bookmarking and curation tools discussed earlier in the book—and in contrast to "free" reference management services that make their money off of ads and freemium models—I encourage the use of a free, openly available tool, Zotero. Created by the Corporation for Digital Scholarship (n.d.-a), which is described on the Zotero website as "a nonprofit organization dedicated to the development of software and services for researchers and cultural heritage institutions," Zotero and the companion tool ZoteroBib (short for Zotero Bibliography) are most often used by students and academics in higher education. Still, I contend that each of them, especially ZoteroBib, can be used by middle and high school students in their efforts to document their sources.

A quick side note: For those who might be interested (and have a good relationship with their IT department), Zotero can be fully integrated with Google Docs and Microsoft Word on Mac and Windows machines. That said, I will not go into elaborate detail on that process here; a link to Zotero's help guides for word processor plug-ins is available on the book's companion website. Instead, the following activity demonstrates use of the web-based tool ZoteroBib, built by the team that developed the freely available Zotero, and shows how we can have students conscientiously document and integrate their sources.

ZoteroBib, according to its home page, "helps you build a bibliography instantly from any computer or device, without creating an account or installing any software," and will allow uses to export their list of citations in MLA, APA, Chicago, or over 9,800 additional styles. The export options include copying to the clipboard for pasting in a word processing document, downloading as an RTF, and saving in a manner that it can be imported by other bibliographic management tools, like Zotero itself. More important than these particular features, however, are the affordances of the ZoteroBib data entry interface, which we explore below.

The ZoteroBib interface, in this sense, serves as a teaching tool, inviting users to add both bibliographic information and notes through the "extra" box at the bottom. One of the challenges in teaching students to find and integrate sources in a meaningful manner comes through decision making about when to quote, when to paraphrase, and when to summarize. As students are in the process of finding and documenting their sources, then, the "extra" box serves as a moment to pause, to ask students to copy/paste key quotes, to write their own paraphrases of those key quotes, or to condense and summarize key ideas. In addition, students could write their own questions about the artifact, capturing their thinking about what they have learned from—and how they might further use—the source.

The screenshots in Figures 6.3.1 and 6.3.2 show two snapshots of the ZoteroBib interface, one in book format (documenting a particular book for which I have an affinity), as well as a second one where I have tried to document as much as I could from the Raritan Valley Community College Library video mentioned above. For my book, I was able to grab the ISBN number from Amazon and then drop it in ZoteroBib's interface to generate the initial citation. Similarly, for the Raritan Valley Community College Library video, I copied and pasted the URL of the YouTube video into ZoteroBib. Then I had to do some additional editing.

For my own book, ZoteroBib captured most of the information needed to create a complete citation in both MLA and APA format. Note in Figure 6.3.1 that the "Item Type" is automatically selected as "Book" and that the title, place of publication, publisher, and date are all included, as well as information about the Library of Congress catalog information. In the "abstract" area there is no information and, in the "extra" area, there is identifying information from OCLC, a major library indexing service. This information is helpful, but these spaces can be used for other purposes, as shown in Figure 6.3.2. In the "Abstract" field I wrote a brief summary (perhaps too brief in terms of what I might expect of a student, but this is just an example!), and in the "Extra" field I transcribed a key quote (and could certainly add more to make my annotated bibliography even more complete).

Having this kind of additional information in the citation is valuable as students synthesize their sources. ZoteroBib offers an additional option to "Link to this version." With this option, the bibliography can be shared via ZoteroBib. Teachers could ask students to create annotations for their entries using the method described above, and subsequently, students could share the link for the teacher to review. In this manner, students can use ZoteroBib as a space to build their annotated bibliography and quickly share it, working on the process of gathering sources well before the final draft of an essay is due. With the bibliographic information from the YouTube video (Figure 6.3.3), some additional editing is needed too. First, ZoteroBib recognized the URL as a web-page (which, technically, it is), though I want to document this source as a video recording on YouTube. Changing the "Item Type" from "Web Page" to "Video Recording," the user is presented with an array of new bibliographic information to complete, including being able to add the director. Again, this provides students with another option for discovering more about their source. While just including the YouTube user's screen name

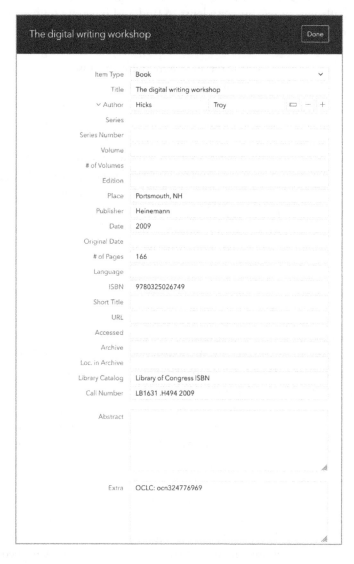

FIGURE 6.3.1. Screenshot of initial book entry in ZoteroBib using ISBN number.

FIGURE 6.3.2.   Screenshot of revised book entry in ZoteroBib.

is an option, the name "RVCCLibrary" is not as complete as we need it to be to produce a full citation. This, in turn, requires some searching, and one can quickly discern that "RVCCLibrary" is the screen name for the Raritan Valley Community College Library, which becomes the director.

At this point, even more cleanup is needed. The "Title" of the video does not need the "- YouTube" at the end of it, and the extended URL will be bulky in a citation. Thus, I need to delete the additional information in the title and return to the original video to get the shorter URL from the "Share" button. ZoteroBib also failed to capture the original date of publication and the "Running Time," so I need to add that information

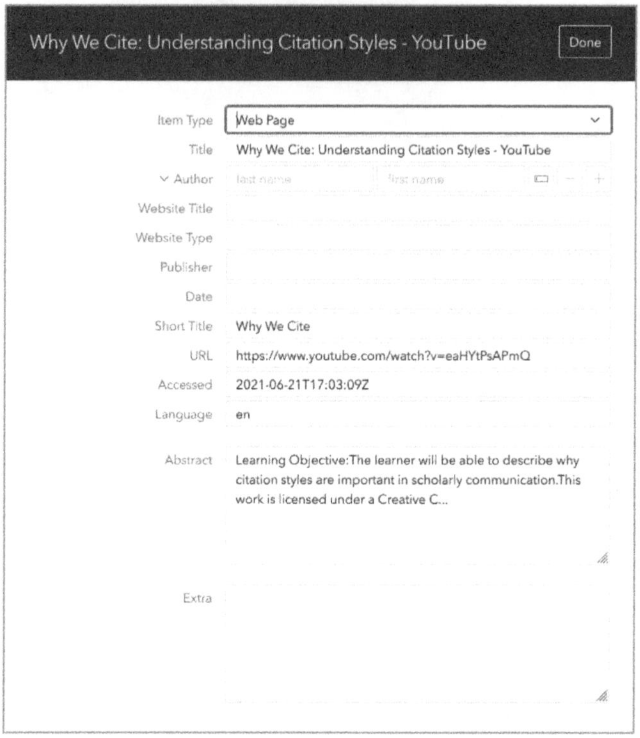

FIGURE 6.3.3. Screenshot of initial video entry in ZoteroBib using YouTube URL.

too. And though I didn't in this example, the options to add an "Abstract" and "Extra" information are present in this entry too. These changes result in an almost entirely new version of the ZoteroBib entry, shown in Figure 6.3.4.

With all these changes in place, the final outputs of my ZoteroBib bibliographies are slightly different. In Figure 6.3.5, I capture the "before and after" versions of the Zotero-Bib reference list, in APA format, for my two citations. The book entry on the surface looks the same, though there is additional information that I added in the "Abstract" and "Extra" sections. The Raritan Valley Community College Library's video, however, is much different, as it has been converted from a webpage to a video recording (with the additional information added and the change in format), so the outputs are quite different.

These are just two examples, and as students cite more and more sources to support a continual conversation about all the bibliographic elements, we can glean a sense of how the tool works. That said, a tool like Zotero or ZoteroBib is not without criticism or concern. Many teachers with whom I have discussed the use of bibliographic management tools are concerned that the tools are not useful because they do not always create accurate citations. I am concerned about this too, yet see this as an advantage, not a detriment. The example of the video entry, for instance, is just one such point to discuss

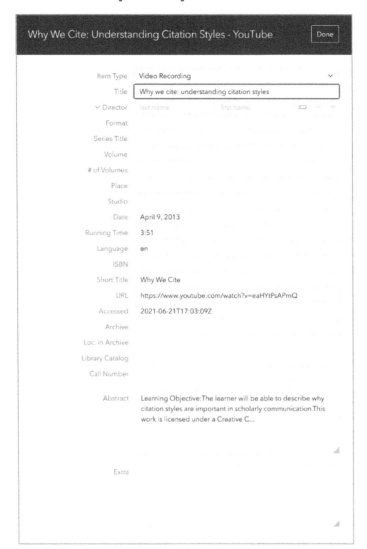

FIGURE 6.3.4. Screenshot of revised video entry in ZoteroBib.

Original ZoteroBib entry output in APA style	Revised ZoteroBib entry output in APA style
Hicks, T. (2009). *The digital writing workshop*. Heinemann.	Hicks, T. (2009). *The digital writing workshop*. Heinemann.
Why we cite: Understanding citation styles—YouTube. (n.d.). Retrieved June 21, 2021, from www.youtube.com/watch?v=eaHYtPsAPmQ	Raritan Valley Community College Library. (2013, April 9). *Why we cite: Understanding citation styles*. https://youtu.be/eaHYtPsAPmQ

FIGURE 6.3.5. Two versions of ZoteroBib reference list, before and after editing.

as we look at ways for students to more accurately document their sources. Moreover, as I prepared to export my bibliography and switch from MLA to APA style in the bibliography, ZoteroBib offers the following pop-up note of warning to me as the user, which is also worthy of conversation:

Converting Titles to Sentence Case

The style you've selected requires titles to be in sentence case rather than title case. When you use this style, ZoteroBib will convert the titles of entries to sentence case for you, but you'll need to manually edit some entries to capitalize proper nouns.

They go on to note, in their FAQs:

We know this is annoying, but we think it's less annoying than manually lowercasing all the other words in titles. Some other tools simply ignore this requirement and generate incorrect, title-cased bibliographies, but we try our best to generate citations according to the style you've chosen. (Corporation for Digital Scholarship, n.d.-b)

Again, this opens up a point of discussion with students where differences in bibliographic style can become opportunities to talk about both how and why various disciplines use their own unique styles. While some of the peculiarities may remain, these are elements of discussion that can be pursued in a larger conversation about source citation.

As I have before, I now return to the NCTE (2019b) definition and consider connections. Immediately, I am drawn back to the "Curate" segment of the "Consume, curate, and create actively across contexts," considering questions such as "Do learners consciously make connections between their work and that of the greater community?" and "Do learners apply ethical practices when using media?" Also, as this process of citing sources then moves into more formal writing, questions from the "Create" segment become pertinent. For instance, by acknowledging the needs of an academic audience, "learners [will] share and publish original content with a consideration of the intended audience" and are "respond[ing] constructively to published work" of others.

By providing complete citations to the work of others—especially work that has been produced and shared online and could be remixed or repurposed easily without attribution—this topic also encourages students to "advocate for their own individual and community's access to texts" and "consider the contributors and authenticity of all sources." At a deeper level, if students are citing primary sources from their own communities—including social media posts and firsthand research through oral histories or other means—they could also document these sources in an academic manner, and thus "amplify the cultural wealth in their communities" and "utilize digital texts and tools to validate their existence and lived experiences." In this manner, citing sources becomes much more than a lesson in the quirks of capitalization and punctuation, moving to more substantive conversations about the principles of digital diligence, especially empathy and intention.

Guiding Questions

When working with students and exploring this topic, consider the following questions when designing lessons, assignments, and assessments:

- What have your previous experiences with learning how to use citation styles been like?
  - What have you learned about different citation styles?
  - What have you learned about *why* we cite the work of others?
- As you are documenting your sources and using the ZoteroBib interface, what do you notice about the many kinds of bibliographic entries that can be added (including everything from art work to books to podcasts)?
  - As you review this list, what additional kinds of sources had you not considered before as the kinds of evidence you could use for an academic argument?
- As you dig deeper into creating your citations, what do you notice about the additional elements that could be added to different kinds of entries?
  - What additional information might you need to discover about your sources to complete your bibliographic entry?
- In the future, how might you go about using tools for bookmarking and curation in conjunction with a tool like ZoteroBib in order to better organize your sources?

Repurposing Existing Materials and a Brief Overview of Copyright, Fair Use, Creative Commons, and the Public Domain

Given that the next two chapters of the book focus in even more detail on students creating digital media—as well as finding existing digital media artifacts and repurposing them—it is worthwhile to offer a quick explanation on copyright and fair use before delving more deeply into the specific tools. As has been the case for decades, one person's use of materials from other writers, painters, musicians, photographers, filmmakers, or any number of creative professionals can be seen as either a sincere form of flattery . . . or as theft.

In the context of teaching students of the 2020s about what it means to produce and publish digital work, ELA teachers can get lost in a morass of legal and academic conversations about intellectual property, citation and plagiarism, and what amount of material can be appropriate for our students (and, for that matter, for us) to use when creating our own projects. To that end, I want to highlight two key influences on my thinking and point to a number of resources that will be useful when exploring the topics in the next two sections of the book.

First, we as ELA teachers need to become familiar with the idea of *remix*. "Whether text or beyond text," says Larry Lessig (2008), "remix is collage; it comes from combining elements of RO [Read/Only] culture; it succeeds by leveraging the meaning created by the reference to build something new" (p. 76). With his book and TED Talk (2010)—as well as his work to develop the Creative Commons licensing system—Lessig brought to the forefront the ideas about imitation that had remained implicit in artistic creation for centuries. The advent of the World Wide Web hastened a revolution from what he defined as the "Read/Only" to "Read/Write" culture and has led tens of thousands of creators and educators to deepen our conversations about the ways we can (and should) be able to use materials in an ethical and responsible manner.

Second, we also need to become familiar with the ideas of *fair use*. Renee Hobbs has, in many places, articulated ideas about the ways in which educators can flex their fair use rights, including her book *Copyright Clarity: How Fair Use Supports Digital Learning* (2010), in a brief video produced by the International Society for Technology in Education (2015), and through a number of resources available through the Media Education Lab (all linked on the book's companion page). For sake of concision, I summarize her points in two ways.

At one level, it is important to know that students and teachers have wide fair use rights, so long as the original materials are used in a transformative manner, which she describes as a "weaving together" of ideas, and notes that "creativity consists of bringing old ideas together in new ways" (Hobbs, 2010, p. 8). As noted above, humans have always been building on the ideas of others, and this is the way in which we communicate through various forms of art and writing. By building on the ideas of others, we continue to make meaning for ourselves; in this sense, legal definitions of "copyright" are relatively new in the scope of human expression as more and more people and corporations work to earn money from their intellectual property. Still, students can take materials and remix them in a variety of ways, so long as the use of the material is "transformative." By taking the words from the page (or, in this case, screen), students can copy and paste them into any number of digital spaces: a word-processed document, a social media post, a slide, a graphic organizer, a timeline, a video, or other multimedia forms. But, there is more to it than a simple copy–paste. Transformative use, in fact, requires more than copying and pasting. By taking the original materials and changing them through analysis, critique, or parody, students are doing more than simply retransmitting the original work.

To Hobbs's second point, this extensive—and relatively easy—use of digital material raises a few additional questions and issues about the *academic* concern of citing our sources as compared to the *legal* question of copyright and fair use. She is careful to note that—no matter what materials we are inspired by or choose to repurpose in our own work—one of the main tenets of scholars who make arguments in academic spaces is to ensure they have given proper attribution to their sources. To properly give that attribution, we create citations. If we do not cite our sources, especially if using verbatim text, then we are considered to be plagiarists. Even though students can copy and transform original work, they still need to give credit where credit is due.

To that end, we need to teach copyright and attribution as complementary principles, whether students are using copyrighted materials in a transformative manner or whether they are reusing materials that are available in the public domain or through a Creative Commons license. So, even if a student is taking a portion of a text, using a clip from a song or a portion of a video, or taking an image found through a Google Search, they should still cite their sources (while using them in a transformative manner).

This interlude is just an introduction to these concepts, ones that are worthy of deeper exploration. In the spirit of providing open access to many resources, it is important to note that Lessig has released his entire book under a Creative Commons license (so it can be read in its entirety online), and—in addition to her book—Hobbs has made dozens of learning resources related to copyright available on the Media Education Lab website noted above, and linked on this book's companion website.

Beyond these resources for providing background on the topics noted above, for educators who want to ensure that students are using only a limited number of copyrighted materials for specific purposes, many additional resources for finding materials that exist in the public domain or with Creative Commons licensing are available (and all are linked on the book's companion website):

- Wikimedia Commons. As one of the largest repositories of materials available in the public domain, the nearly 64 million media objects (as of the time of this writing) are freely available for use. Similarly, the Internet Archive offers access to millions of media items, as does the Library of Congress.

- Creative Commons Search. Providing access to millions of files, the Creative Commons Search portal has recently been refined to focus on images. Access to the old search portal is still available but does not appear to be maintained (so it will likely be limited). In this same spirit, the "Advanced" features in many search engines will allow users to search for materials based on usage rights.

- Unsplash. As a site committed to providing freely available images for use instead of expensive stock photos, Unsplash began in 2013 and has continued to grow from their humble beginnings as a Tumblr blog, keeping all images free and only suggesting that users provide attribution (Unsplash, n.d.). Similar services like Pexels, Pixabay, Raw Pixel, and Videvo allow users to search through free—as well as paid—images and video clips. On these sites, be sure to help students identify the items that are openly available, lest they be asked to enter a credit card number as they prepare to download various items.

- Music and sound effects are a bit trickier to find and use appropriately, though a few sources that seem reliable include YouTube's Audio Library, Incompetech's Royalty Free Music Collection, MusOpen's Royalty Free Music Collection, Audionautix's free production music, and, with attribution, music from CCMixter. For sound effects, FreeSound offers Creative Commons licensed audio files.

With all these conversations about copyright—and the amazing opportunities that the Internet offers us as digital writers and connected readers—we want to remind students of the lessons learned in Topic 6.3. Everything online has a "home" and someone (or a group of someones) who created it. Giving attribution to our sources through citation—whether we call it an homage, a remix, or something else—is a key aspect of being digitally diligent and can permeate all our lessons in ELA.

CHAPTER 7

Extending Opportunities for Digital Writing

While tools like blogs, podcasts, and videos have permeated our conversations about digital writing for more than a decade, we now have opportunities to embrace more complex, nuanced, and immersive forms of multimodal composition through integrated social media campaigns, maps, and timelines.

As an advocate for digital writing, I've been grateful for the many changes that have occurred during the past 10 years or so since my first book. As I shared in my 2018 article "The Next Decade of Digital Writing," it is true that "what it means to teach the English language arts with websites, apps, and social media continues to evolve quickly, both in terms of the tools as well as in terms of the practices" (T. Hicks, 2018, p. 10). To that end, we need to continually think about how we can move students from the kinds of writing tasks that have, in a good way, become almost a perfunctory part of daily life—like Google Docs and emails—toward even more compelling forms of digital writing. Often, this will involve a "mash-up" of various written pieces, where students are working across websites and platforms, and in collaboration with one another.

Connecting to broader themes in the field of ELA instruction, we can see a continual trend toward more multimodal composition being welcomed into our classrooms, curricula, and communities. Still, we have work to do. Just as I closed that piece in 2018, we need to work with our students—and colleagues—to demonstrate how digital writing can be integrated into their "writing lives even more strategically and creatively in the years ahead" (p. 13). NCTE has been at the forefront of this work for decades, and we are reminded—at the beginning of a chapter on digital writing—of the core elements from their definition of digital literacies: "These literacies are interconnected, dynamic, and malleable" (NCTE, 2019b). We are indeed on the path to teaching digital writing in more robust ways, though we still need to emphasize these opportunities as a part of a renewed focus in ELA instruction over the years ahead.

Chapter 7, as the title implies, pushes us to extend the purposes and processes for digital writing. With Topic 7.1, "Sparking Ideas: From Post to Page to Video," I explore one tool with multiple features, Adobe Spark. By taking a single idea and expressing it across many media forms, students are able to summarize and expand their ideas, thinking creatively about various ways to represent a single concept. Next, with Topic 7.2, "Moving Stories with Mapping," I introduce the first of two tools from Northwestern University's Knight Lab, StoryMapJS, which allows students to create interactive maps with embedded media elements. Similarly, with Topic 7.3, "Telling Stories with Timelines," I share another one of Knight Lab's tools, TimelineJS, which works in a similar manner to StoryMapJS, though it moves viewers along a chronological timeline as compared to an interactive map. In each case, I hope to move us toward the kinds of "interconnected, dynamic, and malleable" literacies to which we aspire.

Putting a coda on the introduction to this chapter is especially challenging, as there are so many colleagues to whom and resources to which I could point. Thus, I will instead suggest that educators interested in digital writing and the broader trends that have brought us, as well NCTE as a professional organization, to our current understandings of digital writing consider reviewing the many position statements related to 21st-century literacies, mentioned in Chapter 1, beginning with 1970's "Resolution on Media Literacy" (NCTE, 1970) and stretching up to the present. In particular, I have been fortunate enough to work on some of these documents and continue to find the work of my NCTE colleagues to be valuable. A link to these position statements can be found on the book's companion website: hickstro.org/digitaldiligence.

And, to bring a critical perspective to this history of digital literacies in the teaching of English, I recommend Jason Palmeri and Ben McCorkle's (2017) article in *Kairos*, "A Distant View of *English Journal*, 1912–2012." They recognize that "English teachers can be seen as one node in the complex shifting assemblage that has shaped and reshaped our culture's understanding of new technologies over the past century." Through an extensive coding of 100 years of *English Journal* articles, they create many interactive data visualizations that show, quite literally, how this assemblage has grown and changed. They remind us of the perennial challenge educators face: Everything old is new again when we introduce innovative technologies, and the ways in which we frame the conversation matters. This visual trip through history reminds us that English teachers have been concerned about teaching with new forms of media for well over a century, and that we carry on that tradition still today.

As with all sections of the book, those mentioned here will be gathered on the book's companion website: hickstro.org/digitaldiligence.

TOPIC 7.1. SPARKING IDEAS: FROM POST TO PAGE TO VIDEO

To help them become digitally diligent, we need students to move across multiple forms of expression, employing various media tools to compress and expand their main ideas and make those ideas accessible for audiences that may encounter their work through web searches, social media scrolling, or other networked communication.

Overview

If trends in social media have taught us anything, it is that shorter messages can sometimes be as powerful as lengthy ones, and that having a "brand strategy" can help to make that message stick. Depending on the time they have available, the audience they seek to reach, and the ways in which they plan to compose their work, students can represent their ideas in a variety of forms of digital writing that range from a single social media post and image to a series of posts and images, and then into longer webpages as well as audio/video productions. The best campaigns attract readers/viewers and draw them into a further exploration across a variety of media platforms.

This technique has sometimes been described as "transmedia storytelling," as it was introduced by media scholar Henry Jenkins (2006), or "multiplatform storytelling." In a blog post Jenkins (2007) elaborates on the definition, noting that

> transmedia storytelling represents a process where integral elements of a fiction get dispersed systematically across multiple delivery channels for the purpose of creating a unified and coordinated entertainment experience. Ideally, each medium makes it [sic] own unique contribution to the unfolding of the story.

Though it is a technique that is often applied to fictional narratives or advertising campaigns, students can take the tenets of this technique and apply it to informational and argumentative compositions too.

Using the freely available Adobe Spark, this topic invites students to take one idea and represent it through a social media post/image, a responsive webpage, and/or a brief video. Comparing and contrasting their authorial choices with each tool, students can begin to think strategically about their preferred media, as well as how all three can work in concert with one another. Additional tools are, of course, available for all of these tasks, such as Canva for social media posts; website builders like Weebly, Wix, and Google Sites; and, for videos, tools like WeVideo. Still, the advantage of keeping students connected with Adobe Spark is that they are working within one space and using tools that have a common set of features for similar tasks, such as adding images and changing themes.

Teaching Points

In any single glimpse at our social media feeds, it is possible to see ideas represented through a single image, with a short video, or from a link to more information on a separate webpage. Oftentimes, social media advertising campaigns rely on each of these forms, working across many of them, as noted above, to share a single message related to a particular celebrity, brand, or other unifying factor. Given that our goal should be to move students into increasingly sophisticated uses of digital writing tools, over time and across assignments, Adobe Spark can serve as one-stop shop for a series of tasks.

In the examples shown below, imagine that a student is working on an overall research project, one that culminates in an argumentative essay, and that she is working to represent the information from that project through a variety of formats. By planning intentionally to shape her message through each of the forms in Adobe Spark, this student can create an entire social media campaign by crafting their message across each of the three tools: Spark Post, Spark Page, and Spark Video. For instance, if a student is working on an essay that describes the effects of climate change and the 2020 season of California wildfires, she might attempt to share the message in different ways, from brief, compact posts to ones that are more expansive in the form of a webpage or video. In this case, the student might be making an argument similar to the politicians and forest management professionals in California who contend that the fires—while a regular part of California's ecology—have been exacerbated by the effects of climate change. Having drawn on a number of scientific resources to make her essay complete, it will take some creative design to share this information with an audience of her peers, as well as the wider world.

In some ways, this moves her from a stance of academic argument and into techniques of advertising and propaganda. In working to make her work more accessible to a wider audience, she will need to avoid falling into the traps of creating negative propaganda. Yet, as noted by Hobbs (2020), the student may still rely on techniques to "unlock people's attention, emotions, and values" through the keys of activating strong emotions, simplifying complex ideas, and responding to an audience's needs (p. 70). That said, we will likely encourage students to avoid the fourth pillar of propaganda noted by Hobbs, attacking opponents. Thus, we enter a deeper dialogue about when, why, and how these social media tools might be used to promote positive messages without sounding overly optimistic, naive, or sentimental. Still, she turns to Adobe Spark to begin designing a campaign, thinking about the affordances of each tool.

When first logging in, the Adobe Spark interface is sparse, with the invitation to begin telling your story. As shown in Figure 7.1.1, the main dashboard for Spark provides options for searching through thousands of templates or clicking into the options provided. Also, by clicking the "+" icon in the upper left, below the Adobe Spark logo, the user is presented with options to start creations in a variety of other formats. Clicking into any one of these options provides the user with a variety of templates to build from, each with different fonts, color schemes, filters, and other design options. It is worth noting that there are hundreds of tutorials for Adobe Spark—and other similar programs—so my descriptions here will be concise, knowing that a web search could yield many help guides and how-to videos. In the paragraphs below, I imagine the ways that a student might compose a campaign. First, the student might explore Spark Post.

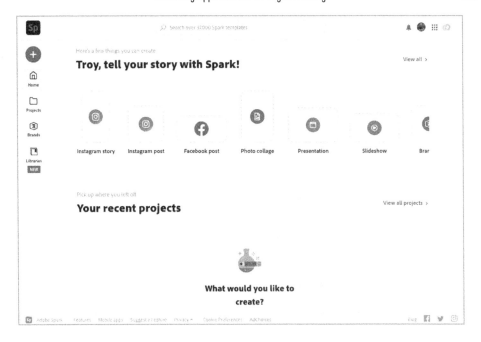

FIGURE 7.1.1. Screenshot of the Adobe Spark dashboard. Used with permission of Adobe.

With Spark Post (see Figure 7.1.2), the student could have a single, unifying theme that uses similar fonts and filters with all photos. With a catchy slogan or hashtag, the student uses images of animals that demonstrate an anthropomorphized feeling of sadness and creates a series of square images with an orange hue on each. Carrying a hashtag that is being used already (or creating anew), the images exemplify a similar feeling and become recognizable as they are shared across various social media platforms. Other images could have some of the statistics from the students' research represented. Using a series of pictures that include different animals and scenes of destruction, the images are designed to rely on the viewer's previous experiences with these common animals to invoke empathy. These social media-style images can then be downloaded as image files or shared directly to social media.

With Spark Video (see Figure 7.1.3), the student could then take these photos and embed them on a timeline with additional written details selected from her essay. Beginning with a question or other hook, the introduction of the video would draw viewers into the same set of photos showing the animals in their natural habitat, and then with the photos of ash and flame brought on by wildfire. Appealing, of course, to emotions, the video does offer some of the starkest of facts from the student's research. The music is foreboding, yet not completely ominous, perhaps even suggesting that taking action soon could result in changed outcomes for these forest creatures. Narration—perhaps even drawn from some of the text of the argumentative essay, or at least adapted from it—provides context for the images and statistics. At the end, the video invites viewers

FIGURE 7.1.2. Screenshot of the Adobe Spark Post interface. Used with permission of Adobe.

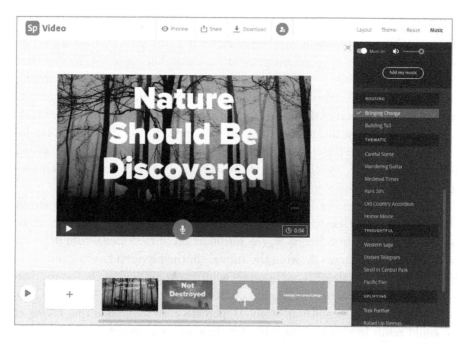

FIGURE 7.1.3. Screenshot of the Adobe Spark Video interface. Used with permission of Adobe.

to post on social media with the hashtag, as well as to visit the campaign's website. Like Spark Post, Spark Video can also be downloaded (to then be shared on YouTube or another service) or published directly from Spark as a video with a unique URL.

Finally, with Spark Page (see Figure 7.1.4), the student uses many of the same photos from the social media posts to populate a single webpage and is also able to embed the video. A dominant banner and webpage title makes the purpose of the site clear; similar fonts, colors, and imagery ensure the viewers/readers of the site that they have landed on the correct page, given the link that was clicked from a social media post, or at the end of a video. On the page, a "call to action" presents itself, where the reader can click to sign an online petition or offer a donation. All references for the project are documented, inviting further exploration. Additionally, conversations about the ways in which hyperlinks can be strategically employed throughout the webpage could be valuable too, encouraging students to think about ways to both document their sources at the end of the webpage and to invite their readers to click over to these resources in the context of reading their overarching argument.

In the screenshot in Figure 7.1.4, I only show a glimpse of the responsive headline and image to give a sense of the way that the Spark Page interface provides additional options for adding photos, text, buttons, video (including those created in Spark), and other photo formats. Of course, the student could add elements from her essay into different segments, each of which could also be accompanied by a media element. All of these items are then part of one longer page, which allows for responsive scrolling on

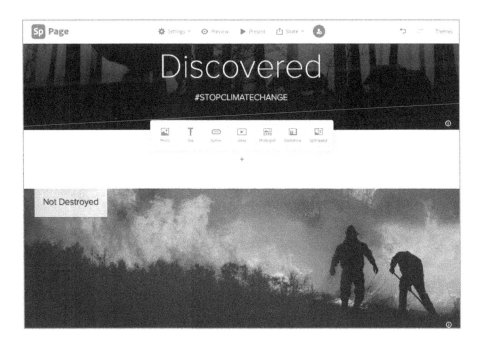

FIGURE 7.1.4. Screenshot of the Adobe Spark Page interface. Used with permission of Adobe.

multiple devices. Like Post and Video, a publishing option is available, and then the URL for the page can be shared.

Taken together, the student has worked to distill a significant amount of information into a campaign that includes a series of image-based posts, a brief video, and a substantive website with links to more information. Moving from smaller, more concise forms of messaging in the posts to longer, more expansive forms of visual communication in the video and, ultimately, through words and images in the website, students have opportunity to express themselves in a variety of ways within one tool where fonts, colors, and media assets remain consistent. As the aphorism goes, writing something short takes a long time, so it could be powerful for students to move through this thinking exercise. Again, we must consider how to help students take their overall argument and transform it from a research-based essay into a website, and then into graphic forms with the video and social media posts.

As we move into these discussions of digital writing, we can see more connections to the NCTE definition of digital literacy. Because the premium version of Spark can be accessed by all K–12 schools, for free (Gragueb & Temerlies, 2018), this tool helps alleviate some of the concerns under the "Advocate for equitable access to and accessibility of texts, tools, and information" section of the statement (NCTE, 2019b). For instance, even though we cannot guarantee that all students have "access to well-funded school and public libraries," the use of Spark and its premium features do allow for a level of creativity for all students that may not be found when using other free or freemium options. Moreover, as students explore various inquiries, they could use the shared functionality of Spark to "collaborate with others whose perspectives and areas of expertise are different from their own" and "work in a group in ways that allow them to create new knowledge or to solve problems that can't be created or solved individually," both parts of the "Build intentional global and cross-cultural connections and relationships" segment of the definition, depending on the goals we might have for this kind of collaborative project.

Guiding Questions

When working with students and exploring this topic, consider the following questions when designing lessons, assignments, and assessments:

When Working with Posts

- Given that posts rely mostly on the power of the photograph and minimal amounts of text, how might you explore various options related to using each element?
  - For photos, how might you use zooming, recoloration, rotation, and mirroring to change the tone of the image?
  - For text, how might you use various fonts, colors, sizes, rotations, shadows, outlines, and backgrounds to change the tone of the words being displayed?

When Working with Video

- Given that videos rely on a combination of image and video clips, spoken narration, captions, music, and transitions, how might you explore various options related to using each element?
  - For instance, how might a consistent—or very different—theme for each segment of the video affect the overall viewing experience?
  - How might having the voice of one narrator be different than having two narrators?
  - How might still images and video clips be combined for maximum effect?

When Working with Pages

- Given that pages also rely on a combination of factors—and that you will likely want to leave your readers with a "call to action"—how can you use images and videos in a strategic manner to keep them paying attention to the page?
  - How, too, might you use buttons and hyperlinks within the text to direct your readers to useful external resources and, ultimately, invite them to take action?

As Students Design a Cohesive Campaign

- How might you begin to develop a cohesive campaign that relies on consistent fonts, colors, imagery, and messages across multiple forms of social media?
  - Based on campaigns that you find compelling from different companies or social media influencers, what can you determine about the strategies that they target their audience?
- For instance, the Texas A&M University Writing Center (n.d.) has a resource with a number of questions related to audience awareness, including general ones like "How much does the audience know about the subject?" and "How does the audience feel about your topic?" as well as more in-depth tips for addressing specific audiences.
  - Other similar resources and question guides can be found through a quick web search and would provide a foundation for initial discussion when beginning an entire campaign.
  - Additionally, a search for "marketing campaign templates" will yield, quite literally, millions of examples of guides that advertising companies use to formulate their own campaigns. With one of these guides, students could create a proposal for their Adobe Spark products and overall theme before beginning the digital writing process.

TOPIC 7.2. MOVING STORIES WITH MAPPING

To help them become digitally diligent, we need students to embrace
tools for digital writing that enhance what they might typically
create with standard, office-style tools (such as word processors and
slideshows), creating more meaningful products that integrate a
combination of skills from multiple disciplines, exploring different forms
of media in the process.

Overview

Geography is generally not in the wheelhouse of the ELA teacher, and yet the effects of space
and place on story—including narratives and dramatic productions, as well as nonfiction
essays, articles, and books—are immense. We can all think of a poem, story, essay, or film
that is reliant on place as a dominant motif. Relying on place as a way to explore the lives of
authors and characters is an established practice in our storytelling culture, and this is one
angle that we can play upon when thinking about the use of maps in our ELA classrooms.

At one level, we can invite students to review maps that others have created. For
instance, Google Earth allows users to create projects that are pinned to places. Building
on this idea, the nonprofit Google Lit Trips was founded as a way for ELA teachers to
demonstrate the power of place as it relates to story (links in this chapter, as with other
chapters, are listed on the book's companion website). In simplest technical terms, a
Google Lit Trip is a collection of places pinned into a cohesive order on Google Earth
related to a specific text, such as *The Diary of Anne Frank* or *The Odyssey*. Additional
information can be layered into the map, including images, videos, and text. These trips,
then, can be explored by outside viewers through sharing, and Google Earth launched
new storytelling tools in 2019 to make this process even more efficient. These trips are
not limited to literature, however, as there are many other kinds of Google Earth tours
that can be found through a simple web search.

Having students explore existing maps is one powerful opportunity. Yet reading—
and writing—maps are never neutral acts, as Walker D. Mills notes. Maps, like any
form of text, are infused with ideology. Mills (2020), a Marine Corps officer, contends
that "every map is an argument about what is important and what is not." And because
he is specifically talking about the politics of military maps, we can point out recent
discrepancies in the way that Google Maps represented an Indian-Pakistani border, and
how this became a controversy as just one example (Bensinger, 2020). These political
discussions of place, of course, infuse a great deal of classic and contemporary literature,
poetry, and nonfiction. For further exploration, a search for the field of "critical cartography" will yield many results, including this brief definition from Cal Poly's Robert E.
Kennedy Library (2020):

> Critical Cartography is a set of mapping practices and lens of analysis grounded in
> critical theory, specifically the thesis that maps reflect and perpetuate relations of
> power, typically in favor of a society's dominant group.

As just one example, the 23rd U.S. poet laureate, Joy Harjo, is leading a project entitled "Living Nations, Living Words: A Map of First Peoples Poetry," sponsored by the Library of Congress, featuring an interactive map of indigenous poets (Lederle, 2020). In her description of the project, she discusses how the map itself becomes an act of critical literacy. She aims to use "this map to counter damaging false assumptions—that indigenous peoples of our country are often invisible or are not seen as human." This stands in contrasts to the rich cultural traditions and oral histories of First Peoples, and the interactive map is designed to demonstrate a poet's perspective on "visibility, persistence, resistance, and acknowledgment." The project is represented in a book too (Harjo, 2021), and the combination of the multimedia map and printed text is especially powerful.

Similar kinds of projects can be enacted with students. Engaging in geographic representations can invite students to build maps of their own communities, bringing in unique perspectives on the people and places therein. A number of creative mapping projects and websites demonstrate the power of images and storytelling. Jon Wargo and Cassie Brownell's (2016) project, Hear My Home, invited students to capture their neighborhood soundscapes as part of their lived lives, and offers yet another unique example of multimodality and mapmaking. Considering tools, the website HistoryPin invites members to upload photos and curate them in a web-based collection, which is then coordinated with a Google Map. As a user browses various images, videos, and stories, the "pin" on the map moves to show where the image/video was taken. In building interactive, multimodal collections, HistoryPin allows digital writers the opportunity to show a story unfolding over space and time. Other tools like Tripline, Sutori, and even Padlet's "map" format invite us to use maps in creative ways too.

As ELA teachers, we must now consider the ways that maps and location services are now a ubiquitous part of web-based experiences. My own children and their friends track one another on "Snap maps" and can see exactly where their friends are at, or traveling to, and geotagged photos help us categorize our experiences in image-sharing apps. Our photo albums can be organized around GPS coordinates and, in turn, quickly made into slideshows and movies. Thus, in the ways that we invite our students to craft their own narratives—as well as informational tours or arguments that rely on place as yet another form of evidence in their reasoning—the process of using maps can be powerful. Our students (as well as their smartphones) know where they are at all times, and from whence they have come. In this sense, we need to help them become situated in both the physical and digital world of maps.

In addition to tools like HistoryPin and Google Earth, the teaching points below introduce a tool used by professional journalists, StoryMapJS, inviting them to consider ways to create academic arguments with maps and other multimedia. StoryMapJS works as a multimedia editor that combines features familiar for building a slide deck (like PowerPoint, Keynote, or Google Slides) with options for placing a marker on a Google Map. The interface allows the user to embed an image, a video, a tweet, or many other kinds of media into the slide. Each slide, then, is tagged to a particular location, and as the user progresses through the slide deck, they will see both the movement along a route in the map itself and the changing media and text on the slide. One note here: This topic explores StoryMapJS, created by the Knight Lab, based at Northwestern University, and is available for free. There is another, similar product, ArcGIS StoryMaps, yet this comes with a subscription cost, so please be sure to follow the link from the book's companion website to get to the right "story-map" software, or look for Knight Lab in a web search.

Teaching Points

Inviting students to create in StoryMapJS can help them revise and, quite literally, "re-see" their digital writing in a number of different ways. Here are a few possibilities.

Using StoryMapJS for Interpretation and Analysis

As a part of reporting on another text they have read, students could use StoryMapJS to outline key places in a particular text. Much like a Google Lit Trip, if students are reading a piece of literature and want to document the journey that a character is experiencing, they can build this journey in StoryMapJS. This could become a kind of virtual book talk. For instance, if students are reading Maya Angelou's (1969) *I Know Why the Caged Bird Sings*, they could create a map that shows the places in which she lived in Arkansas and California, and draw in historical images and video clips from the Library of Congress or other sources to document the civil rights movement. In a similar way, readers of Christopher Paul Curtis's (1995) *The Watsons Go to Birmingham—1963* could track the family's trip from Michigan into the Deep South. These are just two examples, and certainly any book that includes movement through place as a key theme would be worthy of exploration through a story map.

StoryMapJS could be used to examine the places important in the life of a particular author too. For instance, the idea of building from Angelou's first book could be elaborated into a story of her entire life, with images and video clips of key moments, such as reading "On the Pulse of Morning" at President Bill Clinton's inauguration in 1993 and then being awarded the Presidential Medal of Freedom in 2010 by President Barack Obama. Both of these events would land back in Washington, D.C., though other events in her life could certainly bring motion and depth to the map. In this same way, a student could layer in additional ideas from a novelist's life to show how various places were influential to him or her.

Fictional stories, too, could be told, as the places do not need to happen on Earth, limited to using the GPS locations of a Google Map. In StoryMapJS, a user can import an image that becomes a "canvas" on which the map then gets built. Fictional worlds that can already be found through a Google Image search (including examples ranging from Middle Earth to Hogwarts to a map of districts in Panem) could be imported and examined through StoryMapJS. How, for instance, might a student document Katniss Everdeen's journey through all three novels of the original trilogy, drawing in images of the characters from the movies and documenting the key events—and their interpretation of those characters, events, and places—in the text box of the StoryMapJS interface?

For other purposes, StoryMapJS could be used to craft an argument or share information too. Given the events of 2020, a timely topic could be for students to track the exponential spread of the novel coronavirus through a series of slides and map locations, in which they might emulate the multimedia style of *The New York Times,* which has created many such maps using mobile phone location data. Similarly, students could document key locations in social movements, such as the protests for Black Lives Matter, embedding additional images, videos, or multimedia that document the dramatic events across the United States and around the world.

While it is still important for students to write about texts and authors, analyzing and critiquing them in words, a tool like StoryMapJS can bring even more opportunities for students to demonstrate their interpretations. Layering in additional media and locating particular elements of the text in specific places provides students with an opportunity to deepen their knowledge and understanding. The possibilities for building maps on real and imagined characters are all quite powerful, though these are only an introduction to what students could do when thinking about how to tell their own stories through mapping.

Using StoryMapJS for Creating a Digital Story or Essay

In addition to the many opportunities to use StoryMapJS as a tool for analysis, there are also opportunities for creation. I begin with the idea that students could create a digital story, in the classic sense of creating a brief video using basic software in which authors tell their own story through "the digital equivalent of film techniques, stills, audio only, or any of the other forms of non-physical media" (Wikipedia, 2020b). This form of storytelling was popularized by StoryCenter, a California-based nonprofit, beginning in the early 1990s with the advent of movie-making software on personal computers. These kinds of digital stories, certainly, could be created in conjunction with—and integrated into—a story map. In fact, I could see that as a valuable, parallel process. That said, many scholars have written about digital storytelling in other spaces, so I will keep the focus of my attention here on the use of StoryMapJS.

Given the many literacies that can be employed as part of this mapmaking process, the goal in creating such a map is to have digital writers intentionally connect a sense of place to the multimedia. With images and recording, both audio and video, students can become multimedia authors themselves, bringing their own firsthand experiences into the production of the story map. With a combination of their own writing and media elements, they have the potential to compose even more compelling stories and essays. Using their own still images and videos, for instance, students can create a more robust multimedia project, as compared to simply finding random images online.

Having shared StoryMapJS with undergraduate students who could choose to use it as one of the multimedia authoring tools for a broader project on investigating place, I've seen a few creative approaches. For instance, one of my groups of undergraduates used

StoryMapJS to document the "history and legends" of our university campus, which was especially timely given that their project was due during the week of Halloween. Another group documented local galleries and performance venues as a way to share local arts and cultural attractions. These uses were tied to a unit that was meant to expand their notions of inquiry, and I describe them in more detail in my coauthored book *Creating Confident Writers* (T. Hicks & Schoenborn, 2020), with links to these projects provided on this book's companion website.

During a virtual summer camp experience in 2020, I employed a similar approach when working with middle school students. We had offered them a variety of digital storytelling options over the week, including the process of creating a video as well as generating a StoryMapJS project. One student combined the best of both, as he shared a series of trips he had taken with his family while growing up, visiting different zoos around the country, complete with images of his sister and him at each one. He recorded the "tour" of the story map as a screencast and then embedded that screencast on the front page of the story map. And, while I don't have permission to share this particular project, it speaks to the ways in which this student took advantage of the motion that StoryMapJS provided, demonstrating movement across place and, in some cases, time as well.

As just a quick demonstration, the screenshot in Figure 7.2.1 illustrates how I created my own StoryMapJS project emulating George Ella Lyon's (1993) "Where I'm From" poem as a mentor text. I begin my poem with a quick ode to my hometown, Jackson, Michigan. As shown in Figure 7.2.1 and Figure 7.2.2, I began my version of the "Where I'm From" poem with a focus on two local attractions, the Cascades Falls Park and a local ice cream shop, The Parlour, which is famous for its enormous "Dare to Be Great" sundae. Following the general format of Lyon's poem, I open with a nod to Michigan's geography and these two local icons with the lines "I am from the palm of the mitten. | From the city with cascading falls, | And an ice cream parlour that would dare us to be great." A closer look demonstrates the features of the StoryMapJS interface and the public view.

Figure 7.2.1 shows the editing interface of StoryMapJS. On the left, as with other slide deck programs, the space for adding and organizing slides presents itself in a column. Then, after typing in "Jackson, MI," in the map interface, I was taken to that location with a generic marker and in the standard black-and-white map. Using the "Options" menu from the upper left, I was able to change the "map type" to "watercolor," and using the "Marker Options" in the lower right, I was able to upload an icon of a home, which I found available for free from a website with open licenses on icons. I zoomed the map out from the very close street-level view of Jackson to a regional view showing the entire Midwest region.

Then, in the lower portion of the interface, I was able to add both media and text. A web search yielded an antique postcard of the Cascades Falls, available on Wikipedia, so I imported that as the main image for this slide. For the media, I enter the initial words of the poem, "I am from," and my first three lines. As noted above, I could have added

FIGURE 7.2.1. Screenshot of the StoryMapJS interface. Used with permission of Knight Lab.

effects on that text, including bold, italics, or a hyperlink. Clicking the "</>" menu item would allow me to go in to edit the HTML in more detail, if needed (though I have not figured out a way to change the font or background color, so I would likely not share this feature with students to save them from confusion). By clicking on the chain-link icon, I can easily insert a hyperlink and click to force it to open in a new window. For instance, in my poem, if I had wanted to, I could have included a hyperlink to a link on the City of Jackson's website, Trip Advisor, Wikipedia, or other sources.

From there, I add a few more items to my story map to make it more robust, adding a slide for my high school with a schoolhouse icon, as well as another image from Wikipedia for the main page, a snapshot of the historic Michigan Theater. This is a relatively quick example, though it could grow as I add more and more locations. Then, in Figure 7.2.2, I share a preview of what my story map will look like in a public-facing format. Notice the map on the left with the two locations that have been built into the slides, as well as the cover image with the title "Jacktown" and picture of the Michigan Theater. By clicking on the arrow icon on the right, or on the "Start Exploring" button, I would then launch into the first slide, showing the Cascades postcard and "home" icon. It would then progress to the school slide and, had I added more, go on from there.

What is compelling about engaging with StoryMapJS is that the story itself progresses and leads the viewer from one location to the next. With the image for each slide, as well as the text, the viewer of the map feels a sense of motion. In addition to images, other forms of media can be embedded on a slide via URL, such as a link to a YouTube or Vimeo video, a tweet, a SoundCloud audio file, or other sources. The story map could stand on its own, or a student could record a narrated tour of the story map

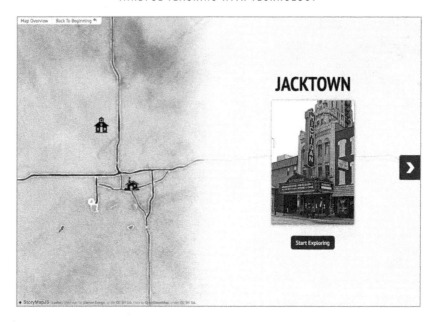

FIGURE 7.2.2. Screenshot of the sample story map in the public view. Used with permission of Knight Lab.

as a screencast. Some of my students have been inventive by recording videos and having those embedded on individual slides within their story map. Mine is just one brief example of what could become a much larger StoryMapJS project, yet it does provide a sense of possibility for what could be accomplished. Even in this quick glimpse of the interface, there are several opportunities for students to consider the audience, purpose, and tone of their story map. For instance:

- Possibilities for map textures, including black and white, a typical open street-map view, a "watercolor" option (as in the example above), and options for even more customization with fee-based tools like Mapbox and Gigapixel
- Options to add citation elements to the media being embedded, including a credit line and a caption (which could include a hyperlink in HTML)
- A headline that will appear in "all caps," which raises points about how much text and what kinds of words are best suited for such a headline
- A space to enter text, which allows, too, for basic HTML coding, including bold, italics, and hyperlinks
- Additional options for markers and backgrounds to add even more detail and customization to the map

Though it could be a challenge to stay focused and not become distracted by so many options, the construction of a story map certainly provides opportunities for students to be purposeful in the composition of their narratives and persistent as they try out different combinations of the various features to achieve the maximum effect. While my own example is only a few slides long (and, thus, not worth posting as an example on the book's companion website), as a reminder I have included a few links to some other examples of student work there.

Connections to the NCTE Definition of Literacy in a Digital Age

In all these ways, StoryMapJS can be used to bring nuance and complexity to the topics under consideration and invite students to explore ideas in relation to both time and place. As noted in the latter portions of the NCTE (2019b) definition of digital literacies, there are expectations for ELA teachers to help students "determine how and to what extent texts and tools amplify one's own and others' narratives as well as counter unproductive narratives" and "recognize and honor the multilingual literacy identities and culture experiences individuals bring to learning environments." From my perspective, there are many opportunities that StoryMapJS provides to fully explore these expectations. In particular, I am encouraged when thinking about how story maps may help students to "engage in participatory literacy practices" and provide them with "opportunities within the curriculum to author multimodal stories in order to examine power, equity, and identities and grow as digitally savvy and civic-minded citizens."

A number of subquestions within these two segments of the definition can be explored in further detail, including the following:

- From the "Determine" section:
  - "Do learners analyze [and create] narratives to address accuracy, power dynamics, equity, monolithic notions of race, ethnicity, culture, gender, sexuality, or ability?"
  - "Do learners explore [and create] multimodal narratives to identify and better understand the cultural practices that inform the creation of these narratives?"
  - "Do learners create and disseminate narratives that leverage the affordances of digital tools?"
- From the "Recognize" section:
  - "Do learners have opportunities to connect them with their textual and historical lineage and narratives?"
  - "Do learners explore and critique the premises, myths, and stereotypes that are often held by the dominant culture?"
  - "Do learners have space in the curriculum to support positive racial and ethnic identity development while pushing back against marginalized narratives?"

With these many connections in mind, I offer a few additional guiding questions to push students' thinking as they analyze and create story maps that serve a variety of purposes.

Guiding Questions

When working with students and exploring this topic, consider the following questions when designing lessons, assignments, and assessments:

Before Creating a StoryMapJS Project

- What are your experiences with maps, both in your own life and as you have experienced both fiction and nonfiction?
  - Are there news reports from the media that you can recall that prominently feature maps?
  - Are there stories that you have read where a map is included as a key part of the text?
- In what ways do maps themselves tell stories?
  - What can we understand about the ways people perceive a particular place based on the way it is represented in a map?

While Creating a StoryMapJS Project

- What is your overarching goal for the StoryMapJS project you are creating?
  - Are you attempting to analyze, inform, argue, or accomplish something else?
- How are your choices related to specific images, videos, and other forms of media influencing the way in which you are designing your map?
- In what ways are you working to move the reader/viewer of your map through a particular arc of story, informational process, or line of argument?
  - What decisions are you making for each slide/map location to ensure it is a clear, concise choice for that particular element of the overall map?

After Creating a StoryMapJS Project

- As you view your StoryMapJS project, what do you notice about the sense of place it represents?
  - Is it limited to a particular state or region? Does it move across states or regions? Around the world?
  - What can this sense of space tell you about the topic you have been researching?
- In what ways might your map be useful for others studying this piece of literature (or this author's life, this social event, etc.)?
  - What have you included that provides your viewers with insights on this topic and leads them to more information?

TOPIC 7.3. TELLING STORIES WITH TIMELINES

To help them become digitally diligent, we need students to envision events across time, exploring sequencing as well as cause and effect with a variety of sources of evidence, drawing valid conclusions and integrating multiple forms of media into their digital writing projects.

Overview

In a similar manner to maps, timelines can also bring an academic argument to life in a compelling manner. In some ways, creating a timeline might feel a little more convenient and familiar to an ELA teacher, as all stories have key elements of time built into them (e.g., exposition, rising action, climax, and falling action). These temporal markers are familiar to us as readers of stories, as viewers of TV or film, or as listeners of podcasts. As we think about how to translate events—in fiction or nonfiction—into projects that can be best served in the form of a timeline, this chronological approach to analyzing and interpreting events can be helpful.

In support of timelines as an academic genre, Danielle Picard and Derek Bruff (2016) of Vanderbilt University's Center for Teaching make the case that

> interactive timelines support visually rich displays of information—text, images, multimedia, hyperlinks, even geospatial data—using spatial arrangements, categories, and color schemes to convey meaning, which make them ideal platforms for achieving a variety of course goals and objectives.

By inviting students to create timelines, Picard and Bruff go on to describe the ways that learners can then analyze relationships between peoples, places, and events, as well as to zoom in on particular events in great detail (minute by minute or hour by hour), or spread out over a longer period that could include years, decades, or centuries. Inviting students to document key moments in a piece of literature or historical era as they develop their own argument can, in turn, offer them a sense of perspective—where causes and effects are tied together chronologically—that simply putting together a slide deck likely will not.

Timelines, like maps, can be contested spaces and ripe for critical examination. As just one example of a timeline that documents a well-known author and piece of literature, the Anne Frank House has produced a multimedia piece that moves users through key moments leading up to the Holocaust, as well as specific events in her life and events following World War II (link on the book's companion website). Though some of the timeline tools noted below, including TimelineJS, would not allow students to emulate the specific multimedia style of the Anne Frank timeline, it is a worthy example because of the level of written detail and purposeful selection of images that it includes on each entry. The Mount Vernon website has a similar timeline for George Washington showing his complicated roles as the "father of our country" and owner of slaves.

Beyond these, countless examples of timelines can be found through web searches, though one other notable curated collection that can become a source for timelines as mentor texts (as well as various other museum-based resources) is a blog post created by the Museum Computer Network (2020) in response to COVID-19-related closures (link on the book's companion website). There are a number of tools for creating time-lines too, each of which has a different pricing model, and I simply provide a list here (with links on the book's companion website) of a few, including actual timeline creators like Preceden, TikiToki, Sutori, TimeToast, Histropedia, Chronoflow as well as graphic design and infographic programs that can be used for timeline creation like Venngage, Creately, Infogram, and Piktochart. With all this in mind, the teaching points below introduce a second tool from the Knight Lab, TimelineJS.

Teaching Points

Using a tool created for professional journalists, TimelineJS can integrate images and words into an interactive experience. Considering events that happen across millennia, or within the span of just a few minutes, students can build a responsive timeline that integrates multimedia into a compelling argument. TimelineJS integrates with Google Sheets and requires that users "publish to the web," and then takes the URL of their published sheet and drops that link into an interface on the Knight Lab website. This, in turn, generates a URL for the timeline itself, which can then be either shared as a direct link or embedded into another website or blog posts.

The TimelineJS Google Sheets template is, in and of itself, an interesting text for students to examine and consider as they prepare to build a project. Because of the expansive nature of the spreadsheet's columns, a close-up image of one would not repro-duce itself well here, so I encourage readers to go to the Knight Lab page and look at the Google Sheets template directly. It consists of six key segments, broken into mul-tiple columns, in which the user enters the dates, main headlines, and their own writ-ten descriptions for each event that will be represented on the timeline. There are also columns to enter information about the media that will be embedded in the particular timeline entry, including a link to the stable URL for the media, the credit for the cre-ator of the media, that caption that will appear underneath the media, and, if desired, a media thumbnail.

At this point, students would then publish their timeline through the Knight Lab website, generating a unique URL for their timeline, or embed code so the timeline could be shared in the context of a blog post or webpage. There are many useful tutorials and how-to videos about using TimelineJS, including one from the University of Notre Dame's Kaneb Center for Teaching and Learning, linked on this book's companion website.

With this background on TimelineJS—and considering the points above about the particular kinds of chronological information and media elements that could be included within a timeline—I consider some additional ideas for exploration. For instance, stu-dents could compose timelines that summarize, examine, and critique the following:

- Events in a piece of literature, documenting key moments in the plot and engaging in analysis related to foreshadowing or other literary elements
- Events in a piece of nonfiction, situating the work within a larger historical context and providing links to additional details
- Events in the life of a particular author that influenced their stance toward writing, including the basics such as birth date and family life, as well as other key personal or historical events that shaped their lives
- Events, artists, and authors from cultures that have provided additional influences on the ways in which an author draws inspiration
- Events in their own lives—and their family's history—as a way of developing their own narratives, perhaps coupled with digital storytelling or links to additional writing that they have produced

In each of these cases, students can create timelines that take advantage of chronology, all in the service of building a narrative, providing information, or developing an argument that recognizes a variety of perspectives and presents topics in a nuanced manner. For instance, students could take an approach to creating their own story, similar to what they might have done with a StoryMapJS project, bringing in images that represent significant moments in their lives and using personal photos to build a "Where I'm From" style timeline. They could also use the timeline to display significant events related to a particular person, place, or topic, focusing mostly on factual information without an overt effort at persuasion. Or, building on this series of events, they could craft a more purposeful argument.

One example from a first-year student at Central Michigan University traces the history of African American athletes, from Jackie Robinson to Muhammad Ali to Colin Kaepernick, leading up to the events of 2020 and the significant number of Black Lives Matters protests around the United States and the world. Throughout his timeline, he makes a similar set of moves. In one moment on the timeline, he shows the protest of a Black athlete and, in the next, some responses from the media or general public. In addition to video clips of commentators providing what can only now be seen as racist statements, dating from the 1940s to the present, he shows how athletes continue to stand firm in 2020. While he employed fair use to draw in a number of copyrighted images and video clips into his timeline—and used them in a transformative manner—it would be too difficult to secure permissions for all these images and to share them here in the book. To that end, I encourage readers to visit the book's companion website where there is a link to his TimelineJS project (as well as a few additional projects from other students). The Knight Lab home page for TimelineJS, too, has links to projects created by professional journalists that could also serve as mentor texts for students to examine.

As we consider these teaching points, we can build assignments and assessments that integrate elements of NCTE's (2019b) definition of literacy in a digital age. As with all the topics presented in this book, there are several approaches one could take here, and I am drawn back to the "Create" questions in the "Consume, curate, and create actively across contexts" section. For instance, timelines offer students opportunity to "publish their work in a variety of ways," ones they most likely had not considered in their K–12 ELA careers. While many students may have represented historical events in slideshows, or made a timeline on paper, few have likely been asked to compose a digital timeline. Moreover, in this process, students will need to make "creative decisions with intention, developing and using skills associated with [the] modality" of timelines, as well as to "communicate information and ideas to different audiences" who may view their timelines.

Also, with both StoryMapJS and TimelineJS, we have opportunity to talk with students about elements in the "Advocate for equitable access to and accessibility of texts, tools, and information" segment of the definition. Regardless of their ability, all students can use the accessibility options built into the Knight Lab tools (image descriptions for screen readers, links to original source material) to consider "adhere[nce] to web accessibility principles" and as an opportunity to create "equitable access to texts, tools, and information." Producing their digital writing with openly available tools that, in turn, generate highly accessible web-based texts can help students build their own digital diligence, embracing empathy as a core value in their composing process.

Guiding Questions

When working with students and exploring this topic, consider the following questions when designing lessons, assignments, and assessments (copied from and slightly adapted from the same types of questions asked of story maps in Section 7.2):

Before Creating a TimelineJS Project

- What are your experiences with timelines, both in your own life and as you have experienced fiction and nonfiction texts?
  - Are there news reports from the media that you can recall that prominently feature timelines?
  - Are there stories you have read where a timeline is included as a key part of the text?
- In what ways do timelines themselves tell stories?
  - What can we understand about the ways people perceive a particular person, series of events, or entire era based on the way it is represented in a timeline?

While Creating a TimelineJS Project

- What is your overarching goal for the TimelineJS project you are creating?
  - Are you attempting to analyze, inform, argue, or accomplish something else?
- How are your choices related to specific images, videos, and other forms of media influencing the way in which you are designing your timeline?

- In what ways are you working to move the reader/viewer of your timeline through a particular arc of story, informational process, or line of argument?
- What decisions are you making for each slide/chronological event to ensure it is a clear, concise choice for that particular element of the overall timeline?

After Creating a TimelineJS Project

- As you view your TimelineJS project, what do you notice about the sense of time it represents?
  - Is it limited to a particular year, decade, or century?
  - Does it move across broader swaths of time?
  - What kinds of events are represented?
  - What can this sense of time tell you about the topic you have been researching?
- In what ways might your timeline be useful for others studying this piece of literature (or this author's life, this social event, etc.)?
  - What have you included that provides your viewers with insights on this topic and leads them to more information?

CHAPTER 8

Embracing Opportunities
for Connected Reading

The sum of human knowledge is in the palms of our hands,
and yet it seems that we read less now than ever before;
using connected reading tools to engage with that knowledge
and participate in shared reading experiences is crucial
as we teach students to be digitally diligent.

As noted throughout the introductory chapters of this book—and largely postponed in the conversation until now—it is clear that our consistent use of the web across a variety of devices is affecting the ways in which we select materials to read, as well as whether we choose to engage fully in that reading process . . . or not. Why and how this phenomenon is occurring is a question for neuroscientists, psychologists, sociologists, and educational scholars who have more experience with and understanding of the ways in which our reading brain operates to continue discussing and debating. Thus, I pause here at the beginning of a chapter on connected reading practices to simply acknowledge that this is an ongoing challenge, with experts weighing in on the ultimate effects of these changed practices ranging from a doomsday scenario in which no one reads anything to a utopian vision of textual expression and engagement.

My hope is that we as ELA teachers fall a little further on the side of the idealistic vision, though with a healthy dose of skepticism and a vision of teaching our students to be digitally diligent about the ways in which they read. Through my work with Kristen Hawley Turner and, more recently, with her and Lauren Zucker, we have worked to articulate a definition of "connected reading." To offer a brief repeat from the introduction, Turner, Zucker, and I have recently defined "connected reading" as a model of print and digital reading comprehension that conceptualizes readers' inter-actions with digital texts through encountering (the ways in which readers seek or receive digital texts), evaluating (the ways in which readers make judgments about the usefulness of digital texts), and engaging (the ways in which readers interact with and share digital texts). (Turner et al., 2020, from the abstract)

The topics in this chapter, then, extend many of the ideas that Turner and I articu-lated first in our coauthored book as well as introduce some updated tools. That said, even as tools change, the principles remain the same. The three key verbs in the con-nected reading framework—encounter, evaluate, and engage—are very much in line with the principles outlined in the NCTE definition of digital literacies.

Topic 8.1, "Creating Multimedia Analyses," reminds us that there are many oppor-tunities for students to use common tools like screencasting and multimedia develop-ment tools like ThingLink to bring their interpretations of literature to life. Topic 8.2, "Creating Space(s) for Talk," then invites students to consider new ways to communicate with one another about texts. As more and more platforms are introduced that can be used for annotation (some built right into e-readers and others available on the web), we need to help students prepare for and participate in meaningful conversations. Finally, Topic 8.3, "Remixing the Classics," takes advantage of the many, many texts that are available in the public domain—and that typically comprise the "literary canon"—and invites students to remix these materials using a tool available to all, Google Slides, as a way to offer critical readings of those texts.

There are many other literacy scholars and educators from whom I have learned more about what reading is, how we read both print and nonprint texts, and what the changing nature of literacy means for us as ELA teachers, as well as for our students. This is a case where there are too many to name, so I focus my attention here on one: my original advisor in graduate school and a leader in our field, Ernest Morrell. At the time I first met him in the early 2000s, he described the process of critically analyzing a text in four steps, which I elaborate on in Topic 8.3. Recently, in a white paper for an educational publisher and in his talk during the 2020 ILA Next event, I have heard him approach this process of critical reading in three steps. In the white paper, he describes the three approaches as "reading behind the text, within the text, and in front of the text" (Morrell, 2019, p. 8). He goes on to describe this reading process as "a rhetorical triangle where there is author-centered, text-centered, and reader-centered approaches." These are useful ways to help students approach texts with a memorable set of prepositions: behind, within, and in front.

More recently, I have been introduced to Earl Aguilera's (2017) interpretation of this, specifically focused on digital literacies, in which he asks three questions: (1) "What's on the screen?"; (2) "What's behind the screen?"; and (3) "What's beyond the screen?" Like Morrell's questions, Aguilera's questions also push students to think critically about both what they are seeing on-screen and how it works. These questions remind us that no texts are neutral and that we need to continually push our students toward digital dili-gence, especially in the sense that they are alert and persistent as they search for materials to read across multiple platforms.

TOPIC 8.1. CREATING MULTIMEDIA ANALYSES

To help them become digitally diligent, we need students to analyze texts—especially texts that are "born digital"—using a variety of tools and perspectives, inviting them to use think-aloud protocols to share their ideas about texts while in the process of reading as well as interactive multimedia to add more sustained, nuanced analysis to texts after deeper study.

Overview

We know—from our own experiences as readers as well as from students' self-reported engagement with reading—that there are many challenges facing our youth as it relates to helping them lead literary and literate lives. On the one hand, we can look at this as a moment of crisis in which we are falling in a downward spiral of students becoming more distracted and less engaged. And while this may in part be true, we can—on the other hand—take this as an opportunity for helping them both find new items to read and to engage more deeply in the process of reading. Moreover, we can invite them to read longer, more substantive online texts with intention, a stance in which they may not always be engaged. So, rather than bemoaning the state of our students' reading, I argue that we need to move beyond the basic reading responses and book talks that we have asked of students in the past and, in the future, provide them with structure and opportunity to more fully engage with their reading through multimedia analysis.

The opportunity for students to take the texts they are reading—especially interactive texts that are specifically designed to be read online, not just conveniently placed there as an alternative to print-based publications—and engage in a multimedia analysis of that text is powerful. As Kristen Turner and I (2015b) argued in our book, "A Connected Reader will engage with digital texts using tried-and-true reading strategies as well as strategies that are unique to reading on a screen" (p. 116). In addition to the relatively commonplace ideas that we can click on a hyperlink and move from one web-based text to another, or that we could highlight a word in an ebook reader for a definition, we can also think about ways to have students read more complex multimedia texts that integrate audio, video, maps, and other forms of interactivity. For instance, the experience of reading the *1619 Project* through *The New York Times Magazine* website that includes additional photo galleries, podcasts, and other media elements (Hannah-Jones, 2019) is one that could not be emulated in print text alone, though it was published as a print text too (Gyarkye, 2019). Showing students these texts—and talking about the affordances they provide for both readers and writers—can be a powerful way to begin an analysis of multimedia.

Knowing there are so many ways to approach these texts, we do need to provide some structure for our students. As a thinking tool, we can invite them to use the kind of comprehension strategies (predicting, questioning, inferring, connecting, and more) that have been a part of reading instruction for quite some time, as well as more recent strategies like the "notice and note signposts" from Beers and Probst (2012, 2015). For instance, a common strategy is to have students make a prediction before they begin reading a text, or to offer a brief summary when done reading. Or, as Beers and Probst suggest with their signposts, readers might look for supporting characters to offer "words of the wiser" to the main character (from which they can infer what might then happen next for the main character). Many of these strategies and resources can be found through a simple web search and can be adapted for guiding students as they offer responses to a text and begin their multimedia analysis.

To find even more "born-digital" texts that are useful for students to read and interpret, I have yet to identify a clear, comprehensive, and ongoing list of updated texts aimed at middle and high school students, though one is likely to exist (and, if you know of one, please contact me to let me know about it through the book's companion website). Still, there are a few trusted sources that we can turn to, including nonfiction from *The New York Times* that, since producing "Snow Fall: The Avalanche at Tunnel Creek" (Branch, 2012), has continued to innovate, with timely and engaging interactives and long-form journalism like the *1619 Project*, noted above. Another example from *The New York Times* provides readers/viewers with a "close read" of Thomas Eakins's 1875 painting, "The Gross Clinic" (Eakins, 1875), in which a piece of art is examined by zooming in and out on elements of the painting, offering a few sentences of analysis alongside, packaged in a responsive, scrolling website (Farago, 2020). I strongly encourage educators to look to *The New York Times* for compelling multimedia content, as well as their resources from *The New York Times* Learning Network.

Other journalistic outlets are producing more multimedia texts too. For instance, in the fall of 2020 a provocative interactive map "What if all COVID-19 deaths in the United States had happened in your neighborhood?" created by *The Washington Post* (2020) forced viewers to imagine the scope of pandemic-related deaths by superimposing that count on a virtual map of their own zip code. From a different angle, there are works of fiction and poetry being created too. For a resource related to electronic literature, the Electronic Literature Organization offers a number of collections of eliterature, as well as a collection of teacher resources (Hayles, 2020). Of course, more and more "born-digital" texts, both fiction and nonfiction, come into existence each day, so sometimes the best strategy is just to keep our eyes open as we scroll through social media and in our casual web browsing.

To find even more ebooks and other online resources, there are many openly available spaces for Lexile-leveled reading materials, including Common Lit, Read Works, and Tween Tribune, among others. These can lead to other sources, such as a school district's or state's own online elibrary, and a tool like Library Extension, which will allow users to search for books quickly through an online book seller and then find a link to available materials in their local library. Also, I credit librarian and Rutgers professor Joyce Valenza (2020) with pointing me to many resources over the years, and highly recommend her blog *NeverEnding Search* (link available on the book's companion website, hickstro.org/digitaldiligence). She, like many other librarians, is consistently posting information about how to move students from "information poverty" to "information privilege," and a recent post highlighted the Google Chrome add-on TeachingBooks (Valenza, 2020). The TeachingBooks site integrates as a Google Chrome extension and will provide links to additional resources from a general web search with their Book Connections plug-in. There are also communities of librarians and teacher readers online in a variety of spaces, and seeking out these groups will likely yield new ideas as well.

No matter how we help our students find "born-digital" or those that are simply "digitally convenient" texts, we can then invite them to respond to those texts in a variety of ways. The first one is relatively quick, and assumes that students have some proficiency with the use of screencasting with tools mentioned in Chapter 2, such as Screencastify, Screencast-o-matic, Loom, or others. (Of note, in the fall of 2020, Flip-grid introduced a screen-recording option that could be employed for these purposes.) The second uses a multimedia design tool, ThingLink, which allows students to import and image and add layers of annotations to it.

Teaching Points

As noted above, there are two main ways to engage students in an analysis of their reading: one that is relatively brief in duration and one that would take more time for them to prepare. They could be done in sequence, or either could be completed as a separate task, depending on the timing of the lesson and one's instructional purposes.

Point 1: Recording a "Think-Aloud" through Screencasting

Once students have a digital text that they have been reading—and have begun to do some initial analysis—it is time to invite them to share their impressions with a "think-aloud," recorded in a screencast. The think-aloud protocol has been used as a tool for qualitative research, adapted as a way for educators to have students describe their thinking process while engaged in academic work, usually reading. The Learning for Justice (formerly Teaching Tolerance) website (2014) describes a number of activities that students might talk about, including the process of "skipping text, rereading, searching back in the text for information, questioning, clarifying, summarizing, making connections, reflecting, predicting and visualizing." In addition, their lesson plan includes a "Think-Aloud Checklist," available as a PDF, which lists specific skills and offers cue words to help readers begin a thinking routine. For instance, with the skill of "clarifying," there are cues like "I got confused when . . ." or "I'm not sure of . . ." With twelve strategies and two dozen cues, this is a useful resource for students as they begin their reading and prepare for their screencast.

Without going into a detailed explanation of screencasting, especially since all the tools vary with their functionality, I will be brief. In order to prepare for their think-aloud, students should have had adequate time to read the text, have a basic understanding of the strategies that are most important for them to demonstrate about their reading, and, perhaps, have two or three additional guiding questions provided by the teacher to reply to as they talk. As they prepare to record, students will need to ensure they are selecting their web browser or ebook reader. If available, they might use some of the tools available for annotation. For instance, Screencastify has tools like the "focus mouse," "show circle on mouse click," "pen," and "eraser." Students can be encouraged to use those tools, sparingly, as a way to augment their think-aloud process, though the main focus should be on them connecting, questioning, and extending their own ideas from the text. Many of the platforms have recording limits (often 5 minutes or less), which is actually a good technical constraint for keeping students focused with a shorter time for response. Once their screencasts are recorded, depending on the platform, they can be shared as links to a Google Drive file or other video published with a unique URL.

Throughout the process, it is important to remind students that the focus is on talking through their thinking. This is needed especially before welcoming students to create recordings in an anytime manner. While a typical think-aloud might be completed with the educator and student side by side in conversation with one another, a few extra reminders about how to stay focused during their screencast could be helpful for students as they prepare to make their recording. Remind students to pick two or three key passages and to go into detail around those passages, pointing—both in spoken word and through the literal pointing and clicking on-screen—to those words that resonated most powerfully for them. Finally, as students work to share their thinking, if they get stuck, remind them they can simply pause the recording and take a breath. This is one of the benefits of anytime learning; while sharing their first draft, one-take thinking is important, if they find themselves completely stuck, they always have the pause button to use if they need it.

For instance, with the example below, a student may have been reading a selection of *Romeo and Juliet* from Project Gutenberg. In this sample that I created using Screencastify, Figures 8.1.1 and 8.1.2 demonstrate how two features of Screencastify could be invitations for students to discuss their interpretations of the text. In Figure 8.1.1, the "Focus Mouse" feature is shown. Students could, for instance, use the focus mouse feature to move across the screen, left to right, top to bottom, showing key moments where they paused and were interested in, confused by, or had a question about the text. Figure 8.1.2 shows a use of the "Pen" tool, where a student could draw a line under a key segment of the text, bringing emphasis to a key quote or making an intentional note about how the author has written the text. There are other annotation tools that could be useful as well, especially the "Show Mouse Click" feature, which would provide clear insights on the navigation of a multimedia text, the rectangle drawing tool (if drawing with the pen tool is awkward) and—with a new release of Screencastify in the spring of 2021—the ability to add emojis. In all these ways, students could continue to annotate their screen during the think-aloud and articulate their response to the text.

Throughout the process, it is important to remind students that the focus is on talking through their thinking. And, with this idea of recording a screencast as one option, we now consider a more complex project that would invite students to analyze a text using a multimedia tool, ThingLink.

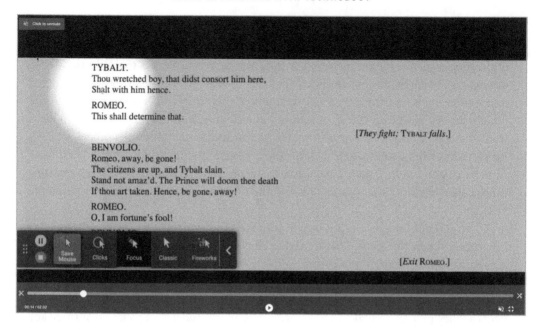

FIGURE 8.1.1. Use of "Focus Mouse" feature during a Screencastify recording. Screencastify interface used with permission. *Romeo and Juliet* text available in the public domain from Project Gutenberg.

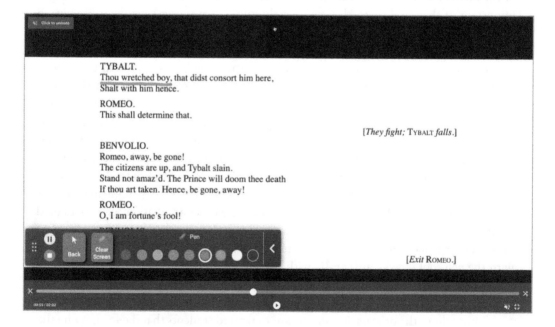

FIGURE 8.1.2. Use of "Pen" feature during a Screencastify recording, with an underlined segment of the text. Screencastify interface used with permission. *Romeo and Juliet* text available in the public domain from Project Gutenberg.

Point 2: Creating a Multimedia Analysis with ThingLink

In addition to providing students with opportunities to share their initial responses through a screencast recording of a think-aloud, they can move into a deeper, more substantive analysis using the affordances of multimedia. A tool that describes itself as "education technology platform that makes it easy to augment images, videos, and virtual tours with additional information and links," ThingLink (2020) allows users to import an initial image or video and then layer on "tags," or multimedia elements, that can lead the viewer to even more information such as links to outside content, embedded videos, or audio commentary. ThingLink, like many tools, works on a freemium model, and educators can create many items for free, yet would need a subscription to embrace all the features of ThingLink, including collaborative editing and useful tools for grading and feedback. Still, the free version is powerful, and the ThingLink interface offers users four options:

- Add text label: The simplest of the tags, only an icon and brief bit of text can be added here (fewer than 100 characters).

- Add text and media: By adding an icon to the image or video, users can then create a title, provide a brief description (no character limit), and invite users to link to an outside resource. They might also add an image, a video, or an audio clip to make this annotation more robust.

- Add content from website: With this feature, students can provide a hyperlink that will embed a YouTube video, a Google Map, or any other type of media that can be included using iFrame code.

- Create tour: Finally, with this option, students can invite their viewers to move through their media in a guided fashion, in a specific order, and, if they wish, with links to additional outside resources.

A quick, extra point here about what students could, or perhaps should, link to. Yes, they can find additional resources that are available online, such as an interview with the author posted to YouTube or a review of the book they are reading. As producers, students could, too, create additional content like Google Docs, a website, or a video in which they further elaborate on the ideas presented in the brief annotation. Educators can encourage students to use the main ThingLink item as a space for an initial explanation and then point their viewers to their own further analysis. With these general points in mind, if additional support is needed, there are several tutorials for ThingLink, available through their website and through a web search.

Inviting students to create an analysis of a multimedia text begins by having them upload an image or a video. Again, this could be an opportunity for students to use a screencast to record their interactions with a particular multimedia text, or it could be a screenshot. After uploading that image or video, students will then be taken into the ThingLink editing interface. Depending on how we might want to structure the task, students could be encouraged to add one of each of the three main tag types ("add text and media," "add text label," and "add content from website"). Once completing this part of their analysis, they could then create a tour. ThingLink (2020) describes the "tour" as an option that will take "the viewer away from the current image, and on to the page of another ThingLink image, video, or 360 image. Use this tag to move from one creation to another." Depending on the level of engagement we would ask of our learners as they create a ThingLink, of just one image or with an entire gallery tour, the levels of complexity can be altered depending on the goals of the analysis assignment.

As just one example, I share a recent textual analysis, based on a media literacy framework, created by one of my first-year students from Central Michigan University, Nick Trombley (link available on the book's companion website). In this analysis, he looked at a sponsored post on *Newsweek* from their Amplify (2020) service, entitled "Here's Everything You Need to Know About Keeping Your Dog Safe from COVID-19." The point that this was a sponsored article—rather than one written by the *Newsweek* reporters—was an initial cue that he should explore this post with a healthy skepticism, which he did. Throughout his ThingLink analysis, he was able to engage in a series of annotations that provided the viewer with fact-checks on the claims in the article, as well as offering some tips on media literacy. In his essay, Trombley begins with these ideas:

> Sometimes pet owners need a little push in order to spark insecurities and worry more about their pets. This concept is exactly what a *Newsweek Amplify* article published amidst the COVID-19 pandemic was attempting to do. This article is full of small lies and misinformation intended to scare pet owners into buying the products that sponsored the article. Throughout the article you will find shoutouts to a pet insurance company, a dog shampoo company, and even an anti-chew spray company. The *Newsweek Amplify* article knew people associated wellbeing with owning a pet and they used this article in an attempt to spark these worries. In particular, three main claims can be seen throughout the article in an attempt to do just that.

From there, he continues to point out how the article accomplishes these goals, and in Figure 8.1.3, Trombley's annotations using ThingLink demonstrate some of these

FIGURE 8.1.3. A screenshot of Trombley's ThingLink analysis of the *Newsweek* Amplify article. Used with permission of Trombley.

concerns about the opening elements of the article (the background of the *Newsweek* article has been blurred due to copyright restrictions).

1. With the first tag, Nick describes *Newsweek*'s founding in 1933, demonstrating its longevity as a source of journalistic quality and noting that AllSides' analysis of *Newsweek* as a source that shows a slight left-leaning bias.
2. With the second tag, Nick provides a direct link to the sponsored article so his viewers can go directly to it.
3. With the third tag, in yellow, Nick draws in a quote about "sponsored content" with a definition from *Business Insider*, noting that many readers do not typically notice the disclosure of sponsored content.
4. With the fourth tag, in red, Nick discusses the propaganda technique of creating a catchy headline and also noting how some important information about how rare it is for a pet to test positive with the virus has been omitted.
5. Finally, with the fifth tag, in red, Nick elaborates more on the label of "Sponsored Article," describing briefly the point that the material in the article is paid for by an advertiser, in this case, a health insurance company for pets.

By the end of his essay—and in verbatim language in an annotation on his ThingLink—Trombley makes a direct appeal to his peers:

> In conclusion, I urge you to be aware of the advertising techniques that companies use to profit off of consumers' insecurities. These techniques are sometimes hard to spot and may even influence you to make questionable decisions or purchases. To be safe it is best to check every webpage that you come across for a sponsored disclosure label that is generally located at the top or end of the article. Additionally, if you are unsure whether a source you are reading is giving you the correct information, try lateral reading and checking more credible sources like peer reviewed articles or from federal organizations.

Throughout the entire ThingLink analysis, Trombley includes a total of just over 20 annotations, all of which connect to his essay "Misinformation about COVID-19 on Pets Featuring Newsweek Amplify." He has given me permission to share his entire essay on the book's companion website (hickstro.org/digitaldiligence), and that text—as well as a link to his full ThingLink project—can be found there. Again, with more than 20 annotations, Trombley examines the misinformation and propaganda techniques used in the sponsored article and demonstrates why a reader should be wary of what has been presented in a piece that appears in what would otherwise be considered a reputable news source.

As with other topics explored so far, we now turn to the NCTE (2019b) definition to think about how students would—through these two forms of analysis—connect to the skills and dispositions that digital readers must possess. By moving through these two forms of analysis, from a more traditional sense of reading, "learners have opportunities to increase engagement with reading and other academic subjects." By sharing their think-alouds and a more formal analysis, they are demonstrating their proficiency in basic reading comprehension and the study of fiction and nonfiction. Also, from a more technical standpoint, by using the original reading materials in a transformative manner, students "respect and follow the copyright information and appropriate licenses given to digital content as they work online" as well as "create products that are both informative and ethical." This topic provides opportunity to have conversation about many aspects of connected reading, all leading students to a deeper, more substantive evaluation of the texts that students are reading, viewing, and listening to.

Guiding Questions

When working with students and exploring this topic, consider the following questions when designing lessons, assignments, and assessments:

For the Think-Aloud/Screencast

- Consider asking students to use protocols from Harvard Project Zero, the Media Literacy Smartphone, Beers and Probst's signposts, or other similar guides as a way to analyze the text.
- Or offer a list of more general questions to guide their work:
  - As you are beginning your analysis, describe the sections of the text that resonate the most with you. What do you connect with? What other texts does this remind you of that you have read or seen before?
  - As you move deeper into your analysis, ask questions of the text. What do you wonder about the content of the text? What do you wonder about the structure of the text?
  - As you conclude your analysis, make predictions about the text. What do you think will happen in the next sections of the text? What other ideas do you feel will be raised?

For the Analysis with ThingLink

- Consider asking students, again, to use protocols noted above to create annotations on the text they are analyzing.
- Or invite them to consider the following:
  - How and where might you add a tag that will include your own voice recording, offering insights on the text?
  - How and where might you add a tag with a link to an outside website or media element, providing more context for a particular segment of the text?
  - How and why might you create a tour of the text, as a way to guide your viewer through your analysis in a particular order in the form of a compelling argument?

TOPIC 8.2. CREATING SPACE(S) FOR TALK

To help them become digitally diligent, we need students to participate
in a variety of conversations about the materials they are reading, across
time and space as well as with different communities of readers.

Overview

Reading is more than just something one person does alone. Indeed, making sense of
what we read—through interpretation, analysis, and critique—is a social act. Conversations about what we read (as well as view and listen to) are essential in order to make
meaning. We also know that meaning making doesn't happen in scripted discussion
forums, where students offer a response to a teacher's initial question and then provide
feedback to two of their classmates. Or, as Morris and Stommel (2013) remind us, "students post because they have to, not because they enjoy doing so. And teachers respond
(if they respond at all) because they too have become complacent to the bizarre rules that
govern the forum." Instead, as many teacher researchers and literacy scholars remind
us, we must encourage dialogue among our students in order to have them more fully
engage in the reading process and, more importantly, to develop a habit of reading that
will carry them forward in life.

In this topic, we explore tools for facilitating online conversation on documents,
images, and videos, moving away from traditional LMS-style discussion forums and
into conversations that happen right alongside the text with a variety of annotation tools.
On one level, annotation is simply putting comments on the side of a document and
could be linked to the traditional reading-comprehension strategies, such as questioning, connecting, and inferring. That said, the possibilities for annotation—in an effort
to have our students become digitally diligent readers—needs to be expanded.

Quoting from an open ebook, *Annotation*, by Remi Kalir and Antero Garcia
(2019)—in which they invited me to offer an initial peer review using an online annotation tool, Hypothes.is—I turn to their words as a way to articulate a more robust definition of annotation:

> Annotation is a form of self-expression, a way to document and curate new knowledge,
> and is a powerful means of civic engagement and political agency.
>
> Annotation provides information, making knowledge more accessible. Annota-
> tion shares commentary, making both expert opinion and everyday perspective more
> transparent. Annotation sparks conversation, making our dialogue—about art, reli-
> gion, culture, politics, and research—more interactive. Annotation expresses power,
> making civic life more robust and participatory. And annotation aids learning, aug-
> menting our intellect, cognition, and collaboration. This is why annotation matters.

Teaching students about the possibilities of annotation—especially in a time when
they are moving across digital and physical spaces—helps get the conversation started
and keep it going. There are a variety of annotation tools we can draw upon when

inviting our students to add their own insights to documents under consideration. I will not provide lengthy explanations here, as there are numerous help guides and video tutorials available for all of them, just a few clicks away in a web search. Thus, I draw from descriptions provided on each tool's main or "about" page and offer links to each on the companion website for this book.

- NowComment is a free site—maintained by Paul Allison, a retired teacher and consultant for the New York City Writing Project and National Writing Project—that "is fast, powerful, and feature-rich," allowing students to comment on text, images, and video, and educators to "sort comments, skim summaries, create assignments, hide comments, reply privately" and more. It is web based and freely accessible across multiple platforms and devices.
- Kami, described as "digital pen and paper" that will invite students "to draw freely and annotate with a selection of colors, shapes and text sizes," is a web-based app that can work across browsers. Students are able to annotate PDFs with many tools, including voice and video responses. Like Kami, another tool, Perusall, offers some unique annotation features in a freemium model too.
- In a similar manner, Edji is a tool that allows users to annotate "a PDF, image, web article, or GIF" in "a collaborative, engaging experience while you get live data." One of the key features is the "heat vision" function, which "will show your students what you see, with the heat map and all of their peers' comments." Another freemium tool, Edji, invites users to annotate with emojis, a well-liked feature.
- Hypothes.is is a web-based tool that allows for digital annotation directly on webpages, in threaded comments. As they state, "Digital annotation also offers new affordances, enabling students to respond to text using different media and empowering them to collaborate on understanding and developing ideas about their readings."
- With an expanded definition of reading, we might also consider Video Ant, designed by the University of Minnesota, and Vialogues, designed by Teachers College at Columbia University. Both offer options for threaded conversation on video clips that can be tied to direct timestamps on the videos themselves (much like a highlight or comment would appear on a specific word, phrase, or sentence in a text).
- Also, for those who have access to Microsoft tools, OneNote allows users to import text and images into notebooks, which can be annotated and shared. Users can type, speak, or hand-draw (with a stylus on a touchscreen) their annotations within OneNote.

Again, there are countless tutorials available to support users as they learn about these tools, so a quick web search will yield many guides and how-to videos.

Regardless of the tool chosen, once the texts are ready for annotation, we need to consider ways in which we can engage students with the text. Morrell's framework (mentioned in the introduction to this chapter and explored in more detail in Topic 8.3) offers one option for inviting students to question the text. With the teaching points below, we will explore two additional resources that provide numerous ways for students to engage with texts, and invite a dialogic response that deepens their own understanding while also welcoming their peers into further conversation: protocols from the National School Reform Faculty and visible thinking routines from Harvard's Project Zero.

Teaching Points

In many of the ways that we set up spaces for online dialogue, we see patterns that replicate what might happen in the classroom. The typical "IRE" (initiate, respond, and evaluate) interaction has been a feature of classrooms for a long time, if not forever (Fisher & Frey, 2010; Mehan, 1979, 1985). In this model of response, three steps typically occur, all of which shut down genuine dialogue and interaction among students:

1. A teacher initiates a question, typically one that requires a "right" answer and is from the lower levels of Bloom's taxonomy.
2. One student is called upon to respond.
3. The teacher evaluates the response and moves on to the next question.

This IRE model has, sadly, translated into the typical model for an online discussion forum, where the teacher posts a question and then students must respond to the original question and offer additional responses to two classmates. This perfunctory exchange is loathed by most students and summed up by one in stating that "if you want students to actively have a discussion about something, then do it. But to just say respond to two other students, it's like talking to a wall" (Hitchan, 2015). With the IRE model moved to a digital space, the outcome is clear: Students are unlikely to build community or engage deeply with content.

Thus, with annotation, we need to encourage dialogic response, in which students are pursuing topics of interest and offering genuine, encouraging responses to their peers. In some cases, this can still happen in discussion forums; however, it seems as if the opportunity to move students into more and more text-based discussions using the annotation tools above can be an effective teaching move. Moreover, when paired with a discussion protocol or visible thinking routine that can scaffold the dialogue, students are more likely to express themselves and push their classmates' thinking.

To that end, two resources I rely on for finding additional tools for structuring effective annotations are the National School Reform Faculty's (NSRF) collection of protocols (2020) and the Harvard Project Zero's collection of visible thinking routines (n.d.). These tools provide us with structures for eliciting students' thinking and, in turn, the opportunity to engage more fully in discussion. Assuming that part of the challenge in responding to a classmate's initial post is that the classmate did not present a compelling answer to the question, we need to scaffold their thinking in productive ways so meaningful dialogue can ensue.

For instance, from NSRF, there are protocols that—while originally designed for face-to-face, real-time conversation—can be adapted for online, anytime conversations. The "ground rules" presented in the "Text-Based Seminar" protocol (Thompson-Grove, 2017) provide some good advice that will, again, need to be adapted slightly for an online, anytime conversation. What it means to "listen actively," to "build on what others say," and to "emphasize clarification, amplification, and implications of ideas" will look different in discussion boards and warrant some attention in early rounds of participation. Perhaps the most important piece of advice from the "Text-Based Seminar" protocol is that we should continue to "refer to the text [and] challenge others to go to the text." By sharing these guidelines with students and creating an example of a thoughtful exchange together, this can begin to set an example for discussions.

For instance, in thinking about how we might have our students write a response to the opening of Curtis's *The Watsons Go to Birmingham—1963*, imagine these two fictionalized responses to something that a classmate had already posted. Exactly what the classmate may have originally posted in response to the first chapter is not as important in thinking about the ground rules from the "Text-Based Seminar" protocol and how the responder might engage fully in the practices outlined above. With that in mind, here are two imagined responses:

- "I like what you said about the introduction to the story. Do you think it could have been better?"
- "As I read your post, I like how you said that 'the introduction to the story was one of the most powerful first paragraphs' you have read. I agree with you, and I really like how Christopher Paul Curtis describes the day where 'your breath kind of hung frozen in the air like a hunk of smoke.' I wonder though, do you think this is an interesting simile? Or could he have used some other literary device to describe the cold?"

In working with students to write more thoughtful responses, we are actually helping them become better readers of both the original text and their classmates' work. When this conversation takes place on the text itself, the process can be even more powerful, as the students are constantly reminded of what it is, exactly, that they are writing a response to (as compared to having a blank box to type in a normal discussion forum). From there, we can provide different structures for them to explore the texts, no matter what annotation tool they are using. Here are a few protocols from NSRF that I find particularly valuable, linked on the book's companion website:

- In the "Save the Last Word for Me" protocol, individuals identify a key passage from the text and then invite group members to share their impression, returning finally to the first person, who gets to summarize and share "the last word."

• In the "Jigsaw Description" protocol, individuals read different portions of a particular text and then bring back a summary to the entire group, answering additional questions that evolve from the conversation.

• The "Making Meaning" protocol can be combined with some of the questions from the "Probing Questions" protocol. Individuals describe what they see in a text, ask additional questions, and in the end, describe what they think is most significant about the text.

• The "Tea Party" protocol can be paired with the "What, So What, Now What" protocol. Individuals bring key quotes from a text and need to describe what they see, what matters in the quotes, and what kinds of interpretations can be drawn in relation to the text as a whole.

• Finally, with the "Text Rendering" protocol, individuals first share one sentence from the text that was powerful, describing why. Then the individuals share a phrase, again describing the importance. Finally, each person chooses just one keyword and discusses the significance of that word in relation to the interpretation of the entire text.

These are just a few examples of how the protocols could be adapted and used in a shared annotation of a given text. In a similar spirit, the visible thinking routines from Project Zero provide a number of useful structures for responding to text. These questions, unlike the protocols from NSRF, need little adaptation, as they are in a "student-ready" form. Each set of questions could be used as a basis for a set of annotations and responses. There are dozens of routines available, and thus I share just a list of a few standbys for me as I structure discussion forums: "See, Think, Wonder"; "I Used to Think . . . Now I Think . . ."; "What Makes You Say That?"; "Think, Puzzle, Explore"; and "The 4 Cs" (which includes the instructions to make connections to the text, challenge the text, identify key concepts, and identify the kinds of changes the text is asking of the reader). Having not explored every single one of the visible thinking routines, I can only imagine there are more that could easily be adapted to annotation activities and peer dialogue.

In thinking about the overlaps between the activities described here and the NCTE (2019b) definition of literacy in a digital age, there are opportunities to explore many of the subsections and questions that have been discussed in earlier chapters, especially related to the goal that they "participate effectively and critically in a networked world" and "explore and engage critically, thoughtfully, and across a wide variety of inclusive texts and tools/modalities." With some extra emphasis from us, I think students could reasonably be expected to respond to some of the questions raised in the "Build and sustain intentional global and cross-cultural connections and relationships with others so as to pose and solve problems collaboratively and strengthen independent thought" segment too.

For instance, with additional scaffolding, students could practice "strategies for interrupting discourse that marginalizes people based on race, culture, sexuality, language, gender, and ability" and—if cross-classroom and school partnerships are established—"have opportunities to collaborate with people/learners from communities that hold different views/ideas/values/beliefs, life experiences, racial, ethnic, and cultural identities, and economic security to address social issues that impact all of our lives" (NCTE, 2019b). These kinds of substantive opportunities for dialogue require an intentional effort from us, as educators, as we might work to set up collaborations through our own professional networks or services, such as PenPal Schools, Generation Global, iEARN, Global SchoolNet, or a Teachers' Guide to Global Collaboration (links available on the book's companion website).

Guiding Questions

When working with students and exploring this topic, consider the following questions when designing lessons, assignments, and assessments:

- Before annotating
  - For you as a reader, what are some of the challenges you face when you prepare to engage with a text?
  - In that same spirit, what are some of the challenges you face when you prepare to have a discussion in class about a text you have read?
  - What has been your experience using annotation tools to highlight and comment upon digital texts? What tools have you used?
  - In what ways have you worked with someone else to collaboratively annotate a text and share an ongoing conversation about it?
- While annotating
  - What are the kinds of questions you are asking of the text as you engage in annotation?
  - How do the digital tools available to you help you to identify segments of the text for annotation?
  - In what ways might you bring in links to outside sources as additional evidence for your annotations?
- After annotating
  - What did other readers have to say about your annotations? How did their responses contribute to your own thinking about the text?
  - What are the qualities of a thoughtful response, based on what you saw others say to you, as well as what you wrote to them?
  - How might you use the responses of others to return to the text for a second reading in order to gain more insights about it?

TOPIC 8.3. REMIXING THE CLASSICS

To help them become digitally diligent, we need students to bring a critical perspective to the texts they read, especially canonical texts that may represent ideologies of times past and can be examined with new scrutiny using technologies and frameworks from the modern era.

Overview

Since the introduction of lists of recommended readings from universities—and the ways in which the Western literary canon has been codified since the mid-1700s to the present—English teachers have continued to question what texts are worthy of study. Just as they have with issues related to digital literacy, NCTE has led the charge on broadening the canon, beginning with 1972's "Resolution on Preparing Teachers with Knowledge of the Literature of Minorities" through the present with ongoing blog posts, Twitter chats, conference presentations, books, and other resources including recent policy documents from NCTE's James R. Squire Office of Policy Research in English Language Arts (in that same spirit, so have many other literacy organizations, such as the International Literacy Association). These conversations have moved us to think about what texts have been valued by educators, parents, and the broader community, as well as the ways in which they have been codified into our curriculum.

As I begin this topic, I offer the humble concession that I am not an expert in canonical literature, historical or current trends in children's and young adult literature, or the continually expanding diversity of literature through authors who identify as BIPOC or LGBTQ+. To better understand these topics, there are numerous resources that can support more critical interpretations of the canon and provide voice to authors who have traditionally been marginalized. First, I recommend the resources provided by Tricia Ebarvia, Lorena Germán, Dr. Kim Parker, and Julia Torres. Their #Disrupt-Texts work both through NCTE's *English Journal* and their website (link available on this book's companion website). A second professional resource for exploring these issues and discovering new approaches for examining these texts is Carlin Borsheim-Black and Sophia Sarigianides's *Letting Go of Literary Whiteness: Antiracist Literature Instruction for White Students* (2019). There are, most certainly, more resources that one could explore in work to broaden the literary canon and choose more diverse texts (e.g., Jago, 2018; Styslinger, 2017; Zapata, Kleekamp, & King, 2018), and I again note my own limitations in not being more active in this area of literacy and literary studies.

That said—and returning to the canonical texts that are the focus for this topic—far from tossing these texts to the trash heap of history, the fact that many of these texts are now openly available on the web through sources like Project Gutenberg gives us opportunities to remix them in more critical, creative, and robust ways (as noted in Topic 8.1, with screencasting, and in more detail below). Even the ones that are not available in the public domain on the web can be worthy of study and analysis, as pictures can be snapped with phone cameras or, in the case of ebooks, screen captures can be made. As students work to examine these texts—and the context in which these texts were produced decades, perhaps centuries, ago—access to these texts through digital means provide us with new opportunities for analysis, interpretation, and critique.

For items in the public domain, teachers and students have the option to copy these materials without any concern. For those that might be copyrighted, I encourage readers to look back to the Interlude that precedes Chapter 7. When using copyrighted materials in a transformative manner, educators and students have wide latitude under provisions of fair use when integrating materials in a transformative way. In this sense, taking a passage from a book and either snapping a picture or retyping the words into a digital form are both reasonable. Though I certainly do not suggest copying and pasting major segments of a text and making it available on the public web, it is possible for students to engage in the kinds of use described in the teaching points below.

Two additional influences have guided my thinking on this set of teaching points. First, the website MyShakespeare provides another model for approaching these kinds of critical approaches, both in a design/technical sense and from the kinds of annotation, questioning, and critical thinking that we would want students to demonstrate. The idea behind MyShakespeare is that, with a mash-up of multimedia, the plays are presented with additional context, analysis, and study tools. More than the study guides we used to be able to purchase to read alongside the text, the design of interwoven elements in MyShakespeare allow students to move seamlessly among the original text, contemporary translations, and additional materials such as interviews, clips of performances, animated explainer videos, and comprehension questions. Figure 8.3.1 shows one example of how MyShakespeare provides context in a pop-up window.

Second, Tom Liam Lynch offers ideas about how to take the corpus of canonical literature and look at it through a more data-driven lens. Mentioned first in Topic 5.2, he offers a lesson on using the entire manuscript of *Romeo and Juliet* to map out the uses of the words *love* and *death* and to invite students to then find those instances in the text (Lynch, n.d.). In doing so, students are encouraged to analyze word frequency counts in tables, word clouds, and graphs, thus creating more nuanced interpretations of the play as a whole, as well as individual characters. In the end, Lynch asks students "to use their graphical data and insight to create a 'mixed literary analysis' that cites both quantitative (i.e., raw word frequencies) and qualitative (i.e., textual evidence) data." He has now provided access to datasets from over a dozen texts on his Plotting Points website, linked from this book's companion page. It is from this idea that I share ideas for how students can remix the classic, canonical texts they have been expected to read, though to do so in innovative ways.

Teaching Points

While there are numerous reports decrying the state of reading, part of the problem lies in the ways we invite students to engage with texts, especially classic works of canonical literature. Since most of these works are available in the public domain, we have the

FIGURE 8.3.1. A screenshot of the MyShakespeare interface highlighting *Romeo and Juliet*, Act I: Prologue, with a contextual comment on screen. Used with permission of MyShakespeare.

opportunity to discover—and remix—existing copies of these classics and consider new ways for students to annotate and respond to these texts. Using the ubiquitous slide deck tools of Google Slides, Microsoft's PowerPoint, Apple's Keynote, or another, similar program, we can invite students to create their own interpretations of canonical texts, in the style of MyShakespeare and with additional, critical analysis through both quantitative and qualitative evidence (as suggested by Lynch).

As a way to help students approach the canonical texts they are interpreting, we can certainly look to literary theories as frames of analysis. As my colleague and coauthor Andy Schoenborn (2020) notes in our book *Creating Confident Writers,* students can approach this analysis using Jim Burke's (2012) guide "The Basics: Critical Theory" from *The English Teacher's Companion* (pp. 188–189), which outlines the key tenets of twelve approaches, including feminist, Marxist, postmodern, and reader's response criticisms. There are teachers who have created similar, shorter lists of these critical theories too, and additional links are available on this book's companion website.

While these critical interpretations are important, so too can be a series of general questions that might be applied across texts. Hearkening back to my acknowledgment at the beginning of Chapter 8, I turn here to a strategy introduced by Ernest Morrell when I was a graduate student. In sharing a process for critically approaching our reading, he used four prepositions to describe how we should approach a text: with, against, upon, and beyond. These heuristics could be applied to any kind of text, from poems to novels and from blog posts to academic articles. Author and coauthor of numerous books, including *Every Child a Super Reader: 7 Strengths to Open a World of Possible* (Allyn & Morrell, 2015), Morrell would encourage us to engage in the following thinking routines:

- Read *with* the text: With this approach, the goal is to read and understand the author's words and to gain a basic level of comprehension about the topic at hand. In the process, students can consider what is happening as the author moves forward with a narrative, presents information, or develops an argument. Annotations and questions for reading with the text might begin with ideas like these:
  - I see a connection between . . .
  - In this context, I think that the word _____ can mean . . .
  - With this literary device, the author is trying to . . .
- Read *against* the text: With this approach, the goal is to push back against the text, as well as the author, working to understand what additional information or interpretations could be offered based on what is missing. With this angle, students can consider counterarguments or critical interpretations that might undermine or otherwise call into question what is being presented as natural or logical. Annotations and questions for reading against the text might begin with ideas like these:
  - I disagree with this idea because . . .
  - From a different perspective, this could be seen as . . .
  - Here, the author should also consider . . .
- Read *upon* the text: With this approach, the goal is to examine the text in context, considering the various perspectives that could have informed the author at the time the text was composed, as well as the ideologies and perspectives the author is imbuing throughout. From this perspective, a reader could employ literary theories, tie them to historical context, and offer new insights about the times in which the text was created. Annotations and questions for reading upon the text might begin with ideas like these:
  - From what I know about the era this was written in, I think . . .
  - Knowing more about _____ as a person, I wonder why the author chose to . . .
  - Using the lens of _____, I wonder how . . .
- Read *beyond* the text: With this approach, the goal is to make connections to other texts (including written texts, of course, yet also multimedia texts, film, and other sources). By drawing in evidence from other sources, students can make even more unique and compelling connections. In the teaching points I outline below, a student could import a still image or brief clip from a movie that demonstrates an important point about the characters, plot, or setting. Annotations and questions for reading beyond the text might begin with ideas like these:

○ Compared to other work from this author, what he or she is doing in this text . . .

○ In their interpretation of this text, we can see how this director . . .

○ This trope has become common in popular culture, as shown by . . .

Using these four prepositional frames—with, against, upon, and beyond—and by encouraging them to add context in a manner similar to MyShakespeare, we can give our students a robust tool set for analyzing, interpreting, and critiquing a canonical text. With the example below, I share a model for how students might take any text—though I focus on a work by Shakespeare—to create their own critical interpretations of that text using a slide deck.

As they move from the page to the screen, there are two specific resources—as well as a two general tips—that students can use to supplement their own analysis. First, students will need to find the canonical texts they are reading in the public domain. The first place to begin is Project Gutenberg, whose goal is to make as many ebooks available as possible, and at the lowest cost (ideally, free). Since many works that are considered canonical were created before modern copyright laws went into place, they are available through Project Gutenberg as HTML or other ebook formats. Students can easily search for the text they need and then copy/paste the segments they need.

Second, to get audio, students can find recordings on LibriVox and then edit those recordings into smaller segments. LibriVox's goal is "to make all books in the public domain available, narrated by real people and distributed for free, in audio format on the internet." Thus, it is possible to download the audio files of various segments and then edit them into even shorter segments using a tool like the free and open-source Audacity or web-based alternatives like Sodaphonic (links available on the book's companion website). The audio files that students generate will need to be saved in a general format (like MP3 or WAV) and in the cloud-based space that makes sense given the tool they are using (e.g., OneDrive for PowerPoint; Google Drive for Google Slides).

Third, we can offer students a general tip as they prepare to build their annotated remix of the canonical text. For many canonical texts that have been transformed into film, chances are that clips of those films are available on YouTube. A simple search is likely to yield clips, though I do suggest that students carefully review the particular links within YouTube that they follow, as some users may also link to other inappropriate content. Still, students can embed entire video clips—or take screenshots from those clips—to include as part of their annotation, as demonstrated below.

A fourth and final tip is that, if we want to have them identify a key theme or motif from the text and build their resource with an aesthetically pleasing design, students can be directed to SlidesCarnival, SlidesMania, or Slidesgo to find templates (links on book's companion website). I emulate this in my own sample of the *Romeo and Juliet* analysis below. With that in mind, we do not want students to lose sight of their main goal—analyzing and responding to a text—in their quest to find the perfect template for their project. To do so, of course, we can always ask them to begin with a completely blank canvas rather than one of the templates, though I contend that it is important to have them think about the ways that the visual elements from a template could contribute to their overall analysis.

Student Sample for "Remixing the Classics"

With their resources in place—the original text from Project Gutenberg and edited audio recording from LibriVox—as well as having had time to adequately discuss and analyze the text, a student (or group of students) can set up a slide deck with a simple two-column design, placing the original text on the left and space for the annotations on the right. There are numerous functions within Google Slides that allow for multimedia annotation, including the following (see Figure 8.3.2):

1. Embedding of audio: In the upper left corner, I have used the "Insert → Audio" feature from the Google Slides menu, linking to the edited audio file that was uploaded from LibriVox. Thus, the viewer of this Google Slide could click on the audio icon to play it, or it could be set to play automatically.

2. Linking to definitions: Using an icon of a book from the end of the Slides-Carnival deck, I have highlighted two particular words that could be tricky for contemporary readers in the context of the play: *consort* and *doom*. These icons are then hyperlinked to another slide in the deck that includes contextual definitions.

3. Arrows connecting original text to analysis: Using the "Curved Connector" line from the "Insert → Line" menu, I literally draw connections from the original text to the two segments of my analysis.

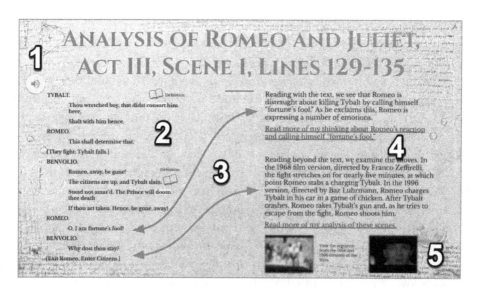

FIGURE 8.3.2. Sample of Remixing the Classics student slide (using "Dolabella" slide template from SlidesCarnival) for a scene from *Romeo and Juliet* (text available in the public domain from Project Gutenberg).

4. Hyperlinks to additional analysis: With the two segments here, "reading with the text" and "reading beyond the text," I offer an initial summary of the ideas, with links to additional writing on later slides in the deck.

5. Additional elements: For this particular analysis of the fight scene, I include links to clips from the two most popular film versions of *Romeo and Juliet,* with the videos embedded from YouTube users. (Images blurred due to copyright.)

As noted, the one slide shown in Figure 8.3.2 is just a sample, modeling the kinds of annotations and connections that are evident in a resource like MyShakespeare. From there, the opportunities for adapting and extending the use of slide deck tools, especially Google Slides, are countless, especially when considering the use of embedded media and hyperlinks, both within the slide deck and to other resources. Considering the teaching points above, students are engaging in a variety of activities that reflect principles from the NCTE (2019b) definition. From the first subsection of the statement, the idea that students can "participate effectively and critically in a networked world," we can push them to "take risks and try new things with tools available to them" and "take responsibility for communicating their ideas in a variety of ways with different modalities and clear intentions." If partnered with another student, or in a small group, this activity provides the opportunity to "independently and collaboratively, persist in solving problems as they arise in their work."

There are connections in the "Consume, curate, and create actively across contexts" section of the definition too. And while I think that intent of this subsection of the document was for students to analyze information presented in contemporary times, I also contend that the idea here for remixing the classics could invite them to "analyze and evaluate the multimedia sources that they consume," even though these are canonical texts presented in a digital form. Similarly, in the "Curate" section, by asking students to compose a more complex and nuanced project, there are also opportunities for them to "evaluate content and develop their own expertise on a topic" and, with scaffolding, "evaluate their own multimedia works" (NCTE, 2019b).

As with many of the topics described throughout the book, this kind of activity could be completed quickly, in just one class period, with only a few annotations or links to external sources. Or the activity could be stretched out to be part of a much deeper and more sustained analysis of a canonical text. I could imagine opportunities for students, as a class, to work on different segments of the text under study and then compile all their analyses and resources into a shared, class-wide slide deck, ultimately creating their own resource in the style of a MyShakespeare-like analysis. This, then, could turn into a space for continued dialogue, as students use commenting features to add even more questions and interpretations to the text itself, as well as their classmates' responses.

Guiding Questions

When working with students and exploring this topic, consider the following questions when designing lessons, assignments, and assessments:

Before Beginning the Analysis of a Text

- What segment of the text will you select to analyze? What is compelling to you about this segment? How does it contribute to the overall story?
- As you zero in on a particular chunk (a few sentences to a paragraph), what literary elements are present?
  - How does this segment change characters and move the plot forward?

While Analyzing the Text

- How will you employ the four stances ("with the text," "against the text," "upon the text," and "beyond the text") to begin your analysis of the text?
  - What questions do these initial perspectives help generate for you?
- What particular words or phrases might need additional definitions and context for your reader?
  - What words or phrases did you struggle with?
- How will you build your slides to provide introductory information and encourage your readers to then click into the further portions of your analysis?
- What other multimedia elements—in addition to the recorded narration of the text—can you add to your remix in order to make it more compelling and useful?

After Sharing the Remix

- How did your classmates respond to your analysis?
  - What resonated for them as they viewed your initial slide and moved into your further analysis through hyperlinks to other slides or outside sources?
- What additional media elements in the slide deck software might you be able to use in future analyses such as these?
- How might you be able to make even more connections between canonical and contemporary texts in future projects?

CHAPTER 9

Conclusion

At the close of this book, I end where I began, with an (ever-emerging) definition that highlights the ways we can be mindful when teaching English language arts. For our students to flourish, I reiterate the following idea:

> *Digital diligence* is an alert, productive stance that individuals employ when using technology (apps, websites, software, and devices) for connected reading and digital writing, characterized by empathy, intention, and persistence.

Throughout the text, I have tried to offer numerous examples of what digital diligence might look like, in practice, and to provide tools for helping accomplish these goals, all tied directly to NCTE's (2019b) "Definition of Literacy in a Digital Age." The authors of this statement have articulated a position that these literacies (plural) are "interconnected, dynamic, and malleable." And, as I think about what I have come to know about being and becoming digitally diligent, I wonder: What can all educators do, personally and professionally, to become more intentional and focused with the ways we use technology in our own lives, and in our classrooms? What might we ask our students to do—to research, to design, and to produce—given the many ideas shared throughout this book? And, finally, in what ways do we begin conversations with colleagues about the technology tools we want to use for teaching, as well as deeper conversations about why and how to use those technologies in purposeful ways?

Before offering a final suggestion about how to accomplish these loftier goals, I look back, briefly, on how my stance has emerged. In the mid-2000s, as I transitioned from my role as a classroom teacher into that of a teacher educator, I knew there were some colleagues integrating technology into teaching and learning, though it was still perceived to be a very content-driven set of activities. My connections during those times to the National Council of Teachers of English, the National Writing Project, my state affiliate of the International Society for Technology in Education, the Michigan Association for Computer Users in Learning, and other professional networks reminded me that, no matter how much technology we were able to bring into the classroom, the pedagogical purposes needed to remain at the core of our work. Put another way, I have always aligned myself with Liz Kolb's philosophy that we put learning first, technology second (Kolb, 2017, 2020), and my hope is that this view is present throughout the entire book. We teach with the needs of our students and their literacy development in mind, and then we make intentional choices about the technologies that we want to use in order to reach those goals.

However, as any educator who checks their email, glances at social media, or has ever attended a conference knows, this goal of staying focused remains a challenge; we continue to be promised more and more opportunities and efficiencies with technology, despite the failures of the past. For instance, as things have continued to become even more "personalized" over time, there has been a push for adaptive technologies guided by a principle of the machines doing the work and letting the algorithms figure out what students needed next. This is done at the cost of failing to focus on the pedagogical principles of engagement and inquiry (Coiro, Castek, & Quinn, 2016). This is just one example, and many more have been noted throughout this book.

And as reports of online learning in the 2020–2021 academic year continue—when millions of students are engaged in remote learning and many more wonder what the future will hold—we are reminded that our students can, quite literally, "game" the virtual learning systems through outright cheating or other creative approaches to getting their work done (Paris, 2020). In many ways, moving our students toward a more mindful approach to using their digital devices for learning took a major turn in 2020. There are great examples of educators doing work in hybrid and fully online spaces, and I have been fortunate enough to work with dozens of them. And, yes, while ubiquitous access is still elusive, we are closer now than ever before to having a device in the hands of every student who needs one. Here, at the beginning of a new decade, there is no more waiting, and we can finally move into a "both/and" world, where educators, from kindergarten to college, need to be producing purposeful arcs of instruction that include substantive activities for anytime learning, as well as for real-time learning.

In short, I contend that a stance of digital diligence is at the core of what it means to be a teacher today and will continue to be for many years as we rethink our K–12 school system and institutions of higher education.

I believe that digital diligence is core to our work not just because a pandemic could shut down schools at a moment's notice or because more families will demand online options. Instead, I believe digital diligence helps us see opportunities for substantive interactions with our students, in both anytime and real-time spaces, if we are intentional about our planning. We know there are ways to use tools in productive ways that can support students before, during, and after a real-time session. We know they are able to use these resources not as a "one-and-done" end point for our lessons or feeble attempts at algorithmic learning, but as a place to begin their own inquiry and continued exploration as they develop real products for authentic audiences. We know that taking a determined position toward our teaching with technology can lead to meaningful arcs of instruction where students, too, become digitally diligent.

Thus, as we think about the uses of digital tools, and come to a close in this book, I look to a mentor text to consider how we might reframe instructional practices. Through four editions of their book, stretching over two decades, Zemelman, Daniels, and Hyde have provided glimpses into "best practices" in America's classrooms, focusing on all content areas and, of particular interest for language arts teachers, reading and writing. Their books provide both practical strategies and provocation, and I lean into their stance here by adapting one of the devices they use in the books. In so doing, I hope to push other educators forward as we all consider, together, what it means to be digitally diligent.

In each chapter, Zemelman and colleagues offer a list of teaching practices that they suggest teachers could "increase" and "decrease." For instance, in the 2012 edition of their book, they offer one "increase/decrease" combination for writing instruction that begins with the idea of increasing "student ownership and responsibility by: helping students learn to choose their own topics" (followed by three other suggestions) and decreasing "teacher control of decision making by: deciding all writing topics" (again followed by three more suggestions). In total, they offer eight broad suggestions for each of the "increase" and "decrease" categories, with about a dozen subsuggestions for each. To find a PDF version of their chapter embedded in a resource from the Center for the Collaborative Classroom, please visit this book's companion website and scroll to page 37 of their resource. Borrowing from Zemelman, Daniels, and Hyde's model, I conclude *Mindful Teaching with Technology* by offering some suggestions for what educators might focus on increasing and decreasing in terms of the practices they employ in their classrooms, as shown in Table 9.1.

Teaching toward digital diligence is about more than just meeting a set of standards or incorporating a few apps to capture students' attention and keep them "engaged" (scare quotes intended!). By teaching toward these broader goals, and by increasing the practices that will support their growth as digitally diligent learners, we can work toward NCTE's (2019b) goal of growing students who become "active, successful participants in a global society" and who will "possess and intentionally apply a wide range of skills, competencies, and dispositions."

Put in an even wider context, I connect here to an article that I coauthored as a supplement in *Pediatrics,* "Developing Digital and Media Literacies in Children and Adolescents" (Turner et al., 2017). In our call for further research, we suggested that "a literate citizenry must read multimodal, hyperlinked texts critically, create these texts, and participate ethically in a networked world" (p. S124). This citizenry will, we can hope, continue to improve equity, access, and inclusion for all, providing more humane spaces for dialogue and collaboration, both face to face and online. So, with these grander ideals in mind, educators can see that there is a great deal of work to do as we enact these principles and practices in our classrooms, schools, and communities, as well as in educational policy, legislation, and the public conversation on K–12 schooling. We have work to do, no doubt, yet it is necessary work that will move our next generation

TABLE 9.1. Practices to Increase and Decrease as We Move toward Digital Diligence

Increase	Decrease
Increase meaningful arcs of instruction that can span multiple days by rethinking: • *Time:* Maximizing real-time and anytime learning, regardless of whether students are face to face, hybrid/concurrent, or online • *Topics and technologies:* Providing choices for students in terms of the learning materials and process, as well as the products they will produce using various apps, websites, and programs • *Teaching techniques:* Moving toward more social, interactive work and encouraging students to document their learning throughout the entire process through written, spoken, and visual reflections	Decrease isolated series of discrete lessons that are completed within one class session by: • Expanding limited conceptions of "flipped" learning in which video tutorials and explanations are a key mode of instruction • Moving beyond "digital dittos" that engage students in only the lower levels of Bloom's taxonomy (e.g., "remember" and "understand" types of questions), as compared to tasks where students "evaluate" existing resources and "create" new products • Using only multiple-choice, true/false, and short-answer questions during formative assessments activities in the form of online quizzes, tests, games, or flashcards
Increase intentional instructional moments in real-time class sessions by: • Modeling processes, engaging in "think-alouds," and encouraging students to generate questions that will move them into further inquiry • Structuring small groups to engage students in purposeful problem solving and dialogue by using visible thinking routines and discussion protocols • Tasking groups with specific, deliverable products from their collaboration using tech tools that enhance teamwork, invite creativity, and are readily accessible by all students	Decrease impulsive instruction in real-time class sessions by: • Using lecturing and note taking as the main or only form of instructional delivery • Asking "initiate–respond–evaluate" style questions of students during real-time interactions • Forcing cooperative learning structures that do not involve meaningful collaboration and problem solving between students • Relying on assessment practices that only involve quizzes/tests or written responses that require defining and summarizing without synthesis
Increase the blend of accessibility, aesthetics, and pedagogy in anytime learning by: • Choosing consistent designs for course materials, including layouts for items in learning management systems (e.g., folders, discussion forums) and formats for other student-facing resources (e.g., assignment descriptions, slide decks, and instructional videos) • Choosing a semi-structured, yet still flexible, format for ongoing class interactions that extend beyond real-time conversations via discussion forums and annotations tools • Structuring lessons with the principles of Universal Design for Learning to "chunk" materials and present them in an accessible format (e.g., appropriate HTML headings for organization and "alt tags" to describe media elements like images)	Decrease irregular practices for organizing anytime learning by: • Surprising students with expectations for class participation in discussion forums or other anytime activity without both adequate instructional scaffolding and time for response • Pushing students to identify other classmates with whom they can collaborate and rely on for social support in asynchronous learning spaces without adequate opportunities for building classroom community and individual relationships • Using a large variety of technologies only once or twice each, without demonstrating their functions or encouraging students to use the technologies to demonstrate higher-order thinking

of students forward on a path toward more mindful uses of their devices in personal, academic, professional, and civic contexts.

Finally, in the spirit of inquiry, exploration, and collaboration, I would welcome further conversation about these recommendations—as well as the other topics presented in the book—by inviting readers to contact me through the information provided in my biography and on the book's companion website. My goal both in writing this book and by inviting further dialogue is to move us all toward the kinds of alert, productive, empathetic, intentional, and persistent stances that promote a mindful use of technology in the English language arts classroom. My hope is that—as we each develop our own stance of digital diligence—we will continue to embrace and enact these principles for ourselves, our colleagues, our communities, and, most importantly, our students.

References

Aguilera, E. (2017, December). More than bits and bytes: Digital literacies on, behind, and beyond the screen. *Literacy Today, 35*(3), 12–13.

Alba, D., & Nicas, J. (2020, October 18). As local news dies, a pay-for-play network rises in its place. *The New York Times*. https://www.nytimes.com/2020/10/18/technology/timpone-local-news-metric-media.html

Albergotti, R. (2019, October 15). Teens find circumventing Apple's parental controls is child's play. *The Washington Post*. https://www.washingtonpost.com/technology/2019/10/15/teens-find-circumventing-apples-parental-controls-is-childs-play

Alim, F., Cardozo, N., Gebhart, G., Gullo, K., & Kalia, A. (2017, April 13). *Spying on students: School-issued devices and student privacy*. Electronic Frontier Foundation. https://www.eff.org/wp/school-issued-devices-and-student-privacy

Allyn, P., & Morrell, E. (2015). *Every child a super reader: 7 strengths to open a world of possible*. New York: Scholastic.

American Psychiatric Association. (2013). *Diagnostic and statistical manual of mental disorders* (5th ed.). Arlington, VA: Author.

Angelou, M. (1969). *I know why the caged bird sings*. New York: Ballantine Books.

Apple Inc. (2019, July 11). *Use screen time on your iPhone, iPad, or iPod touch*. Apple Support. https://support.apple.com/en-us/HT208982

Association of College and Research Libraries (ACRL). (2015, February 9). *Framework for information literacy for higher education*. http://www.ala.org/acrl/standards/ilframework

Averette, P. (2017, March 30). *Save the Last Word for Me*. School Reform Initiative. https://www.schoolreforminitiative.org/download/save-the-last-word-for-me

Bali, M. (2020, June 22). About that webcam obsession you're having . . . *Reflecting Allowed*. https://blog.mahabali.me/educational-technology-2/about-that-webcam-obsession-youre-having

Baron, N. S. (2015). *Words onscreen: The fate of reading in a digital world*. New York: Oxford University Press.

Bauerlein, M. (2008). *The dumbest generation: How the digital age stupefies young Americans and jeopardizes our future.* New York: Tarcher.

Beers, K., & Probst, R. E. (2012). *Notice and note: Strategies for close reading.* Portsmouth, NH: Heinemann.

Beers, K., & Probst, R. E. (2015). *Reading nonfiction: Notice and note stances, signposts, and strategies.* Portsmouth, NH: Heinemann.

Bensinger, G. (2020, February 14). Google redraws the borders on maps depending on who's looking. *Washington Post.* https://www.washingtonpost.com/technology/2020/02/14/google-maps-political-borders

Blackburn, M. V., Clark, C. T., & Schey, R. (2018). *Stepping up! Teachers advocating for sexual and gender diversity in schools.* New York: Routledge.

Borsheim-Black, C., & Sarigianides, S. T. (2019). *Letting go of literary whiteness: Antiracist literature instruction for white students.* New York: Teachers College Press.

Bowles, N. (2018a, October 26). A dark consensus about screens and kids begins to emerge in Silicon Valley. *The New York Times.* https://www.nytimes.com/2018/10/26/style/phones-children-silicon-valley.html

Bowles, N. (2018b, October 26). Silicon Valley nannies are phone police for kids. *The New York Times.* https://www.nytimes.com/2018/10/26/style/silicon-valley-nannies.html

Bowles, N. (2018c, October 26). The digital gap between rich and poor kids is not what we expected. *The New York Times.* https://www.nytimes.com/2018/10/26/style/digital-divide-screens-schools.html

Brame, C. J. (2012, December 7). *Writing good multiple choice test questions.* Vanderbilt University. https://cft.vanderbilt.edu/guides-sub-pages/writing-good-multiple-choice-test-questions

Branch, J. (2012). Snow fall: The avalanche at Tunnel Creek. *The New York Times.* http://www.nytimes.com/projects/2012/snow-fall

Bravin, J. (2020, September 19). Ruth Bader Ginsburg, a pioneering justice on Supreme Court, dies at 87. *The Wall Street Journal.* https://www.wsj.com/articles/ruth-bader-ginsburg-dies-11600472623

Burke, J. (2012). *The English teacher's companion: A completely new guide to classroom, curriculum, and the profession* (4th ed.). Portsmouth, NH: Heinemann.

Burke, J. (2018). *The six academic writing assignments: Designing the user's journey.* Portsmouth, NH: Heinemann.

Burnett, R. E., Frazee, A., Hanggi, K., & Madden, A. (2014). A programmatic ecology of assessment: Using a common rubric to evaluate multimodal processes and artifacts. *Multimodal Assessment, 31*(0), 53–66. https://doi.org/10.1016/j.compcom.2013.12.005

Carr, N. (2008, July 1). Is Google making us stupid? *The Atlantic.* http://www.theatlantic.com/magazine/archive/2008/07/is-google-making-us-stupid/6868

Carr, N. (2010). *The shallows: What the Internet is doing to our brains.* New York: Norton.Carr, N. (2020). *The shallows: What the Internet is doing to our brains* (2nd ed.). New York: Norton.

Catalano, F. (2017, December 6). *Google Chrome OS maintains dominance in US schools, but Microsoft Windows gains ground globally.* GeekWire. https://www.geekwire.com/2017/google-chrome-os-maintains-dominance-us-schools-microsoft-windows-gains-ground-globally

Caulfield, M. (2017a). Go upstream to find the source. In *Web literacy for student fact-checkers.*

Self-published. https://webliteracy.pressbooks.com/chapter/go-upstream-to-find-the-source

Caulfield, M. (2017b). *Web literacy for student fact-checkers*. Self-published. https://webliteracy.pressbooks.com

Caulfield, M. (2019, May 12). *Introducing SIFT, a four moves acronym*. Hapgood. https://hapgood.us/2019/05/12/sift-and-a-check-please-preview

Center for Applied Special Technology. (n.d.). *About universal design for learning*. http://www.cast.org/our-work/about-udl.html

Center for Humane Technology. (n.d.). *Home*. https://humanetech.com

Center for Media Literacy. (n.d.). *Five key questions form foundation for media inquiry*. https://www.medialit.org/reading-room/five-key-questions-form-foundation-media-inquiry

Clay, R., A. (2018). Treating the misuse of digital devices. *Monitor on Psychology, 49*(10), 76.

Code Spaces. (2020, July 29). *Power searching with Google*. https://www.codespaces.com/power-searching-with-google.html

Coiro, J., Castek, J., & Quinn, D. J. (2016). Personal inquiry and online research. *The Reading Teacher, 69*(5), 483–492. https://doi.org/10.1002/trtr.1450

Coiro, J., Dobler, E., & Pelekis, K. (2019). *From curiosity to deep learning: Personal digital inquiry in grades K–5*. Portland, ME: Stenhouse.

Coiro, J., & Hobbs, R. (2021). *Digital learning anytime and real time: Elementary school* (A Norton Quick Reference Guide). New York: Norton.

Conniff, R. (2011, March). What the Luddites really fought against. *Smithsonian Magazine*. https://www.smithsonianmag.com/history/what-the-luddites-really-fought-against-264412

Copeland, M. (2005). *Socratic circles: Fostering critical and creative thinking in middle and high school*. Portland, ME: Stenhouse.

Corporation for Digital Scholarship. (n.d.-a). *Zotero*. https://www.zotero.org

Corporation for Digital Scholarship. (n.d.-b). *ZoteroBib FAQ*. Zotero Bibliography. https://zbib.org/faq

Crash Course. (2018, December 18). *Crash Course navigating digital information* (executive producers, John Green & Hank Green). https://thecrashcourse.com/courses/navigatingdigitalinfo

Crowe, J. (2020, September 19). Supreme Court Justice Ruth Bader Ginsburg dead at 87. *National Review*. https://www.nationalreview.com/news/supreme-court-justice-ruth-bader-ginsburg-dead-at-87

Cuban, L. (1986). *Teachers and machines: The classroom use of technology since 1920*. New York: Teachers College Press.

Cuban, L. (2001). *Oversold and underused: Computers in the classroom*. Cambridge, MA: Harvard University Press.

Cuban, L. (2020a, October 12). Will pandemic-driven remote instruction alter familiar teaching practices in American schools? *Larry Cuban on school reform and classroom practice*. https://larrycuban.wordpress.com/2020/10/12/will-pandemic-driven-remote-instruction-alter-familiar-teaching-practices-in-american-schools

Cuban, L. (2020b, October 25). Does classroom use of computers cause gains in students' academic achievement? *Larry Cuban on school reform and classroom practice*. https://larrycuban.wordpress.com/2020/10/25/does-classroom-use-of-computers-cause-gains-in-students-academic-achievement

Curtis, C. P. (1995). *The Watsons go to Birmingham—1963* (anniversary ed.). New York: Yearling.

Daniels, H. (2002). *Literature circles: Voice and choice in book clubs and reading groups* (2nd ed). Portland, ME: Stenhouse.

Deleon, N. (2018, June 19). What your web browser's incognito mode really does. *Consumer Reports*. https://www.consumerreports.org/internet/incognito-mode-web-browser-what-it-really-does

DeNisco Rayome, A. (2020, January 9). Brain tech is here: These gadgets from CES 2020 rely on your brainwaves to work. *CNET*. https://www.cnet.com/news/brain-tech-is-here-these-gadgets-from-ces-2020-rely-on-your-brainwaves-to-work

Dickinson, T., & Stuart, T. (2020, September 18). Ruth Bader Ginsburg, Supreme Court justice and pioneer of gender equality, dead at 87. *Rolling Stone*. https://www.rollingstone.com/politics/politics-news/ruth-bader-ginsburg-dead-777835

Dogpile. (n.d.). *About Dogpile.com*. https://www.dogpile.com/support/aboutus

DuckDuckGo. (n.d.). *About DuckDuckGo*. https://duckduckgo.com/about

Eakins, T. (1875). *Portrait of Dr. Samuel D. Gross (The Gross Clinic)* [Oil on canvas]. https://philamuseum.org/collections/permanent/299524.html

Ebarvia, T., Germán, L., Parker, K., & Torres, J. (2018, May 13). *What is #Disrupt Texts?* https://disrupttexts.org/lets-get-to-work

ELATE Commission on Digital Literacy in Teacher Education. (2018). *Beliefs for integrating technology into the English language arts classroom*. National Council of Teachers of English. http://www2.ncte.org/statement/beliefs-technology-preparation-english-teachers

Electronic Freedom Foundation. (n.d.). *Panopticlick*. https://panopticlick.eff.org

Espana, C., & Herrera, L. Y. (2020). *En comunidad: Lessons for centering the voices and experiences of bilingual Latinx students*. Portsmouth, NH: Heinemann.

Evon, D. (2020, November 25). Is the CDC setting up "green zones" or COVID-19 containment camps? *Snopes*. https://www.snopes.com/fact-check/cdc-green-zones-covid

Facing History and Ourselves. (n.d.). *Chunking*. https://www.facinghistory.org/resource-library/teaching-strategies/chunking

Farago, J. (2020, May 28). Taking lessons from a bloody masterpiece. *The New York Times*. https://www.nytimes.com/interactive/2020/05/28/arts/design/thomas-eakins-gross-clinic.html

Fisher, D., & Frey, N. (2010). Chapter 2: Questioning to check for understanding. In *Guided Instruction: How to Develop Confident and Successful Learners*. Alexandria, VA: ASCD. http://www.ascd.org/publications/books/111017/chapters/Questioning-to-Check-for-Understanding.aspx

Fisher, D., Frey, N., & Hattie, J. (2020). *The distance learning playbook, grades K–12: Teaching for engagement and impact in any setting*. Thousand Oaks, CA: Corwin.

Framke, C. (2017, December 29). Black Mirror's "Arkangel" takes parental surveillance to its darkest, most obvious extreme. *Vox*. https://www.vox.com/culture/2017/12/29/16791518/black-mirror-arkangel-recap-season-4-review

Friedman, R. A. (2018, September 8). The big myth about teenage anxiety. *The New York Times*. https://www.nytimes.com/2018/09/07/opinion/sunday/teenager-anxiety-phones-social-media.html

Gallagher, H. A., Woodworth, K. R., & Arshan, N. L. (2015). *Impact of the National Writing Project's College-Ready Writers Program on teachers and students*. SRI International. https://

www.sri.com/publication/research-brief-impact-of-the-national-writing-projects-college-ready-writers-program-%e2%80%a8on-teachers-and-students

Gallagher, K., & Kittle, P. (2018). *180 days: Two teachers and the quest to engage and empower adolescents*. Portsmouth, NH: Heinemann.

Gamestorming. (n.d.). *Home*. https://gamestorming.com

Gardner, T. (2011). *Designing writing assignments*. Urbana, IL: National Council of Teachers of English. https://wac.colostate.edu/books/gardner

Garfield, B. (2005, July 8). *Get me rewritem*. https://www.wnycstudios.org/story/129250-get-me-rewrite

Gatto, J. T. (2005). *Dumbing us down: The hidden curriculum of compulsory schooling*. Gabriola, British Columbia, Canada: New Society Press.

Gatto, J. T. (2008). *Weapons of mass instruction: A schoolteacher's journey through the dark world of compulsory schooling*. Gabriola, British Columbia, Canada: New Society Press.

Gergen, K. J., & Dixon-Román, E. J. (2014). Social epistemology and the pragmatics of assessment. *Teachers College Record, 116*(11). http://www.tcrecord.org/library/content.asp?contentid=17625

Golden, J. (2001). *Reading in the dark: Using film as a tool in the English classroom*. Urbana, IL: National Council of Teachers of English.

Golden, J. (2006). *Reading in the reel world: Teaching documentaries and other nonfiction texts*. Urbana, IL: National Council of Teachers of English.

Gonçalves, M. (2017). Fact-checking on Wikipedia: An exercise with journalism undergraduate students. *The Second Coming of Journalism? Rebirth, Resurrection, Renewal, Resistance, Resurgence*. https://jeraa.org.au/wp-content/uploads/2019/11/JERAA-2017-Conference-book-v2.pdf

Gonchar, M. (2017, March 1). 401 prompts for argumentative writing. *The New York Times*. https://www.nytimes.com/2017/03/01/learning/lesson-plans/401-prompts-for-argumentative-writing.html

Google in Education. (n.d.). *Google Search Education*. https://www.google.com/insidesearch/searcheducation

Gragueb, A., & Temerlies, J. (2018, April 9). *Adobe launches Spark with premium features for every student, free of charge*. https://news.adobe.com/news/news-details/2018/Adobe-Launches-Spark-With-Premium-Features-for-Every-Student-Free-of-Charge/default.aspx

Graham, S., Fitzgerald, J., Friedrich, L., Greene, K., Kim, J. S., & Booth Olson, C. (2016). *Teaching secondary students to write effectively (NCEE 2017-4002)*. National Center for Education Evaluation and Regional Assistance, Institute of Education Sciences, U.S. Department of Education. https://ies.ed.gov/ncee/wwc/PracticeGuide/22.

Graff, G., & Birkenstein, C. (2021). *"They say / I say": The moves that matter in academic writing* (5th ed.). New York: Norton.

Grant, A., & Grant, A. S. (2020, September 7). Kids can learn to love learning, even over Zoom. *The New York Times*. https://www.nytimes.com/2020/09/07/opinion/remote-school.html

Graves, L. (2017, August 17). "The most dangerous US company you have never heard of": Sinclair, a rightwing media giant. *The Guardian*. http://www.theguardian.com/media/2017/aug/17/sinclair-news-media-fox-trump-white-house-circa-breitbart-news

Griffiths, M. (2016, July 27). Internet gaming disorder vs. Internet addiction disorder. *Psychol-*

ogy Today. https://www.psychologytoday.com/blog/in-excess/201607/internet-gaming-disorder-vs-internet-addiction-disorder

Gyarkye, L. (2019, August 18). How the 1619 Project came together. *The New York Times.* https://www.nytimes.com/2019/08/18/reader-center/1619-project-slavery-jamestown.html

Haiken, M. (2019). *New realms for writing: Inspire student expression with digital age formats.* Washington, DC: International Society for Technology in Education.

Hannah-Jones, N. (2019, August 14). The 1619 Project. *The New York Times.* https://www.nytimes.com/interactive/2019/08/14/magazine/1619-america-slavery.html

Harjo, J. (Ed.). (2021). *Living nations, living words: An anthology of First Peoples poetry.* New York: Norton.

Harris, T. (2017). *How a handful of tech companies control billions of minds every day.* https://www.ted.com/talks/tristan_harris_the_manipulative_tricks_tech_companies_use_to_capture_your_attention

Harvard Graduate School of Education Project Zero. (n.d.). *PZ's thinking routines toolbox.* https://pz.harvard.edu/thinking-routines

Harvard Project Zero. (2019a). *I used to think . . . now I think . . . : A routine for reflecting on how and why our thinking has changed.* Cambridge, MA: Harvard Graduate School of Education Project Zero. https://pz.harvard.edu/sites/default/files/I%20Used%20to%20Think%20-%20Now%20I%20Think_1.pdf

Harvard Project Zero. (2019b). *See, think, wonder: A routine for exploring works of art and other interesting things.* Cambridge, MA: Harvard Graduate School of Education Project Zero. https://pz.harvard.edu/sites/default/files/See%20Think%20Wonder_2.pdf

Harvard Project Zero. (2019c). *The 4 C's: A routine for structuring a text-based discussion.* Cambridge, MA: Harvard Graduate School of Education Project Zero. https://pz.harvard.edu/sites/default/files/The%204%20Cs_1.pdf

Hayles, K. (2020). *Teaching electronic literature.* Teaching Electronic Literature. https://teach.eliterature.org

He, S., Liu, Z., Mo, V., & Zong, J. (2016). PolitEcho. https://politecho.org/

Herold, B. (2014, March 19). "Ocean" of digital data to reshape education, Pearson report predicts. *Education Week—Digital Education.* http://blogs.edweek.org/edweek/DigitalEducation/2014/03/ocean_of_digital_data_to_resha.html?cmp=SOC-SHR-FB

Hicks, J., Winnick, L., & Gonchar, M. (2018, April 19). Project audio: Teaching students how to produce their own podcasts. *The New York Times.* https://www.nytimes.com/2018/04/19/learning/lesson-plans/project-audio-teaching-students-how-to-produce-their-own-podcasts.html

Hicks, T. (2009). *The digital writing workshop.* Portsmouth, NH: Heinemann.

Hicks, T. (2013). *Crafting digital writing: Composing texts across media and genres.* Portsmouth, NH: Heinemann.

Hicks, T. (2018). The next decade of digital writing. *Voices from the Middle, 25*(4), 9–14.

Hicks, T. (2019a). Hypertext and hypermedia writing. In R. Hobbs & P. Mihailidis (Eds.), *The International Encyclopedia of Media Literacy* (pp. 1–9). Hoboken, NJ: Wiley. https://doi.org/10.1002/9781118978238.ieml0088

Hicks, T. (2019b, July 12). Substantive and sustainable digital pedagogies: The hidden curriculum. *The Educator Collaborative Community.* https://community.theeducatorcollaborative.com/hidden-curriculum-dig-ped

Hicks, T. (2020, August 24). Designing breakout rooms for maximum engagement. *Digital writing, digital teaching.* https://hickstro.org/2020/08/24/designing-breakout-rooms-for-maximum-engagement

Hicks, T., Murchie, S., Neyer, J., Schoenborn, A., & Schwartz, B. (2020). *Teaching English from a distance, grades 6–12* (A Norton Quick Reference Guide). New York: Norton.

Hicks, T., & Schoenborn, A. (2020). *Creating confident writers: For high school, college, and life.* New York: Norton.

Highfill, L., Hilton, K., & Landis, S. (2016). *The HyperDoc handbook: Digital lesson design using Google apps.* Irvine, CA: EdTechTeam.

Hi From The Other Side. (2017). *Conversation guide.* https://www.hifromtheotherside.com/guide

Hi From The Other Side. (n.d.). *Home.* https://www.hifromtheotherside.com

Hitchan, K. (2015, September 21). *Reasons why online classes are the worst.* Odyssey. http://theodysseyonline.com/point-park/reasons-why-online-classes-are-the-worse/167904

Hobbs, R. (2006). *Reading the media in high school: Media literacy in high school English.* New York: Teachers College Press.

Hobbs, R. (2010). *Copyright clarity: How fair use supports digital learning.* Thousand Oaks, CA: Corwin Press.

Hobbs, R. (2011). *Digital and media literacy: Connecting culture and classroom.* Thousand Oaks, CA: Corwin Press.

Hobbs, R. (2017). *Create to learn: Introduction to digital literacy.* Hoboken, NJ: Wiley-Blackwell.

Hobbs, R. (2020). *Mind over media: Propaganda education for a digital age.* New York: Norton.

Hodges, C. B., Moore, S., Trust, T., & Bond, M. A. (2020, March 27). *The difference between emergency remote teaching and online learning.* Educause. https://er.educause.edu/articles/2020/3/the-difference-between-emergency-remote-teaching-and-online-learning

Horowitz, M. (2016, May 25). A web page consumes a constant 25% of the CPU—after it has loaded. Computerworld. https://www.computerworld.com/article/3075472/a-web-page-consumes-a-constant-25-of-the-cpu-after-it-has-loaded.html

Hyler, J., & Hicks, T. (2014). *Create, compose, connect! Reading, writing, and learning with digital tools.* New York: Routledge.

HyperDocs. (n.d.). *Get started.* https://hyperdocs.co/start

Hypothes.is. (n.d.). *About us.* Hypothesis. https://web.hypothes.is/about

International Society for Technology in Education (ISTE). (2015, July 2). *Renee Hobbs—Copyright clarity: How fair use supports digital learning.* https://youtu.be/M7OUftHrOzI

International Society for Technology in Education (ISTE). (2016a). *ISTE Standards for students.* https://www.iste.org/standards/for-students

International Society for Technology in Education (ISTE). (2016b). *ISTE Standards for students: A practical guide for learning with technology* (ebook). International Society for Technology in Education. https://id.iste.org/resources/product?id=4073&childProduct=4074

International Society for Technology in Education (ISTE). (2017). *ISTE Standards for educators.* http://www.iste.org/standards/for-educators

International Society for Technology in Education (ISTE). (n.d.). *About ISTE.* https://www.iste.org/about/about-iste

Iowa State University Center for Excellence in Learning and Teaching. (n.d.). *Revised Bloom's taxonomy.* Ames, IA: Author. https://www.celt.iastate.edu/teaching/effective-teaching-practices/revised-blooms-taxonomy

Ito, M., Baumer, S., Bittanti, M., Boyd, D., Cody, R., Herr-Stephenson, B., . . . Tripp, L. (2009). *Hanging out, messing around, and geeking out: Kids living and learning with new media.* Cambridge, MA: MIT Press.

Jago, C. (2018). *The book in question: Why and how reading is in crisis.* Portsmouth, NH: Heinemann.

Jenkins, H. (2006). *Convergence culture: Where old and new media collide.* New York: New York University Press.

Jenkins, H. (2007, March 21). *Transmedia storytelling 101.* Confessions of an Aca-fan. http:// henryjenkins.org/blog/2007/03/transmedia_storytelling_101.html

Jenkins, H. (2009). *Confronting the challenges of participatory culture: Media education for the 21st century.* Cambridge, MA: MIT Press. https://www.macfound.org/media/article_pdfs/ JENKINS_WHITE_PAPER.PDF

Jiang, J. (2018, August 22). *How teens and parents navigate screen time and device distractions.* Pew Research Center: Internet, Science & Technology. http://www.pewinternet. org/2018/08/22/how-teens-and-parents-navigate-screen-time-and-device-distractions

Johansen, D., & Cherry-Paul, S. (2016). *Flip your writing workshop: A blended learning approach.* Portsmouth, NH: Heinemann.

Johnson, A. (2014, July 31). *The ethics of retweeting and whether it amounts to endorsement.* National Public Radio. http://www.npr.org/sections/ombudsman/2014/07/31/336921115/ the-ethics-of-retweeting-and-whether-it-amounts-to-endorsement

Juarez, K., Thompson-Grove, G., & Feicke, K. (2017, March 30). *The Charette Protocol.* School Reform Initiative. http://schoolreforminitiative.org/doc/charrette.pdf

Kahneman, D. (2011). *Thinking, fast and slow.* New York: Farrar, Straus & Giroux.

Kalir, R., & Garcia, A. (2019). Chapter 1. In *Annotation.* Cambridge, MA: MIT Press. https:// mitpressonpubpub.mitpress.mit.edu/pub/926svib6/release/1

Koenig, S. (2014). Season 1. *Serial.* https://serialpodcast.org

Kohn, A. (1993). *Punished by rewards: The trouble with gold stars, incentive plans, A's, praise, and other bribes.* Boston: Houghton Mifflin.

Kohn, A. (2000). *The case against standardized testing: Raising the scores, ruining the schools.* Portsmouth, NH: Heinemann.

Kohn, S. (2014, July). *Don't like clickbait? Don't click.* TED. https://www.ted.com/talks/sally_ kohn_don_t_like_clickbait_don_t_click

Kolb, L. (2017). *Learning first, technology second: The educator's guide to designing authentic lessons.* Washington, DC: International Society for Technology in Education.

Kolb, L. (2020). *Learning first, technology second in practice: New strategies, research and tools for student success.* Washington, DC: International Society for Technology in Education.

Kreiner, J. (2019, April 24). How to reduce digital distractions: Advice from medieval monks. *Aeon.* https://aeon.co/ideas/how-to-reduce-digital-distractions-advice-from-medieval-monks

Ladd, T. (2020, June 19). Optimizing concurrent classrooms: Teaching students in the room and online simultaneously. *Forbes.* https://www.forbes.com/sites/tedladd/2020/06/19/ optimizing-concurrent-classrooms-teaching-students-in-the-room-and-online-simultaneously

Lakoff, G., & Johnson, M. (2003). *Metaphors we live by.* Chicago: University of Chicago Press.

Learning for Justice. (2014, July 19). *Think aloud.* https://www.tolerance.org/classroom-resources/teaching-strategies/close-and-critical-reading/think-aloud

Lederle, C. (2020, November 24). Poet laureate Joy Harjo gets a third term; Launches "Living Nations, Living Words." *Teaching with the Library of Congress*. https://blogs.loc.gov/teachers/2020/11/poet-laureate-joy-harjo-gets-a-third-term-launches-living-nations-living-words

Lessig, L. (2008). *Remix: Making art and commerce thrive in the hybrid economy*. New York: Penguin.

Lessig, L. (2010). *Re-examining the remix*. https://www.ted.com/talks/lawrence_lessig_re_examining_the_remix

Levin, D. (2019, October 22). Mimicking local news, a network of Michigan websites pushes politics. *The New York Times*. https://www.nytimes.com/2019/10/21/us/michigan-metric-media-news.html

Levy, D. M. (2017). *Mindful tech: How to bring balance to our digital lives*. New Haven, CT: Yale University Press.

LibriVox. (n.d.). *About LibriVox*. https://librivox.org/pages/about-librivox/

Living Room Conversations. (n.d.). *Conversation agreements*. https://livingroomconversations.org/conversation_agreements

Lortie, D. C. (2002). *Schoolteacher: A sociological study*. Chicago: University of Chicago Press.

Lynch, T. L. (2017a). *The hidden role of software in educational research: Policy to practice*. New York: Routledge.

Lynch, T. L. (2017b). *Strata and bones: Selected essays on education, technology, and teaching English*. CreateSpace Independent Publishing Platform.

Lynch, T. L. (n.d.). *Plotting plots*. Google Docs. https://docs.google.com/document/d/1zbYvpdW8R_dssw5hOZe0RwBxG2I6zhzsvbpIx4WW6Sc/edit?usp=drive_open&ouid=100066929429605942678&usp=embed_facebook

Lyon, G. E. (1993). *Where I'm from*. http://www.georgeellalyon.com/where.html

Marchetti, A., & O'Dell, R. (2015). *Writing with mentors: How to reach every writer in the room using current, engaging mentor texts*. Portsmouth, NH: Heinemann.

McDonald, J. P., Mohr, N., Dichter, A., & McDonald, E. C. (2013). *The power of protocols: An educator's guide to better practice* (3rd ed.). New York: Teachers College Press.

McGrew, S., Breakstone, J., Ortega, T., Smith, M., & Wineburg, S. (2019). How students evaluate digital news sources. In W. Journell (Ed.), *Unpacking fake news: An educator's guide to navigating the media with students* (pp. 60–73). New York: Teachers College Press.

McLeod, L. (n.d.). 5 ways you don't realize you're being negative. *The Muse*. https://www.themuse.com/advice/5-ways-you-dont-realize-youre-being-negative

Media Education Lab. (n.d.). *Media literacy smartphone*. https://mediaeducationlab.com/media-literacy-smartphone

Mehan, H. (1979). *Learning lessons: Social organization in the classroom*. Cambridge, MA: Harvard University Press.

Mehan, H. (1985). The structure of classroom discourse. In T. A. van Dijk (Ed.), *Handbook of Discourse Analysis: Vol. 3. Discourse and Dialogue* (pp. 119–131). London: Academic Press.

Menchen-Trevino, E. (n.d.). *FAQ*. Web Historian. https://www.webhistorian.org/faq

Mills, W. D. (2020, August 31). The map is never neutral. *The Strategy Bridge*. https://thestrategybridge.org/the-bridge/2020/8/31/the-map-is-never-neutral

Mindful Staff. (2014, October 8). What is mindfulness? *Mindful*. https://www.mindful.org/what-is-mindfulness

Minor, C., & Hicks, T. (2020). "Go back to better": An interview with Cornelius Minor. *Michigan Reading Journal*, 53(1). https://scholarworks.gvsu.edu/mrj/vol53/iss1/5

Mintz, V. (2020, May 5). Why I'm learning more with distance learning than I do in school. *The New York Times.* https://www.nytimes.com/2020/05/05/opinion/coronavirus-pandemic-distance-learning.html

Montgomery, J. (2020, September 29). All you need to know about using Zoom breakout rooms. *Zoom Blog.* https://blog.zoom.us/using-zoom-breakout-rooms

Morrell, E. (2019). *New directions in literacy teaching: Engaging readers and writers in 21st century K–12 classrooms.* New York: Pearson.

Morris, S. M., & Stommel, J. (2013, May 8). The discussion forum is dead; Long live the discussion forum. *Hybrid Pedagogy.* http://hybridpedagogy.org/the-discussion-forum-is-dead-long-live-the-discussion-forum/

Moynihan, D. P. (2010). An American original. *Vanity Fair.* https://www.vanityfair.com/news/2010/11/moynihan-letters-201011

Murchie, S. A., & Neyer, J. A. (2018). What is the story? Reading the web as narrative. In C. Goering & P. L. Thomas (Eds.), *Critical media literacy and fake news in post-truth America* (pp. 39–52). Leiden, Netherlands: Brill. https://doi.org/10.1163/9789004365360_004

Museum Computer Network. (2020, March 15). *The ultimate guide to virtual museum resources.* https://mcn.edu/a-guide-to-virtual-museum-resources

National Association for Media Literacy Education (NAMLE). (2007, November). *Core principles of media literacy education.* http://namle.net/publications/core-principles

National Association for Media Literacy Education (NAMLE). (n.d.). *NAMLE's history.* https://namle.net/about-namle/namles-history

National Council of Teachers of English (NCTE). (1970, November 20). *Resolution on media literacy.* http://www2.ncte.org/statement/medialiteracy

National Council of Teachers of English (NCTE). (1972, November 30). *Resolution on preparing teachers with knowledge of the literature of minorities.* https://ncte.org/statement/teachlitbyminorites

National Council of Teachers of English (NCTE). (2019a, July 11). *Position statements on 21st century literacies.* http://www2.ncte.org/resources/position-statements/all

National Council of Teachers of English (NCTE). (2019b, November 7). *Definition of literacy in a digital age.* https://ncte.org/statement/nctes-definition-literacy-digital-age

National Council of Teachers of English (NCTE). (n.d.). *About us.* NCTE. http://www2.ncte.org/about

National Council of Teachers of English (NCTE) & International Reading Association. (2012). *NCTE/IRA Standards for the English Language Arts.* https://ncte.org/resources/standards/ncte-ira-standards-for-the-english-language-arts

National Institute for Civil Discourse. (2021). *Engaging differences | Home.* https://engagingdifferences.org

National Public Radio. (2018, November 15). *Starting your podcast: A guide for students.* https://www.npr.org/2018/10/30/662070097/starting-your-podcast-a-guide-for-students

National School Reform Faculty. (2020). *What are protocols? Why use them?* https://nsrfharmony.org/whatareprotocols

National Writing Project. (2018). *NWP teacher-consultant badge framework: A product of the building new pathways to leadership initiative.* https://lead.nwp.org/wp-content/uploads/2018/08/nwp-badging-framework-social-practices.pdf

National Writing Project. (n.d.-a). *College, career, and community writers program.* https://sites.google.com/nwp.org/c3wp/home

National Writing Project. (n.d.-b). *What is a claim?* College, career, and community writers program. https://sites.google.com/nwp.org/c3wp/instructional-resources/what-is-a-claim

National Writing Project, DeVoss, D., Eidman-Aadahl, E., & Hicks, T. (2010). *Because digital writing matters: Improving student writing in online and multimedia environments.* San Francisco: Jossey-Bass.

National Writing Project Multimodal Assessment Project Group. (2013). Developing domains for multimodal writing assessment: The language of evaluation, the language of instruction. In H. A. McKee & D. N. DeVoss (Eds.), *Digital writing assessment and evaluation.* Logan, UT: Computers and Composition Digital Press/Utah State University Press. http://ccdigitalpress.org/dwae/07_nwp.html

Newport, C. (2019). *Digital minimalism: Choosing a focused life in a noisy world.* New York: Portfolio.

Newsweek Amplify. (2020, August 15). *Here's everything you need to know about keeping your dog safe from COVID-19.* https://www.newsweek.com/amplify/dogs-can-now-get-covid-19-how-keep-your-pet-safe

Nield, D. (2020, August 2). Incognito mode may not work the way you think it does. *Wired.* https://www.wired.com/story/incognito-mode-explainer

Noble, S. U. (2018). *Algorithms of oppression: How search engines reinforce racism.* New York: New York University Press.

Novak, K. (2017, February 1). UDL vs DI: The dinner party analogy. *Novak Educational Consulting.* https://www.novakeducation.com/udl-vs-di-dinner-party-analogy

One Small Step. (2020, July 1). *Take one small step with Ideastream and StoryCorps.* Ideastream. https://www.ideastream.org/take-one-small-step-with-ideastream-and-storycorps

Orlowski, J. (Director). (2020, September 9). *The social dilemma.* Netflix.

Otero, V. (2020). Methodology summary: How Ad Fontes ranks news sources. *Ad Fontes Media.* https://www.adfontesmedia.com/how-ad-fontes-ranks-news-sources

Palmeri, J., & McCorkle, B. (2017). A distant view of *English Journal,* 1912–2012. *Kairos: A Journal of Rhetoric, Technology, and Pedagogy, 22*(2). http://technorhetoric.net/22.2/topoi/palmeri-mccorkle

Pang, A. S.-K. (2013). *The distraction addiction: Getting the information you need and the communication you want without enraging your family, annoying your colleagues, and destroying your soul.* New York: Little, Brown.

Paris, F. (2020, September 3). Gaming the grade: How one middle schooler beat a virtual learning algorithm. *Here & Now | WBUR.* https://www.wbur.org/hereandnow/2020/09/03/online-learning-algorithm

Pariser, E. (2011a, March). *Beware online "filter bubbles."* https://www.ted.com/talks/eli_pariser_beware_online_filter_bubbles

Pariser, E. (2011b). *The filter bubble: What the Internet is hiding from you.* New York: Penguin.

Pear Deck. (n.d.). *Pear Deck for Google Slides.* https://www.peardeck.com/googleslides

Peck, T., & Boutelier, N. (n.d.-a). *About.* ISideWith. https://www.isidewith.com/about

Peck, T., & Boutelier, N. (n.d.-b). *Frequently asked questions.* ISideWith. https://www.isidewith.com/faqs

Pernice, K. (2017, November 12). F-shaped pattern of reading on the web: Misunderstood, but still relevant (even on mobile). *Nielsen Norman Group.* https://www.nngroup.com/articles/f-shaped-pattern-reading-web-content

Peterson-Veatch, R. (2017, March 30). *Affinity mapping.* School Reform Initiative. https://www.schoolreforminitiative.org/download/affinity-mapping

Pew Research Center. (2017a). *Political typology quiz*. https://www.pewresearch.org/politics/quiz/political-typology

Pew Research Center. (2017b). *Political typology reveals deep fissures on the right and left*. https://www.people-press.org/2017/10/24/political-typology-reveals-deep-fissures-on-the-right-and-left

Pew Research Center. (2019). *Internet/broadband fact sheet*. https://www.pewinternet.org/fact-sheet/internet-broadband

Picard, D., & Bruff, D. (2016, April 20). *Digital timelines*. Vanderbilt University. https://cft.vanderbilt.edu/guides-sub-pages/digital-timelines

Playmeo. (n.d.). *Fun group games*. https://www.playmeo.com/about-playmeo

Pocket. (n.d.). *Pocket*. Mozilla. https://getpocket.com

Raphael, R. (2017, November 6). Netflix CEO Reed Hastings: Sleep is our competition. *Fast Company*. https://www.fastcompany.com/40491939/netflix-ceo-reed-hastings-sleep-is-our-competition

Rathje, S. (2017, July 20). The power of framing: It's not what you say, it's how you say it. *The Guardian*. https://www.theguardian.com/science/head-quarters/2017/jul/20/the-power-of-framing-its-not-what-you-say-its-how-you-say-it

Reed, D., & Hicks, T. (2015). *Research writing rewired: Lessons that ground students' digital learning*. Thousand Oaks, CA: Corwin.

Right Question Institute. (2019). *What is the QFT?* https://rightquestion.org/what-is-the-qft

Ritchhart, R., Church, M., & Morrison, K. (2011). *Making thinking visible: How to promote engagement, understanding, and independence for all learners*. San Francisco: Jossey-Bass.

Robert E. Kennedy Library, California Polytechnic State University. (2020, October 16). *Critical cartography*. https://guides.lib.calpoly.edu/c.php?g=262000&p=5992741

Roose, K. (2019, June 8). The making of a YouTube radical. *The New York Times*. https://www.nytimes.com/interactive/2019/06/08/technology/youtube-radical.html

Roose, K. (2020). *Rabbit hole. The New York Times*. https://www.nytimes.com/column/rabbit-hole

Saul, I. (n.d.). *Tangle*. https://tangle.substack.com/

Schena, J., Almiron, N., & Pineda, A. (2018). Mapping press ideology: A methodological proposal to systematise the analysis of political ideologies in newspapers. *Observatorio (OBS*), 12*(3), 17–47.

School and College Legal Services of California. (2020, September 21). Legal update memo no. 53-2020—Recording classroom instruction and legal issues with virtual "breakout" rooms (K-12). *School & College Legal Services of California*. https://sclscal.org/legal-update-memo-no-53-2020-recording-classroom-instruction-and-legal-issues-with-virtual-breakout-rooms-k-12

School Reform Initiative. (n.d.). *Protocols*. https://www.schoolreforminitiative.org/protocols

School Reform Initiative, adapted from Spencer Kagan. (2017, March 30). *Jigsaw Description*. School Reform Initiative. https://www.schoolreforminitiative.org/download/jigsaw-description

Shirky, C. (2005). *Institutions vs. collaboration*. TED. https://www.ted.com/talks/clay_shirky_institutions_vs_collaboration

Shirky, C. (2008). *Here comes everybody: The power of organizing without organizations*. New York: Penguin.

Shirky, C. (2011). *Cognitive surplus: How technology makes consumers into collaborators*. New York: Penguin.

Society of Professional Journalists. (2014, September 6). *SPJ code of ethics*. https://www.spj.org/ethicscode.asp

Spring, J. (2012). *Education networks: Power, wealth, cyberspace, and the digital mind*. New York: Routledge.

Stanford Design School. (n.d.). *About*. Stanford d.School. https://dschool.stanford.edu/about

Stanford History Education Group (SHEG). (n.d.). *Civic Online Reasoning*. https://cor.stanford.edu

StatCounter. (2019, July 4). *Mobile operating system market share worldwide*. StatCounter Global Stats. http://gs.statcounter.com/os-market-share/mobile/worldwide

Stillman, D. (2018, May 14). Introducing ZoteroBib: Perfect bibliographies in minutes. *Zotero Blog*. https://www.zotero.org/blog/introducing-zoterobib

Stone, E. (2020, August 19). Advice for how to make Zoom classes energizing and community-building. *Inside Higher Education*. https://www.insidehighered.com/advice/2020/08/19/advice-how-make-zoom-classes-energizing-and-community-building-opinion

Stone, L. (2008, February 8). Just breathe: Building the case for email apnea. *The Huffington Post*. https://www.huffpost.com/entry/just-breathe-building-the_b_85651

Stone, L. (2009, November 29). Continuous partial attention. *Linda Stone*. https://lindastone.net/qa/continuous-partial-attention

StoryCorps. (n.d.-a). *About StoryCorps*. https://storycorps.org/about

StoryCorps. (n.d.-b). *Great questions*. https://storycorps.org/participate/great-questions

Styslinger, M. E. (2017). *Workshopping the canon*. Urbana, IL: National Council of Teachers of English.

Sulleyman, A. (2017, November 20). If you use incognito mode, you should read this. *The Independent*. https://www.independent.co.uk/life-style/gadgets-and-tech/news/incognito-mode-chrome-safari-firefox-meaning-privacy-nsfw-content-who-can-see-google-a8064876.html

TechStacker. (2018, June 22). *How to stop Chrome from using all your CPU*. https://www.techstacker.com/how-to-stop-chrome-from-using-all-your-cpu/Lfi7yNPXnTtxAJSzG

The privacy project. (2019, April 10). *The New York Times*. https://www.nytimes.com/interactive/2019/opinion/internet-privacy-project.html

The Washington Post. (2020, September 24). What if all covid-19 deaths in the United States had happened in your neighborhood? *The Washington Post*. https://www.washingtonpost.com/graphics/2020/national/coronavirus-deaths-neighborhood/

ThingLink. (2020, November 23). Tag types. https://support.thinglink.com/hc/en-us/articles/360021312294-Tag-Types

Thompson, Carol. (2019, October 20). Dozens of new websites appear to be Michigan local news outlets, but with political bent. *Lansing State Journal*. https://www.lansingstatejournal.com/story/news/local/2019/10/21/lansing-sun-new-sites-michigan-local-news-outlets/3984689002

Thompson, Clive. (2010, December 10). How tweets and texts nurture in-depth analysis. *Wired*. http://www.wired.com/magazine/2010/12/st_thompson_short_long

Thompson, Clive. (2013). *Smarter than you think: How technology is changing our minds for the better*. New York: Penguin.

Thompson-Grove, G. (2017). Text-based seminar. *School Reform Initiative*. https://www.nsrfharmony.org/wp-content/uploads/2017/10/text_based_seminar_0.pdf

Training for Change. (n.d.). *Tools*. https://www.trainingforchange.org/tools

Tucker, C. (2020a, June 21). *Station rotation in an era of social distancing.* Catlin Tucker. https://catlintucker.com/2020/06/station-rotation-in-an-era-of-social-distancing

Tucker, C. (2020b, August 19). *Asynchronous vs. synchronous: How to design for each type of learning.* Catlin Tucker. https://catlintucker.com/2020/08/asynchronous-vs-synchronous

Tucker, C. R. (2020). *Balance with blended learning: Partner with your students to reimagine learning and reclaim your life.* Thousand Oaks, CA: Corwin.

Turkle, S. (2011). *Alone together: Why we expect more from technology and less from each other.* New York: Basic Books.

Turkle, S. (2012). *Connected, but alone?* TED. http://www.ted.com/talks/sherry_turkle_alone_together.html

Turkle, S. (2015). *Reclaiming conversation: The power of talk in a digital age.* New York: Penguin Press.

Turner, K. H., & Hicks, T. (2015a). Connected reading is the heart of research. *English Journal, 105*(2), 41–48.

Turner, K. H., & Hicks, T. (2015b). *Connected reading: Teaching adolescent readers in a digital world.* National Council of Teachers of English.

Turner, K. H., & Hicks, T. (2016). *Argument in the real world: Teaching adolescents to read and write digital texts.* Portsmouth, NH: Heinemann.

Turner, K. H., Hicks, T., & Zucker, L. (2020). Connected reading: A framework for understanding how adolescents encounter, evaluate, and engage with texts in the digital age. *Reading Research Quarterly, 55*(2), 291–309. https://doi.org/10.1002/rrq.271

Turner, K. H., Jolls, T., Hagerman, M. S., O'Byrne, W., Hicks, T., Eisenstock, B., & Pytash, K. E. (2017). Developing digital and media literacies in children and adolescents. *Pediatrics, 140* (Suppl. 2), S122–S126. https://doi.org/10.1542/peds.2016-1758P

Twenge, J. M. (2017a). *iGen: Why today's super-connected kids are growing up less rebellious, more tolerant, less happy—and completely unprepared for adulthood—and what that means for the rest of us.* New York: Atria Books.

Twenge, J. M. (2017b, September). Have smartphones destroyed a generation? *The Atlantic.* https://www.theatlantic.com/magazine/archive/2017/09/has-the-smartphone-destroyed-a-generation/534198

Tyack, D. B., & Cuban, L. (1995). *Tinkering toward utopia: A century of public school reform.* Cambridge, MA: Harvard University Press.

University Writing Center, Texas A&M University. (n.d.). *Audience awareness.* https://writingcenter.tamu.edu/Students/Writing-Speaking-Guides/Alphabetical-List-of-Guides/Brainstorming-Planning/Audience-Awareness

Unsplash. (n.d.). *The history of Unsplash.* https://unsplash.com/history

Valenza, J. (2020, November 8). TeachingBooks launches free Chrome extension. *NeverEnding Search.* http://blogs.slj.com/neverendingsearch/2020/11/08/teachingbooks-launches-free-chrome-extension

van Alstyne, J. (2020, February 7). *Likes and retweets are endorsements on social media.* The Academic Designer. https://theacademicdesigner.com/2020/likes-and-retweets-are-endorsements

Vedantam, S. (2019). *Facts aren't enough: The psychology of false beliefs.* Hidden Brain | National Public Radio. https://www.npr.org/2019/07/18/743195213/facts-arent-enough-the-psychology-of-false-beliefs

Wardle, C. (2017, February 16). Fake news. It's complicated. *First Draft News*. https://medium.com/1st-draft/fake-news-its-complicated-d0f773766c79

Wardle, C. (2019, September 1). Misinformation has created a new world disorder. *Scientific American*. https://doi.org/10.1038/scientificamerican0919-88

Wargo, J., & Brownell, C. (2016). *#hearmyhome*. http://hearmyhome.matrix.msu.edu

Watters, A. (2019, December 31). *The 100 worst ed-tech debacles of the decade*. Hack Education. http://hackeducation.com/2019/12/31/what-a-shitshow

Watters, A. (2020, January 3). *The history of teaching machines*. The History of Teaching Machines. http://teachingmachin.es/timeline.html

Wewers, D. (2007). *A brief guide to writing the history paper*. Writing Center at Harvard. https://hwpi.harvard.edu/files/hwp/files/bg_writing_history.pdf

Whittaker, Z. (2019, May 7). *What Chrome's browser changes mean for your privacy and security*. TechCrunch. http://social.techcrunch.com/2019/05/07/chrome-privacy-security-changes

Wikipedia. (2020a). Black Lives Matter. https://en.wikipedia.org/w/index.php?title=Black_Lives_Matter&oldid=990177151

Wikipedia. (2020b). Digital storytelling. https://en.wikipedia.org/w/index.php?title=Digital_storytelling&oldid=987732652

Wikipedia. (2020c). Web syndication. https://en.wikipedia.org/w/index.php?title=Web_syndication&oldid=988535005

Wikipedia. (2020d). Wikipedia: Neutral point of view. Wikipedia. https://en.wikipedia.org/w/index.php?title=Wikipedia:Neutral_point_of_view&oldid=967336587

Wineburg, S. (2018). *Why learn history (when it's already on your phone)*. Chicago: University of Chicago Press.

Wineburg, S., & McGrew, S. (2017). *Lateral reading: Reading less and learning more when evaluating digital information* (SSRN Scholarly Paper ID 3048994). Social Science Research Network. https://papers.ssrn.com/abstract=3048994

Wolf, M. (2018). *Reader, come home: The reading brain in a digital world*. New York: HarperCollins.

Writtenhouse, S. (2019, June 18). *5 Xmarks alternatives to sync bookmarks across devices and browsers*. MakeUseOf. https://www.makeuseof.com/tag/4-great-ways-sync-bookmarks-favorites-computers-phones/

Wurfel, S. (2011, April 27). *Snyder unveils plan to reinvent Michigan's educational system*. Former Governors | Michigan.gov. https://www.michigan.gov/formergovernors/0,4584,7-212-96477_90815_57657-255197—,00.html

Zapata, A., Kleekamp, M., & King, C. (2018). *Expanding the canon: How diverse literature can transform literacy learning* (Literacy Leadership Brief No. 9444). International Literacy Association. https://www.literacyworldwide.org/docs/default-source/where-we-stand/ila-expanding-the-canon.pdf

Zemelman, S., Daniels, H., & Hyde, A. (2012). *Best practice: Bringing standards to life in America's classrooms* (4th ed.). Portsmouth, NH: Heinemann.

Zhao, Y. (2009). *Catching up or leading the way: American education in the age of globalization*. Alexandria, VA: Association for Supervision & Curriculum Development.

Zhao, Y. (2012). *World class learners: Educating creative and entrepreneurial students*. Thousand Oaks, CA: Corwin.

Ziemke, K., & Muhtaris, K. (2019). *Read the world: Rethinking literacy for empathy and action in a digital age*. Portsmouth, NH: Heinemann.

Zomorodi, M. (2015). *Bored and brilliant: The challenges.* WNYC. https://www.wnyc.org/series/bored-and-brilliant

Zomorodi, M. (2017a). *Bored and brilliant: How spacing out can unlock your most productive and creative self.* New York: St. Martin's Press.

Zomorodi, M. (2017b, August 15). *How boredom can lead to your most brilliant ideas.* TED. https://www.ted.com/talks/manoush_zomorodi_how_boredom_can_lead_to_your_most_brilliant_ideas

Index